Y0-BXI-708

Religious Conversion and Disaffiliation

Religious Conversion and Disaffiliation

Tracing Patterns of Change in Faith Practices

Henri Gooren

RELIGIOUS CONVERSION AND DISAFFILIATION
Copyright © Henri Gooren, 2010.

First published in 2010 by
PALGRAVE MACMILLAN®
in the United States – a division of St. Martin's Press
LLC, 175 Fifth Avenue, New York, NY 10010.

Where this book is distributed in the UK, Europe and the rest of the world,
this is by Palgrave Macmillan, a division of Macmillan Publishers Limited,
registered in England, company number 785998, of Houndmills, Basingstoke,
Hampshire RG21 6XS.

Palgrave Macmillan is the global academic imprint of the above companies
and has companies and representatives throughout the world.

Palgrave® and Macmillan® are registered trademarks in the United States, the
United Kingdom, Europe and other countries.

ISBN: 978–0–230–10453–2

Library of Congress Cataloging-in-Publication Data

Gooren, Henri Paul Pierre, 1967–
    Religious conversion and disaffiliation : tracing patterns of change in faith
practices / Henri Gooren.
        p. cm.
    Includes bibliographical references and index.
    ISBN 978-0-230-10453-2 (alk. paper)
    1. Conversion.   I. Title.
    BL639.G66 2010
    204'.2—dc22

                                                            2010001770

A catalogue record of the book is available from the British Library.

Design by MPS Limited, A Macmillan Company

First edition: September 2010

10 9 8 7 6 5 4 3 2 1

Printed in the United States of America.

Dedicated to my father, Henk Gooren

Born: Pematang Siantar, Indonesia, November 9, 1930

Died: Oosterhout, the Netherlands, April 30, 2008

I feel his absence every day.

Contents

List of Figures xi

Acknowledgments xiii

Introduction The Appeal of Conversion **1**

A Hothead in a Disordered World 1
The Conversion Career 3
A Resurgence of Religion? 5
Secularization, Globalization, and Transnational Religion 6
The Religious Perspective: Distinguishing Form and Function 8
Conversion in Christianity 10
Conversion and the Religious Organization 11
Conversion and Disaffiliation in Modern Fiction 15
Methodology and Caveats 16
Aim and Structure of the Book 18

1 Approaches to Conversion **19**

Introduction 19
William James: Conversion as the Healing of a Divided Self 20
Lofland and Stark: The Original Process Model of Conversion 22
Travisano: Conversion as the Disruption of Identity 24
Straus: Active Conversions by Religious Seekers 25
Greil: A Socialization-and-Social-Networks Approach
 to Conversion 26
Heirich: Conversion as a Paradigm Shift 27
Bromley and Shupe: A Role Theory of Conversion and
 Commitment 28
Long and Hadden: Conversion and Commitment as
 Specific Types of Socialization 29
Snow and Machalek: The Convert Role Within a Specific
 Universe of Discourse 30
Richardson: Paradigm Conflict between Active and Passive
 Conversion Approaches 33

Rational Choice Conversion Models: Gartrell and
 Shannon, Stark and Finke   35
Rambo: A Holistic, Interdisciplinary, and Open Process
 Model of Conversion   37
A Critique of Conventional Conversion Approaches   40

2 **The Conversion Career**   **43**

The Need for a New Approach to Conversion   43
The Bias of Scholarly Discipline   45
Synthesizing Conventional Conversion Approaches   46
The Conversion Career   48
The Methodology of the Conversion Career Approach   52

3 **Conversion and the Religious Market**   **53**

Introduction   53
The Micro-Level: The Rationalist Actor   54
The Meso-Level: The Competitive Religious Organization   56
The Macro-Level: The Religious Economy and the
 Religious Market   59
The Religious Market Model and Conversion   63
Conclusion: Connecting Religious Demand and Supply   65

4 **Stories of Conversion and Disaffiliation**   **69**

Introduction   69
Parental Religion   70
Seekers and Shoppers   77
Committed Converts   86
Confessing Leaders   96
Disillusioned Disaffiliates   102
Conclusion   110

5 **Conversion Careers in Latin America**   **115**

Introduction   115
Pentecostal Conversion Careers in Latin America   116
Charismatic Catholic Conversion Careers in Latin America   120
Mormon Conversion Careers in Latin America   122
Pentecostal Disaffiliation   124
Mormon Disaffiliation   125
Catholic Disaffiliation   126
Conclusion   127

6 Conclusion   131

  Introduction   131
  Conversion and the Religious Organization   131
  The Converting Subject   135
  Levels and Patterns of Religious Activity   136
  The Religious Factor in Conversion   138
  General Conclusions and Recommendations   140

Notes   143

References   157

Index   171

List of Figures

2.1 Movement between levels of religious activity in the
     conversion career approach   50

6.1 Levels and requirements of individual religious
     participation in the conversion career approach   133

6.2 Movement between levels of religious activity in the
     conversion career approach   137

6.3 Factors in religious activity   139

Acknowledgments

First of all, the members of the Conversion Careers Research Team must be singled out for special thanks: André Droogers, Marjo de Theije, Anton Houtepen, Miranda Klaver, Birgit Meyer, Ikuya Noguchi, João Rickli, Carlos Sediles, Regien Smit, Linda van de Kamp, Rijk van Dijk, and Peter Versteeg. Our meetings and discussions of our texts at the Department of Anthropology at the Vrije Universiteit, Amsterdam, were always very helpful and stimulating.

I also benefited greatly from the help I received from my former colleagues at the Center IIMO for Intercultural Theology and the Department of Theology at Utrecht University: Freek Bakker, Jeannette Boere, Martha Frederiks, Hervé Jamin, Jan Jongeneel, Willemien Otten, Marian Oude-Griep, Marcel Sarot, Karel Steenbrink, Henk Tieleman, Wil van den Bercken, Geert van Oyen, Peter van Rijn, and Huub Vogelaar.

At various meetings in Birmingham and Amsterdam of the Global Network on Pentecostalism (GLOPENT), I received extremely valuable feedback from scholars like Allan Anderson, Michael Bergunder, Simon Coleman, Jörg Haustein, Bernice Martin, David Martin, and Cees van der Laan.

Many friends and colleagues associated with the Society for the Scientific Study of Religion (SSSR) commented on my ideas or on parts of this book: Andrew Chesnut, Chris Chiappari, Ryan Cragun, Mara Einstein, Carlos Garma Navarro, Virginia Garrard-Burnett, David Knowlton, Rick Phillips, and Timothy Steigenga. I thank Armand Mauss especially—he commented on the whole manuscript. Other friends and colleagues in the United States who offered valuable help and feedback are Edward Cleary, Mark Grover, and Lewis Rambo.

In the Netherlands, the discussions on religion with my fellow editors of the journal *Religie and Samenleving* (Religion and Society)—Durk Hak, Lammert Jansma, Erik Sengers, and Monique van Dijk-Groeneboer— were always stimulating and fun. I also thank Johan Roeland, Wouter van Beek, and Anton van Harskamp for their fresh ideas. Richard Singelenberg provided valuable comments on various chapters of the book.

I am deeply grateful to the Netherlands Organization for Scientific Research (NWO) in The Hague for funding our international research program "Conversion Careers and Culture Politics in Global Pentecostalism: A Comparative Study in Four Continents." Its special program "The Future of the Religious Past" (sponsored by Humanities, Social Sciences, and Wetenschappelijk Onderzoek in de Tropen: WOTRO Tropical Research made this research project possible. A special thanks to the NWO staff members Bernice de Jong Boers, Cora Govers, Marc Linssen, Cécile Raat, and Ruud Strijp.

I am extremely grateful for the support provided by the editors Chris Chappell and Burke Gerstenschlager at Palgrave Macmillan in New York. Three anonymous peer reviewers critically evaluated the entire manuscript for an East Coast University Press. Their detailed comments were very helpful in making this a better book, even though that press declined to publish the book one year later.

My new colleagues in the Department of Sociology and Anthropology at Oakland University in Rochester, Michigan, provided just the right social and intellectual environment for finishing the revision of the original manuscript. I would like to especially single out Peter Bertocci, Graham Cassano, James Dow, Jay Meehan, George Sanders, Scott Smith, Gary Shepherd, Suzanne Spencer-Wood, and Richard Stamps for the wonderful exchanges of ideas we have had over the last year(s). I trust many more will follow.

Rochester Hills, Michigan   April 28, 2010
Henri Gooren

Introduction

The Appeal of Conversion

There is no happiness in the world comparable to that of the experience known as conversion.

(*Robert Hugh Benson, an Anglican convert to Catholicism, 1903*).[1]

A Hothead in a Disordered World[2]

Hassan Butt, a twenty-five-year-old man from Manchester, helped recruit Muslims to fight in Afghanistan. Just like most of the [July 2005] London bombers, he is a British Pakistani who journeyed from rootlessness to radical Islam: "I grew up in a very open-minded family; there are only four of us. My parents never made us pray, never sent us to the mosque, which was very different from the average Pakistani family who would make sure that the child learned something. I learned absolutely nothing."

The world Butt describes before he was first approached, aged seventeen, by members of the Islamist group, Hizb ut-Tahrir, was a disordered one. I met many in Beeston (Leeds)[3] with his makings: small, rootless lives, seeking bigger things. Butt says: "I was seventeen when I really started practicing ... it was through individuals I met, who started speaking a language that I understood, who went beyond just the prayer. I understand the huge importance of that."

He claims to have undergone a profound conversion-like experience:

> Even before I was a practicing Muslim, I was very hotheaded. That hotheadedness was leading us down a path of destruction. A lot of people I grew up among were on drugs, were involved in crime, prostitution, at very young ages ... the first Muslim who talked to me about Islam in a language I understood ... pointed out that I had a lot of anger and frustration that I should direct in a more

productive manner ... Islam is a complete system, a complete way of life.

Taseer: How do you pass the day?

Butt: Daily routine would be getting up to pray the *fajr*[4] without failure, staying awake for as long as I can, for at least an hour, an hour and a half, reciting the Koran, purely in Arabic ... I would agree to being called a radical and one day may even be called to be a terrorist, if Allah permits me. That is something it would be an honor to be called.

Every Muslim must work for the Shari'a to be implemented as a political way of life. They can do that physically, by involving themselves in revolutionary coups, or through political means. As long as they don't attack or compromise other Muslims who are doing something different from them, I have no problem with any of these ways of establishing the Shari'a.

Islam is a way of life, a way of life superior to communism and capitalism. Christianity is a mere religion and can't cater for people's way of life, but Islam can. With the fall of the Soviet Union, people started turning to Islam as a way of life, whereas America wanted to spread capitalism across the world. That's why Islam became the enemy.

Taseer: Why is it that an attack on Muslims in another part of the world affects British Muslims?

Butt: Because Allah is the way of love. Racism has infiltrated Christianity and Judaism. It is inbred in the people. Christians never see themselves as one brotherhood, but rather many dominions,[5] whereas Muslims, no matter what color they are, no matter what race they are, no matter what nationality they are, see themselves as one brotherhood.

Ultimately this is what Islam teaches; that black, white, brown, red, green—if there were aliens in Mars—these people are brothers ... And that is why when Muslims are being attacked, the majority of Muslims kick up a fuss, because they are their brothers and sisters ... Ultimately, if your brothers and sisters were being killed in any part of the world, you would make your utmost effort to try to help them.

I would say the majority of Muslims in this country care about neither moderate nor radical Islam; they care about living their day-to-day life. They're happy with that. But of those people who are practicing, the majority of them hold my views. The difference is that some people come out publicly and others keep quiet.

Taseer: You don't see this rise of extremism among British Muslims as rooted in economic disadvantage?

Butt: I think that's a myth, pushed forward by so-called moderate Muslims. If you look at the nineteen hijackers on 9/11, which one of them didn't have a degree? ... These people are not deprived or uneducated; they are the peak of society. They've seen everything there is to see and they are rejecting it outright because there is nothing for them. Most of the people I sit with are in fact university students, they come from wealthy families ... Even Osama himself, Sheikh Osama, came from wealth that I could never dream of and he gave it all up because it had no value to him. Who can say he came from an economically deprived condition? It's rubbish.

Hassan Butt's family is astonished at the changes in his behavior. The older generation of Beeston is mystified as to where some of their children found this identity. By all accounts, it was not in the mosque.

The Conversion Career

Hassan Butt's story seems incredible. Why do people like him suddenly become religiously active? Is it possible that a religious conversion experience turns someone into a completely different person? Or, alternatively, is conversion merely the outward confirmation of a new line of thinking that is congruent with the convert's earlier experiences of religious upbringing?

To help answer these questions, this book offers a new way of looking at conversion as the start of a dynamic process: the *conversion career*.[6] The conversion career includes all episodes of higher or lower participation in one or more religious organizations during a person's life.[7] It is a tool to analyze the interplay of factors between the individual actor, the religious organization, and the wider social and cultural context. To carry out this analysis, the approach distinguishes various levels of increasing religious participation: preaffiliation, affiliation, conversion, confession, and finally disaffiliation. These levels provide a better yardstick to gauge what conversion means, and they allow me to shed a new light on the increasing worldwide importance of religious seekers and religious shoppers.[8]

I define *conversion* as a comprehensive personal change of religious worldview and identity, based on both self-report and attribution by others. These others obviously include people from the same religious group, but may also include significant others who are not members. *Preaffiliation* is the term used in the conversion career approach to describe the worldview and social background of potential members of a religious group in their first contacts to assess whether they would like to affiliate themselves on a more formal basis. Some Christian churches and sociologists of religion use terms like "visitor," "investigator," or "seeker" instead. The term *affiliation* denotes formal membership of a religious group that is not a central aspect of one's identity. *Confession* is a term from theology for a core member identity, involving a high level of participation inside the new religious group and a strong missionary attitude toward nonmembers of the group. Finally, *disaffiliation* refers to (the process of) detaching one's involvement in an organized religious group.

Coining the concept of the conversion career is a way of synthesizing a century of approaches to conversion in the social sciences and of moving beyond monocausal explanations (see Chapter 1). It offers a unique way of analyzing conversion, building especially upon the work of Richardson and Rambo.[9] The conversion career, which is fully developed in Chapter 2, combines conversion—that is, religious demand—with the religious supply of organizations positioning themselves on the religious market (Chapter 3). However, to achieve this requires making some changes to conventional religious market theory. Offering a framework of five different levels of religious participation, the conversion career approach makes it possible to critically review and situate not only stories of conversion, but also the stories of disillusionment and backsliding (Chapter 4).

The conversion career approach is a general heuristic tool to understand conversion all over the world. Much of the earlier literature was biased in dealing only with conversion in the United States and Western Europe. Moreover, the early literature almost invariably studied adolescents, who converted to Christian groups or New Religious Movements (NRMs). To move beyond these limitations, I follow various strategies.

First, I use a life cycle approach to look at conversion in various age groups. However, I have to depend on the available literature here. Second, I sometimes make comparisons by referring to the literature on conversion to Islam, (orthodox) Judaism, and NRMs. I am, of course, aware that these religions sometimes use other concepts to describe a conversion-like experience, but I will attempt to show that there are interesting parallels. Third, I apply the conversion career approach toward the literature on conversion to specific cases of Pentecostalism,[10] Mormonism (see below), and the Catholic Charismatic Renewal[11] in Latin America (Chapter 5). I occasionally refer to my earlier fieldwork research in Costa Rica and Guatemala.[12]

The story of Hassan Butt from Manchester shows that conversion nowadays occurs under the influence of various factors and processes, many of which now take place at an accelerated rate worldwide. I first discuss the most important of these processes: transnational religion, secularization, globalization, the privatization of religion, and the religious perspective. The so-called subjective turn in religion refers to the growing importance of experience—often the embodied religious experience—and emotion. Some scholars argue that this leads to the increased importance of non-institutionalized spirituality over organized religion.[13]

Afterwards, this introduction analyzes conversion in Christianity, the etymology of religion and conversion, the role of the religious organization in conversion, and the conversion story in modern fiction. I then describe the methodology I follow in the chapters and end with the aim and structure of the book.

A Resurgence of Religion?

When I started preparing for this book in 2004, I realized that I did not need to justify the choice of the theme to colleagues from different fields of study anymore. This was different from my earlier studies of Mormonism and Pentecostalism in Central America in the 1990s. To most sociologists and anthropologists at that time, religion seemed to be a dead end, most likely bound for extinction in the coming decades—at least in Western Europe. Even in the Southern Hemisphere, formerly called the Third World, anthropologists preferred to study fashionable themes like democratization, civil society, poverty, the informal sector, or agricultural reforms. It was hard to obtain funding to conduct research on religion anywhere in the world, because in academia religion was definitely *not* in fashion in the 1990s.

So what happened?

In recent years, especially after 2001, it has become common to hear about the supposed "resurgence of religion."[14] But I remember reading about this in the early 1980s.[15] The key issues at that time were Khomeini's Islamist Revolution of 1979 in Iran (which completely surprised experts on religion *and* the CIA), the Islam-inspired guerrilla movement against the Russians in Afghanistan, the rise of the Moral Majority movement in the United States, and the presidency of Ronald Reagan (1980–1988). One can safely add to this a host of other phenomena that emphasize the increased—or perhaps *continued*?—worldwide importance of religion in the 1980s: the vigorous political and religious charisma of Pope John Paul II, the role of Catholicism in mobilization against communism in Poland, the surprise success of Pentecostalism in Catholic Latin America and elsewhere,[16] the civil war between Christians and Muslims in Lebanon, and the rise of Hindu fundamentalism in India that culminated in the bloody conflict with Muslims over the temple in Ayodhya.[17]

Most of these phenomena continued well into the 1990s—some, in fact, are still relevant today. Pentecostalism also started growing rapidly in sub-Saharan and southern Africa in the 1990s.[18] New evidence for the political relevance of religion was added by the consolidation of Islamic fundamentalism in the Middle East and Afghanistan (the Taliban), and the start of Al Qaeda. This culminated in the destruction of the Twin Towers in New York City on September 11, 2001. In the early twenty-first century, the social and political force of religion is no longer contested in the academic debate.

Looking back, it is possible to see the pattern. First, there is the expected demise of religion: a sequence starting with industrialization, modernization, Weber's inevitable disenchantment with the world, and the subsequent juggernaut of secularization in the Western world—all building up to the neglect of religion in research. Second, there are the contemporary phenomena, mentioned above, that clearly show the increased—or continued—importance of religion since the 1970s. Combine the two and you get a resurgence of religion. To gauge whether the importance of religion has increased or, alternatively, simply continued much in the same way as before, the main question of this book is: why do people become religiously active?

Secularization, Globalization, and Transnational Religion

A first step toward addressing this question is analyzing what is new about religion today. To do this requires a historical perspective, focusing especially on the second half of the twentieth century.

Peter Berger originally defined secularization as:

> the process by which sectors of society and culture are removed from the domination of religious institutions and symbols ... [A]s there is a secularization of society and culture, so is there a secularization of consciousness. Put simply, this means that the modern West has produced an increasing number of individuals who look upon the world and their own lives without the benefit of religious interpretations.[19]

Secularization theory had a strong predictive value in the 1950s and 1960s. Much of the evidence to support the theory about secularization in the Western world seemed to be already present: growing religious pluralism, the undermining of religious plausibility structures, and the erosion of tradition and/or coercive religion.[20] The visible and measurable effect was a decline in church attendance rates, which continued in Western Europe and the United States until the 1970s. Peter Berger accurately predicted in the late 1960s that all of these factors combined would lead to (1) increased religious pluralism and "hence" secularization, (2) the privatization of religion, and (3) increased interreligious competition for members between different religious organizations, leading to (4) a religious economy and local religious markets.[21]

In the second half of the twentieth century, religion increasingly became a matter of private personal choice and not of tradition.[22] This privatization of religion also implied a gradually increasing acceptance of people who were not religiously affiliated or not religious at all (atheists and agnostics). In Western Europe, church attendance rates went down more rapidly and more sharply than in the United States.[23] The influence of antireligious secular perspectives and the increased economic security and well-being resulting from the expanding welfare states were possibly responsible for this. Especially in Western Europe, many mainstream churches gradually became less "religious" and more involved in progressive politics, in solidarity with the Third World, and in ecumenical cooperation—for example in the World Council of Churches. Cooperation and even mergers between churches became commonplace. People looking for spiritual solace had to find it in other religious organizations. Some European states, however, put up barriers to make it harder for NRMs to establish themselves (a process that is continuing until today).[24]

In the United States, increased education and increased religious pluralism at first also led to a drop in church attendance in the 1960s and 1970s. But this trend was reversed in the 1980s, possibly because of a countercultural offensive by the same conservative evangelicals who helped Reagan to the presidency. Already in the 1970s, many Americans had felt attracted to strict churches, and the first evidence had been visible that born-again Christians were increasing in ever-greater numbers.[25] Ample religious freedom and a minimum of government interference provided a fruitful context for the working of a free U.S. religious economy.[26] Interreligious competition became an important phenomenon in the 1970s United States and provided the fuel for a variety of new phenomena: the increase in born-again and Pentecostal Christians, the growth of Mormons and Jehovah's Witnesses, the rise of televangelists (Roberts, Swaggert, Bakker), and the beginning of religious marketing or "faith branding."[27]

I find it interesting, and quite telling, that all of these phenomena right from the start included a transnational or global dimension. In fact, all of these phenomena were soon visible in many parts of Latin America.[28] This means that the globalization process was already in full swing in the 1980s—although the term itself was not commonly used until the 1990s.

Of course, it is now a commonplace to note that the globalization process by itself is nothing new. The circulation of technology, people, and ideas all over the globe has been going on for millennia and has certainly accelerated since the sixteenth century. Globalization and especially global capitalism became common terms in the 1990s, after the fall of the Berlin Wall marked the formal end of state communism. New computer communication technologies—Internet, email, and satellite television—made the exchange of ideas and technology more efficient and more rapid. Hence, the defining characteristic of contemporary globalization is its speed, aided by technology (mass media, computerization) and mass migration from the Southern to the Northern Hemisphere.[29]

There is certainly no lack of literature on globalization and religion, or, more broadly, on transnational religion.[30] All the religions mentioned above as successful in terms of membership growth (Pentecostalism, Mormonism, Witnesses, and some Muslim groups) include transnational dimensions. I think that the following are the four main dimensions of the contemporary relationship between religion and globalization:

First, religions currently follow *intercontinental immigration networks*, making their presence and recruitment now truly global.[31] This is an important factor in many contemporary religious conflict zones, especially where these conflicts are based on economic and political power imbalances.

Second, the construction of *global religious networks and global religious identities* is new. This is connected to the first dimension, but it goes beyond that. The global spread of religions implies increased contact between religions, and, where allowed by national states, increased interreligious competition for members. This often makes the dialogue between them more complicated.

Third, the increased use of *mass media*—especially television, Internet, and email—in both religious practice and religious recruitment is noteworthy. Again, this is connected to the first and second factors, but it also has a dynamic of its own. Some religions, like Pentecostalism, prefer to use certain mass media (radio and television), but there is almost always an influence following from this use on the religious organization itself.[32] Their liturgical styles often change, the "health and way" gospel often becomes more important, and the religious organization continuously needs more funds to finance its mass media operations.

Fourth, I showed above that another possible dimension—*political religion* or religious fundamentalism—was already on the rise in the 1970s, culminating in the guerrilla insurgency against the Russians in Afghanistan and the Islamic Revolution of Iran in 1979. Political religion was visible during the starting phase of all world religions, but the current pace of globalization has intensified global religious competition and hence global religious conflict. In some areas, especially in the Middle East and South Asia, this tendency has led to armed conflicts that are framed in religious terms. The influence of ethnic, cultural, and even geopolitical factors is important here. However, these factors receive less attention in this book.

The Religious Perspective: Distinguishing Form and Function

The English word "religion" is derived from the Latin word *religare*, which implies a tying back together of what has been torn asunder.[33]

It is imperative to distinguish analytically between the form and the function(s) of religion, between what religion *is* and what it *does*. Almost since the establishment of the separate field of study called religious studies (or alternatively, the sociology of religion and the anthropology of religion), the line separating these two has been blurred. It is easy to give a quick listing of various *functions of religion*, as these have been identified and discussed thoroughly by some great thinkers in the field:

1. Religion as a source of *legitimation* of politics—Many thinkers consider this to be a prime function of religion. The trajectory goes from Karl Marx's famous "opium of the people"[34] to Stark and Finke's sacralization of politics.[35]

2. Alternatively, religion may become a source of political or cultural *critique*—Famous examples are liberation theology from Latin America and Minjung theology from South Korea. But one could also think of innovative prophets or charismatic leaders and countercultural prophetic movements.[36]

3. Whether used for legitimation or critique, religion can be very efficient as a resource for political *mobilization*. Religion has the power to cross the usual fault lines of education, class, income, ethnicity, and nationality. Durkheim identified religion as the main factor in establishing and maintaining social cohesion.

4. Religion also has the power to provide people with *meaning* and structure in their lives through its stories, rituals, and symbols, but especially through its rules and codes of conduct. In anthropology, the late Clifford Geertz developed this perspective analytically.[37]

5. Finally, religion may also be used as a resource for *wealth accumulation*—This function sometimes happens in a very direct way. Religious entrepreneurs may earn a living with the contributions of their adherents, perhaps by promising them "health and wealth" in a prosperity gospel. But it can also happen indirectly: through the religious code of conduct, people may be able to save money.[38]

The religious perspective is essentially a worldview, a life philosophy, which combines elements from the form and function of religion.[39] The five functions of religion are certainly important, although they depend heavily on the historical, geographical, social, cultural, economic, and political context. Other factors that relate especially to the form of religion, including mystical experiences and developing a personal relationship with the supernatural (or God), come into play as well. These elements are part and parcel of a wider process that in Christianity has come to be known as "conversion."

Conversion in Christianity

The prophetic movements of ancient Israel propagated a strict universal religion, monotheism,

> for the *oikoumenè*, the whole inhabited earth. The change of mind and heart ... and the worship of this one God above and beyond all other gods and the entrance into the covenant of Israel with JHWH ... was called by the prophets *teshubah: to return, to come back*, with strong post-exilic overtones.[40]
>
> The English word "conversion" is derived from the Latin *convertere* which means "to revolve, turn around" or "head in a different direction." This basic meaning also holds for the biblical Hebrew word *shub* ("to turn, to return") and the Greek words *strepho* and *epistrepho*. Two other Greek words [are mentioned] in the New Testament... *metamelomai* ("to be anxious, regretful") describes the state of the subject undergoing a conversion experience... *metanoia* ("change of mind") describes the positive state or attitude of one who has undergone conversion.[41]

The original meaning of the word conversion thus is a turn in a different direction, a turning to and a turning from. This turning can be an anxious or stressful process, judging by one Greek word (*metamelomai*) used in the New Testament. The end result is supposed to be a change of mind and a change of heart. Perhaps we could call this, in contemporary terms, a change in identity.

However, conversion can also turn around the other way again—perhaps through the very same regret alluded to above—and become *deconversion* or disaffiliation. The word apostasy refers especially to the extreme cases: "Apostasy is derived from Greek *apostasies*, 'a standing away from, a defection, a revolt.'"[42] I show throughout this book that conversion and deconversion are two sides of the same coin. How this coin will fall, heads or tail, is not up to chance (not entirely anyway).

If conversion is to remain a useful concept for scholars, however, it has to be carefully distinguished from its original religious—Christian—context and meanings. Conversion needs to be thoroughly differentiated and nuanced to move it beyond the early Christian idea of a unique and once-in-a-lifetime experience. This idea is originally based on the classical example of Biblical conversion: Saint Paul on the road to Damascus, as described in the Book of Acts (9: 1–22).[43]

Saul of Tarsus was a ruthless persecutor of the early Christians in Jerusalem. However, on the road to Damascus, Saul had a terrifying vision: "suddenly a light shone around him from heaven. Then he fell to the ground, and heard a voice saying to him, 'Saul, Saul, why are you persecuting me?' And he said, 'Who are You, Lord?' Then the Lord said, 'I am Jesus, whom you are persecuting'" (Acts 9: 3–5). Saul "was three days without sight, and neither ate nor drank" (ibid 9). Ananias, a Christian from Damascus, told him: "'Brother Saul, the Lord Jesus, who appeared to you on the road as you came, has sent me that you may receive your sight and be filled with the Holy Spirit.' Immediately there fell from his eyes something like scales, and he received his sight at once; and he arose and was baptized. So when he had received food, he was strengthened. Then Saul spent some days with the disciples at Damascus" (Acts 9: 17–19). Later, Saul receives the name Paul (ibid 13: 9) and becomes an Apostle. He is to spread the gospel among the gentiles in many lands.

The Pauline conversion is spectacular, a once-in-a-lifetime experience, fraught with miracles, and brought on by a higher authority.[44] The Pauline conversion experience greatly influenced both theological conversion models and psychologists of religion. Many of its principal elements—especially the bright light and the idea of surrender—still turn up in the conversion stories of believers all over the world, as becomes clear in the following chapters. The Pauline conversion concept clearly illustrates the importance of the religious organization in developing, framing, legitimizing, and finally shaping conversion among its affiliates.[45]

Conversion and the Religious Organization

Conversion in early Christianity was about repentance and rebirth, but it was not merely a personal process: "The emphasis was on the communal character of conversion: the gospel of Jesus being accepted by Samaritans, Phoenicians, Greeks and Romans in renewed communities of children of Adam (Gal. 3:28–29). People were baptized 'together with their house' (*oikos*), that is, their families, relatives and servants."[46] The entrance in the new community of Christian believers was the public sign of conversion, demonstrated by baptism and the sharing of the Lord's Supper. Their social life interactions with pagans "created new situations for believers in Jesus and required Christian choices to be made on a daily basis... Converts have to be constantly, relentlessly turning their ways of thinking, their education and training, their ways of working and doing things, toward Christ."[47] In the beginning, the hostile non-Christian social context made the social costs of conversion high.

Following the conversion of Emperor Constantine, however, Christianity first became the dominant religion and finally the state religion. Forced conversions started in the fifth century, at the same time as mass conversions of entire tribes or nations followed the conversion to Christianity of their rulers. As the Church became more powerful, "*conversio* gradually became synonymous to living a devout and religious life, not only for monks, but for lay people as well, who began to imitate the rules of monastic life."[48] Most mendicant religious orders started in the thirteenth and fourteenth centuries. Thomas à Kempis's book *Imitatio Christi* summarized the medieval ideas of a lifelong conversion by lay people as part of a new spiritual movement in the fifteenth century.

With the early Protestant Reformation of the sixteenth century, even more radical ideas of conversion developed. The Protestant reformers abhorred the corruption and the priestly emphasis on ceremonial customs in the Catholic Church. They propagated a more personal form of the Christian faith, which allowed ample room for more individual conversion experiences. But there were differences between the followers of Luther and Calvin that would resonate throughout the Reformation and the later awakenings of the eighteenth and nineteenth centuries:

> For Luther, conversion was not a one time dramatic event but a daily struggle to fulfill the promises of one's baptism and to live from the grace of God in a permanent attitude of contrition and penance. Calvin, however, describes his personal conversion to the confession of the Reformers, stressing the absolute sovereignty of God in the order of salvation, as a *subita conversio*: a sudden experience of grace and salvation from sin by God.[49]

In other words, Luther's concept of conversion remained closer to that of the Roman Catholic Church, while Calvin's conversion ideal was more sudden and more individual.[50] As the new Protestant churches gradually became dominant in some European countries, more radical dissenting groups emerged. Fighting the control of state churches, the Puritans, Pietists, and Methodists of the seventeenth and eighteenth centuries once again emphasized the importance of a personal conversion and *heartfelt religion*.[51]

The Puritan conversion ideal was a stern forerunner of the contemporary individualized conversion concept in evangelical and Pentecostal churches.[52] Consider this quote by Lovelace:

> Dealing with the subject of conversions which are really genuine, most of the Puritan works seem to imply a standardized progression of experience toward salvation, beginning with legal terrors and proceeding through various stages of humiliation and contrition toward a final application of the promises in behalf of one's own redemption, after having "sold all" in fully yielding one's life to God's rule.[53]

Lovelace mentions all the Puritan signs of a genuine conversion: "continuing true grief and hungering for grace, the performance of works, the role of Scripture, the work of the Spirit, the sanctifying effect of his presence, the impulse toward prayer, a spirit of freedom from legal bondage and fear, a spirit of gentle mourning for sin, the infusion of longings to be with Christ, and boldness in coming to God." But the Puritan concept of salvation is a gloomy one: "it invariably assures unbelievers that all their efforts to reach God are vain and sinful, but that nevertheless they had better keep trying and that perhaps God will choose arbitrarily to lift them out of these strivings if they persist."[54]

However, scholars have demonstrated that the conversions in the Great U.S. Awakening of 1730–1750 were above all a *family* phenomenon, a social phenomenon like in early Christianity, much more than a personal conversion.[55] "The family, not the individual, is the central motif of Jonathan Edwards' *A Faithful Narrative of the Surprising Work of God in the Conversion of Many Hundred Souls in Northampton* (1737)":[56]

> There were remarkable tokens of God's presence almost in every house. It was a time of joy in families on account of salvation being brought unto them; parents rejoicing over their children as new born, and husbands over their wives, and wives over their husbands.[57]

Houtepen quotes Charles Finney (1792–1875), a major figure in the Second Awakening (since the 1810s) in the United States: "Regeneration: the same as the new birth, ... the making of a sinner holy ... God's agency induces the change: ... the change of moral character in the subject." Houtepen continues: "This must be experienced and felt, both by the person converting and by the surrounding community. Testimonies to such experiences became the core-narratives of rallies and mass-meetings, parish missions and spiritual exercises, underpinned by tracts, prayer diaries and organizations for spiritual guidance."[58]

The Second Awakening is also the time of the start of Mormonism, following the young prophet Joseph Smith's First Vision and the subsequent founding of the Church of Jesus Christ of Latter-day Saints in 1830.[59] Mormon Church meetings in the 1830s were highly ecstatic, with people shouting, crying, and even speaking in tongues.[60] Like in the First Awakening, most Mormon conversions in the nineteenth century happened within entire families.[61] But the distinct features of Mormonism— the gathering of members in a U.S. Zion, the living prophet Joseph Smith, and the theological innovations (especially polygamy)—gave the conversion stories of nineteenth-century Mormon converts a different flavor from the evangelical Protestant ones.[62]

I would argue that the modern individual concept of conversion in Christianity can be traced back to the Second Awakening in the

United States. Flinn describes the Cane Ridge Revival in Kentucky (1805) as an early triggering event, where emotional phenomena like barking, dancing, and falling started: "The 'falling' phenomenon later came to be known as 'being slain in the Spirit.'"[63] The tent revivals and mass rallies of the 1810s and 1820s were later followed by a less emotional Third Awakening in the 1880s and continued as the Billy Graham crusades of the twentieth century. The conversions that took place here conformed to the general evangelical model of repentance and accepting Christ as a personal savior, followed by baptism. This model came about in the Holiness movement, which dominated the Third Awakening. During emotional mass rallies, people who felt the Holy Spirit began to shout, dance, or cry. Accepting Jesus Christ as one's personal savior was supposed to be the start of a sanctification process, allowing "holiness" to fill the born-again convert's life.

Pentecostalism further refined a concept of conversion that eventually became highly influential in the United States and in much of the (non-Western) world since at least the 1980s.[64] Pentecostal churches derive their name from the second chapter of Acts in the New Testament, in which the Spirit came over the Apostles in "tongues, as of fire."[65] Some Holiness pastors already adopted the new idea of the Spirit as a force capable of changing individual lives in the 1890s. "Significantly, the key founders of the Pentecostal movement, Charles F. Parham and William J. Seymour, both came from a Methodist Holiness tradition … The first recorded evidence of Pentecostal conversion took place when Agnes Ozman began speaking in tongues at Charles F. Parham's Bible school in Topeka, Kansas, on New Year's Day, 1901."[66]

The Pentecostal conversion concept thus drew from the nineteenth century Holiness model, but expanded it theologically: "Most varieties of Pentecostalism have placed unusual emphasis on the second baptism in the Spirit which bestows the nine gifts of the Spirit listed in 1 Corinthians 12 and 14, including speaking in tongues (*glossolalia*) and healing of physical ailments. The nine gifts are: wisdom, prophecy, knowledge, discernment of spirits, faith, speaking in tongues, healing, interpretation of tongues, and the working of miracles."[67] Moreover: "Pentecostal conversions are typically more intense than those experienced by evangelicals."[68] The evangelistic fervor is also often stronger in Pentecostalism, because of the eschatological urgency: Jesus may return soon, so accept Him today! Many of these elements return in the rich conversion stories of Pentecostals in the United States, Europe, and Latin America, which are described and analyzed in Chapter 4 and Chapter 5.

Conversion and Disaffiliation in Modern Fiction

One could easily devote a whole book on conversion and disaffiliation in fiction alone. In a highly secularized society like the Netherlands, disaffiliation is an important theme in most modern literature. The whole oeuvre of many contemporary Dutch fiction writers—for example, W. F. Hermans, Jan Wolkers, Maarten 't Hart, and perhaps even Jan Siebelink—is ultimately based on the fundamental premise of the deconversion story: the sudden insight that the oppressive Calvinist religion of their parents was humbug. The sense of liberty that they experienced after rejecting this religious heritage was overwhelming.

Deconversion has a long history in modern Western fiction, of course, going back at least to Sinclair Lewis's *Elmer Gantry* (1927), which ridiculed the emotional campaigns of the Third Awakening. Converts were often expected to be zealous fanatics, "more royal than the king."[69] Thus, Catholic converts, for example, were expected to act holier than the pope, and the first converts to Protestantism in Latin America burned images of the saints and harshly denounced the evils of the Catholic Church.[70]

One contemporary author with a detached cost-benefit view of religion is Czech fiction bestseller Milan Kundera. Consider this quote from his *The Unbearable Lightness of Being*:

> I used to admire believers. I thought they had an odd transcendental way of perceiving things, which was closed to me. Like clairvoyants, you might say. But my son's experience proves that faith is actually quite a simple matter. He was down and out, the Catholics took him in and before he knew it, he had faith. So it was gratitude that decided the issue, most likely.[71]

Many other writers, however, especially from the United Kingdom, have experienced the appeal of conversion themselves—and have written vividly about it.[72] A fascinating book exists on the conversion stories of famous fiction writers.[73] Oscar Wilde, Evelyn Waugh, J. R. R. Tolkien, and C. S. Lewis[74] all followed their own idiosyncratic conversion careers, which in the early twentieth century often led them to join the Roman Catholic Church.[75] However, none of these converts could be described as acting "more zealous than the pope" (although they may show that Protestant conversion models were beginning to influence Roman Catholic approaches to conversion at that moment in time).

Conversion is even a major theme for fiction writers who have not experienced it themselves. At the time of writing this book, the (de)conversion theme has cropped up at some expected and unexpected places, like

Dan Brown's *Da Vinci Code* (see quote at the beginning of Chapter 3), in the haunting stories of science fiction author Philip K. Dick,[76] or in recent novels by Douglas Coupland,[77] DBC Pierre,[78] and David Mitchell.[79]

It is no coincidence that the conversion theme is overrepresented in both modern fiction and scholarly literature from the United States. Dan P. McAdams argues in *The Redemptive Self: Stories Americans Live By* (2006) that American culture and society constantly invite people to reinvent themselves in the lives they live and in the stories they tell others about it. McAdams analyzes some typical examples, like Horatio Alger[80] and more recently Oprah Winfrey.[81] I think pop singer Madonna is the typical U.S. model of the continuous reinvention of the self.

Some contemporary mass media celebrities are among the world's most famous converts, of course. They include pop singer-songwriters like Cat Stevens (an early convert to Islam in the 1970s) and salsa singer-songwriter Juan Luis Guerra (Pentecostalism) from the Dominican Republic or actors like Tom Cruise, Kirsty Alley, and John Travolta: three converts to Scientology with a strong missionary attitude. In almost all of these cases, these celebrities' religious quest, their conversion career, and the ultimate act of (re)affiliating with the religious organization were clearly reflected in their tendency to give testimony of their conversion experience in their artistic work or in their acting as spokespersons for the religious organizations they converted to. They are active at the *confession* level: the highest level of the conversion career typology of religious activity (see Chapter 2).

Methodology and Caveats

This book represents a theoretical elaboration of my conversion career approach. It is based on the available scholarly conversion and disaffiliation literature. I perused a huge number of articles, books, and Internet sources, hunting for detailed stories of conversion and disaffiliation. My main criteria were the quality of the story, the quality of the methodology, and the quality of the research. I looked for conversion stories that were at the same time also life histories: oral histories describing people's religious background, how they ended up in religious organizations, and why they left or stayed there. I was always trying to piece together the puzzle of the individual conversion career: what were the main factors that influenced it and how were these factors in turn interconnected?

Although my main aim here is not a psychological analysis,[82] studying conversion careers always requires analyzing individual life histories. To fully "understand religious conversion,"[83] one must get under the informants' skin as much as possible. Fundamental to the life history method is one central idea: "In order to exist in the social world with a comfortable sense of being a good, socially proper, and stable person, an individual needs to have a coherent, acceptable, and constantly revised life story."[84] It is a commonplace that life stories are formative of one's identity and that "discourse mediates between the fate of the individual and the larger order of things."[85]

Hence, conversion and deconversion stories are both essentially *self-narratives*: individual life histories shaped by personal experience and sociocultural context. The narrative approach in conversion research explicitly addresses this feature. Ulrike Popp-Baier indicates two main currents in narrative conversion research: "one emphasizing the aspects that can be observed and described in the process of telling conversion stories" and the other one analyzing "a new narrative conceptualization of conversion."[86] Throughout this book I frequently refer to authors that Popp-Baier puts in the second current.[87] These authors interpret conversion as a change in the informant's *universe of discourse*, a concept that goes back to George Herbert Mead. A "genuine" conversion experience changes people's self-image; this self-transformation is then reflected in an important indicator for conversion: (auto)biographical reconstruction.[88] People who undergo a conversion experience literally reconstruct their lives, giving new meanings to old events, and putting different emphases in the big "plot" of their life story.[89] Hence, I use these stories as indicators of the conversion process and as illustrations of recurring themes all over the world.

Considering all of the above and fully recognizing that conversion is such a broad concept, I offer three warning caveats.

First, this book is about religious change as a personal *choice*. It deals with people who have the freedom to change their religion in a local context of (increasing) religious pluralism. I do not address so-called mass conversions[90]—if these exist at all and are not mythical[91]—or forced conversions. Similarly, it is not about conversion to secular (political) ideologies either.

Second, the emphasis is generally on conversion to *Christianity* or so-called *NRMs* like the Unification Church or Scientology. I wonder if the process of recruitment to Islam really follows such a different path from conversion to Christian churches;[92] the comparison may certainly bring out interesting parallels. That is why I started with the story of Hassan Butt, who will return in Chapter 4.

Third, the literature and conversion stories used here rarely go back more than thirty years. This book deals with conversion as a *contemporary* phenomenon. Our general concept of conversion is clearly an early modern invention. Conversion stories were important following the Reformation in the sixteenth century and gained ever more importance after the revivals of the seventeenth (Calvinism, Puritanism, and Pietism), eighteenth (Methodism), and nineteenth (Holiness, Pentecostalism) centuries. The oldest literature used here goes back a century,[93] but most conversion stories I found in the literature were collected in the 1970s, 1980s, or 1990s. Some conversion stories I used, like the one of Hassan Butt, are even more recent. Hence, this book analyzes the contemporary relevance of conversion in an age of accelerated globalization, modern mass media, and political uses of religion.

Aim and Structure of the Book

The book's aim is to better understand both conversion and deconversion (disaffiliation), without imposing a single (monocausal) explanation. In the past, social scientists studying religion often tended to equate the act of joining a church with religious conversion. Chapter 1 develops a critique of the conventional conversion approaches. The five-tier typology of religious participation, which forms the basis of the conversion career approach, allows for greater refinement in distinguishing people's involvement in church throughout their lifetime. The conversion career approach is fully elaborated in Chapter 2. It classifies the various types of influences (social, cultural, institutional, individual, and contingency factors) that affect changes in individual religious activity.

Chapter 3 provides a critical discussion of religious market theory and proposes an alternative use of it. This alternative links the options individuals find on the religious market with socialization and role model theory from the conversion approaches in Chapter 1. Chapter 4 discusses the new conversion career approach in detail, stressing particularly the interconnections between the various types of factors. This is done by a detailed analysis of five different conversion careers that can be distinguished in the general literature. These are: successful socialization in the original religion, religious seekers and shoppers, satisfied converts, confessing leaders, and religious disaffiliates. Since most of this literature deals with studies from the United States and (Western) Europe, Chapter 5 contains further exploration by analyzing conversion careers in Latin America. Finally, Chapter 6 concludes the book by reviewing the evidence in support of the conversion career approach. It shows that the approach can systematically explore and better explain processes of religious change than the conventional approaches to conversion.

The book is written for all students and scholars of religion: sociologists, anthropologists, theologians, mission experts, psychologists, historians, and philosophers. It can easily serve as a handbook for college and university courses on religious conversion. Moreover, the book also aims to interest people who are fascinated by the current success of the evangelical and Pentecostal movements, the continuing appeal of New Age spirituality, and the perceived rise of Islam.

I

Approaches to Conversion

The man who embraces a new paradigm at an early stage must often do so in defiance of the evidence provided by problem-solving. He must, that is, have faith that the new paradigm will succeed with the many large problems that confront it, knowing only that the older paradigm has failed with a few.

(*Thomas Kuhn,* The Structure of Scientific Revolutions, *1970: 158*).

Introduction

The central question throughout this book is: *Why do people become religiously active?* At least since William James, this question was almost always defined in a rather limited sense in terms of *conversion.* The question then becomes: Why do certain people convert to a certain religious group? But I think that conversion is only part of the story of people's varying levels of religious involvement during their entire lifetime. I address this in the next chapter on the conversion career.

This chapter is a critical discussion in chronological order of thirteen twentieth-century approaches to individual conversion in the social sciences, as well as their subsequent revisions and elaborations.[1] They were developed by the psychologist William James (1958 [1902]), the sociologists John Lofland and Rodney Stark (1965), the psychologist Richard Travisano (1970), the sociologist Roger Straus (1976, 1979), Arthur Greil (1977), Max Heirich (1977), the sociologists David Bromley and Anson Shupe (1979), Theodore Long and Jeffrey Hadden (1983), David Snow and Richard Machalek (1983, 1984), James Richardson (1985), two pairs of rational choice sociologists Gartrell and Shannon (1985) and Stark and Finke (2000), and the psychologist Lewis Rambo (1993). All the approaches are evaluated with regard to their scope, range, claims, methods, subjects, underlying assumptions, and internal consistency. Subsequent sections present a critique of these conventional approaches and a synthesis of their best elements, leading toward a new approach: the conversion career. I will occasionally refer to the conversion career typology of five levels of religious activity, which is presented in detail in the next chapter.

William James: Conversion as the Healing of a Divided Self

The psychologist and philosopher William James (1842–1910) had no interest in "your ordinary believer," whose religion has been "made for him by others, communicated to him by tradition, determined to fixed forms by imitation, and retained by habit" (*The Varieties of Religious Experience*, 1958 [1902]: 24). He was fascinated by the extreme cases, the "acute fever" of the "original experiences" of religion in first-hand descriptions.[2] He was interested in "personal religion pure and simple" (ibid.: 41), ignoring the "institutional branch."

For James, all individuals were either "'once-born,'" with no element of compunction or crisis (ibid.: 79), or "twice-born." James supposed that the twice-born had a "sick soul" (James 1958: 112 ff.), leading to radical pessimism, melancholy, and depression. They often reached a point where life seemed to lose meaning (cf. Tolstoy in James 1958: 129–30), because their "incompletely unified moral and intellectual composition" (ibid.: 141) led to a "divided will" (ibid.: 145). To be converted, then, is "the process, gradual or sudden, by which a self hitherto divided ... becomes unified" (ibid.: 157). "To say a man is 'converted' means ... that religious ideas, previously peripheral in his consciousness, now take a central place, and that religious aims form the habitual centre of his energy" (ibid.: 162). Conversion thus appears to be a highly individualistic form of healing.

Following Starbuck (*The Psychology of Religion*, 1899: 224, 262), James (1958: 164) writes:

> Conversion is in its essence a normal adolescent phenomenon, incidental to the passage from the child's small universe to the wider intellectual and spiritual life of maturity ... The age is the same, falling usually between 14 and 17. The symptoms are the same: sense of incompleteness and imperfection; brooding, depression, morbid introspection, and sense of sin; anxiety about the hereafter; distress over doubts, and the like. And the result is the same—a happy relief and objectivity.

Although James's emphasis was clearly on conversion in adolescence, his text's quotes from converts included people from all ages. Most were Christians, although there were also some Muslims and Hindus.

James was not interested in simple membership in a religious organization, judging from his quote above on ordinary believers. Although he wrote about backsliding and deconversion (ibid.: 205–6), he did not consider this essential. Conversion was his key concept, and it has influenced generations of scholars. James (1958: 169–78) distinguished between two types of conversion: volitional conversion, which is gradual, and instantaneous conversion. The latter form is sudden and dramatic: "a complete division is established in the twinkling of an eye between old life and new." The supreme example here, of course, was Saint Paul's conversion experience on the road to Damascus in Acts 9. The conversion of Saint Paul has become an almost "paradigmatic model" for many Christian churches and many conversion scholars (see below, for example, Lofland and Stark 1965, cf. Richardson 1985).

James (1958: 195–204) described four *indicators of conversion*, the "feelings which immediately fill the conversion hour": a sense of higher control, peace and harmony, a sense of perceiving truths not known before, a sense of the clean and beautiful newness of life and the world in general, and an "ecstasy of happiness." Their extreme subjectivity makes them very difficult to operationalize. James (1958: 194) provides this summary:

> if you should expose to a converting influence a subject in whom three factors unite: first, pronounced emotional sensibility; second, tendency to automatisms; and third, suggestibility of the passive type; you might then safely predict the result: there would be a sudden conversion ... what is attained is often an altogether new level of spiritual vitality ... in which impossible things have become possible, and new energies and endurances are shown. The personality is changed, the man *is* born anew.

Modern studies, however, doubt whether having a conversion experience is capable of changing one's personality (Paloutzian, Richardson, and Rambo 1999: 1073; Downton 1980: 395; see also my discussion of Rambo 1993 below).

William James's extreme case studies expressed an excess of emotions and often bordered on the pathological, establishing a link between conversion and pathology that would prove very hard to overcome for generations of future scholars (especially in psychology). His conclusions that religious experiences ranked among the best that an individual could have (James 1958: 207, 348) and that they were ultimately grounded in the subliminal unconsciousness (ibid.: 201, 366 ff.) seem biased and reductionist from a contemporary perspective. His individualistic bias makes it seem that people with "sick souls" (James 1958: 112) need only surrender to a higher power to be healed. There is no critical analysis of the conversion narratives of his informants. But *The Varieties of Religious Experience* is a fascinating book and his conversion stories are still rich and illuminating.[3]

Lofland and Stark: The Original Process Model of Conversion

The Lofland/Stark process model is quoted in almost all of the conversion literature. In 1962–1963, the authors interviewed converts to "a small, millenarian cult in Bay City" (Lofland and Stark 1965: 862) that was later revealed to be the Reverend Moon's Unification Church in San Francisco. Lofland and Stark conducted extensive participant-observation and also interviewed the converts' acquaintances, families, and workmates; people who were interested in the cult but who did not convert; as well as "clergymen, officials, neighbors, employers" (ibid.: 863). They said "the converts were primarily white, Protestant, and young (typically under 35); ... most were Americans of lower middle-class and small-town origins."

Lofland and Stark (1965: 874) summarized their motivational model, which they presented as a sequential "funnel" (ibid.: 863), in the following manner:

For conversion a person must:

1. Experience enduring, acutely felt tensions,
2. Within a religious problem-solving perspective,
3. Which leads him to define himself as a religious seeker;
4. Encountering the D.P. [the cult] at a turning point in his life,
5. Wherein an affective bond is formed (or pre-exists) with one or more converts;
6. Where extra-cult attachments are absent or neutralized;
7. And, where, if he is to become a deployable agent, he is exposed to intensive interaction.

Lofland and Stark presented a four-level typology of religious commitment, of which they only defined and developed two levels. Conditions 1 to 3 were called background factors or "pre-disposing conditions" (ibid.: 864); and conditions 4 through 6 were "situational contingencies" (ibid.: 870). Factors 1 through 6 sufficed to turn the unspecified "pre-converts" (ibid.: 865) into "verbal converts, who professed belief and were accepted by core members as sincere" , and "total converts exhibited their commitment through deeds as well as words" (ibid.: 864). The fourth level was made up by unspecified "core members," who decided which converts were "sincere" and which were not.

The influence of James is visible in the emphasis on tension, deprivation, and subsequent frustration (factor 1) as the underlying foundations for conversion. The importance James placed on religious experience, however, is completely absent. Lofland and Stark (1965: 864) gave examples of frustrations such as the "longing for unrealized wealth, knowledge, fame, and prestige; frustrated sexual and marital relations; homosexual guilt; disabling and disfiguring physical conditions." The model is clear and systematic in outlining the prime factor in conversion: social networks, both involving members of the cult (factor 5) and significant others such as family and friends (factor 6). The second most important factor is personality, which forms the basis of the acutely felt tensions (factor 1), the religious problem-solving perspective (2), and the self-definition of a religious seeker (3). The third most important factor in conversion is the contingency element: the turning-point experience (factor 4).

The conceptualization of the individual that appears in the Lofland/ Stark model contains both active and passive elements responsible for conversion. Young, frustrated Protestants come to define themselves as seekers and happen to meet a religious group they like. If emotional bonds with nonmembers like peers and relatives are stronger than those with cult members, they will most likely not convert. On the other hand, if the emotional bonds with cult members are stronger, conversion is likely to follow.

The Lofland/Stark model has been criticized as being too specific and without empirical foundations (Snow and Machalek 1984: 184) and as too static and individualistic (Richardson and Stewart 1978: 28, 31). The role of prior socialization is mostly ignored (see Greil 1977; Long and Hadden 1983; and my discussion below). Alienation and frustration are only measured after people become members; "variability in social availability of potential recruits" (Bromley and Shupe 1979: 168) is ignored; and there is a tendency "to explain away affiliation with marginal groups as the result of irrationality or emotional instability."[4]

Snow and Philips (1980) make a rigorous empirical examination of the Lofland/Stark model by using data on the Buddhist group Nichiren Shoshu in the United States. They confirm that cult-affective bonds and intensive interaction are "essential for conversion" (ibid.: 444). However, their findings "are especially at odds with the contention that personal tension, ideological congruence, and religious seekership are necessary predisposing conditions for conversion" (ibid.: 443). Their results also call into question the necessity of the turning point and that of weak or severed extracult attachments. Another rigorous testing of the Lofland/Stark model among Dutch adolescents, which included a control group, confirmed most of the model's conditions—but again with some caveats.

> Evidently, a religious problem-solving perspective is not an independent condition for conversion … The contribution of the turning point

[condition 4] identified as 'job change' runs counter to expectation ... In contrast to Lofland and Stark's theory, the conditions are largely independent of each other. No significant correlations were found among the five conditions. This finding contradicts the supposed cumulativity of the Lofland and Stark model.

(Kox, Meeus, and 't Hart 1991: 237)

The model is also blind to the influence of gender (aside from mutual attractions between members and preconverts).

Travisano: Conversion as the Disruption of Identity

Richard Travisano's social psychological model departs from the notion that our personal histories are constantly remade under the influence of "interaction within shared *universes of discourse*" (Travisano 1970: 594). The latter concept is derived from George Herbert Mead (1934): "a system of common or social meanings." Travisano distinguishes between two different kinds of personal transformation: alternation and conversion. *Conversion* involves the "complete disruption" of an older identity; "anything less signals *alternation*" (ibid.: 598).

His case studies involve interviews with Hebrew Christians and Jewish Unitarians in their twenties and thirties, many of whom are married. Travisano (1970: 599) concludes: "The Hebrew Christian has broken with his past, the Jewish Unitarian has not." The Hebrew Christians experienced a *conversion*: "the adoption of a pervasive identity which rests on a change ... from one universe of discourse to another" (ibid.: 600). He adds that "conversion often involves a period of emotional upset." Jewish Unitarians, however, experienced only an *alternation*: "relatively easily accomplished changes of life which do not involve a radical change in universe of discourse ... Alternations are transformations to identities which are prescribed or at least *permitted* within the persons' established universes of discourse" (ibid.: 601).

Alternation, which might be equated with simple membership or affiliation, and conversion are the only dimensions in Travisano's typology of religious activity. Conversion "involves the ubiquitous utilization of an identity," meaning that converts strive "to make their new identity central to almost all interactions" (ibid.: 605). Individual choice, strongly shaped by personality, is considered to be the primary factor in conversion; the influence of social networks is secondary.

Hence, the conceptualization of the individual in this model is again quite individualistic: these converts are active agents shaping their own identities. If they adopt an identity that is not compatible with their former identities, a rupture results that is called conversion. This rupture is often accompanied by a period of depression or confusion. However, the accompanying "emotional upset" is not seen as the cause of the change in identity. Travisano provides a useful way to carefully define the identity change that is crucial to conversion, but his model does not address the causes of this change.

Travisano's model is strongly influenced by his fieldwork experiences. When Jews become Christians, it is often very traumatic, because they split with family and Jewish friends. Conversion is often seen as a betrayal of the Jewish community. The central problem with Travisano is that he takes his fine research in that context and projects that experience as being normative for all conversions and alternations.[5]

Kox et al. (1991: 228) maintain that "conversion implies both an objective and a subjective break in one's life." They use Travisano for their definition of conversion: "a revision of one's world view such that one's self-image and notions as how to deal with others undergo radical change ... To join a group without undergoing radical change in world view is to 'alternate' rather than convert." Unfortunately, they only review the implications of their results for the Lofland/Stark model and not for Travisano's model.

Straus: Active Conversions by Religious Seekers

The sociologist Roger Straus (1976, 1979: 158–59) is highly critical of the "passivist" conventional approach to conversion, which he describes in terms strongly reminiscent of a "brainwashing model" as "depicting the convert as driven into the arms of a group that manipulates him or her so as to exact cognitive and behavioral commitment to its belief system and institutional structure." Straus (1979: 161) focuses on individual action: "how a person comes to be a seeker and then how the seeker goes about finding a more adequate world of everyday life."

The author never answers his first question, which is fundamental to the conversion process: how do certain (but not all) people become seekers? In his model, Straus (1979: 162–63) systematically outlines the typical patterns of religious seekers: first instrumentally combing for clues through their social networks and the mass media, gradually refining the nature of their quest, experimenting with a certain religious group (*preaffiliation*), "learning the appropriate language, set and interpretation schemes" (*affiliation*), following the institutionalized "bridge-burning acts" (*conversion*), and sometimes becoming an "agent or representative of the group" seeking new converts (what I will call *confession* or core membership in the conversion career approach). There is no attention devoted to the life-cycle stages of the seeking individual.

In this chronological review of conversion literature, the trend toward increasingly individualistic models is continued with Straus, who was a student of Lofland.[6] Straus conceptualized the individual as a free, active seeker, instrumentally combing "through social networks, chance encounters, mass media … looking for leads to prospective means of help" (ibid.: 162). People who want to change themselves use religious groups as a vehicle for personal transformation. Here, we already begin to see the contours of a rational choice approach to conversion (see below). However, Straus (1979: 160) is quite balanced in his treatment of active and more passive approaches to conversion: "There is great tactical utility in treating collective behavior *as if* humans were passive objects of social forces and interactive pressures … The two approaches are complementary, not antagonistic." Unfortunately, he does not provide a clear answer of how the two approaches could be united in a single model. Arthur Greil attempted to do just that.

Greil: A Socialization-and-Social-Networks Approach to Conversion

By attempting to combine a socialization with a social networks approach, Arthur Greil (1977: 120) is able to answer the question why certain people become religious seekers: "If we are willing to accept that man is a meaning-seeking animal who cannot endure the sense of being bereft of a viable world view, then we may also accept that those whose identities have been spoiled become 'seekers' who search for a perspective to restore meaning." The concept of spoiled identity is derived from Goffman (1959, 1963). Identities become "spoiled" under the influence of significant others (via social networks) or "when that perspective is perceived as not dealing with the problems that the individual encounters in everyday life" (ibid.: 119). This leads to a dissatisfaction and happens especially in times of "rapid social change."

Socialization ("previous dispositions") influences religious seekership: "The stock of knowledge developed out of the sedimentation of his past experiences sets limits to the range of perspectives he may find plausible" (ibid.: 122). Direct face-to-face contact, however, tends to limit the influence of previous dispositions. Greil (1977: 124) concludes "that—other things being equal—an individual in a situation of social strain will be attracted only to those movement perspectives whose intellectual style is compatible with the cognitive style of the social group in question."

Concerning the levels of religious activity, the author only distinguishes between recruitment or "membership" (ibid.: 116, 121) and conversion that is "a radical change in the perspective of the recruited individual" (ibid.: 116). The conceptualization of the individual would seem to determine the importance of the factors in conversion. For the more active converts, the seeker's personality comes first, followed by social networks. For the more passive converts, whose identities become "spoiled" through the influence of significant others, social networks obviously come first and individual factors are only of secondary importance. Greil's model is not based on a concrete case study; neither does he address the influence of stages in the life cycle (adolescence, etc.). This severely limits the scope of his model. His main contribution is in conceptualizing and modeling the importance of (religious) socialization in the conversion process and in linking it to spoiled identity and seekership.

Heirich: Conversion as a Paradigm Shift

Heirich (1977: 662–63) offers no new model, but tests the older models by looking at the importance of stress, socialization, and social networks among a sample of Catholic Pentecostals in Michigan and a control group of Catholic respondents. Heirich is one of the first scholars of conversion to use a control group that enables him to show that converts and nonconverts *both* suffer from stress and tensions (ibid.: 664). Partly challenging Greil (1977), Heirich (1977, 669) concludes that "immediate personal influences have more impact than does one's psychological state or prior socialization." However, social networks are very important, but only "for those already oriented toward a religious quest" (ibid.: 673). Social encapsulation was often an important factor in conversion, but not always. Heirich concludes that he has shown "the *route* that conversion takes within a population, but ... cannot explain what lies behind the religious quest."

The author argues that the basis for conversion seems to be the destruction of the clarity about our "root reality" (Heirich 1977: 674–75). This happens when life's problems cannot be solved within the conventional perspective (cf. Greil 1977), because of individual stress and tensions (cf. James 1958; Lofland and Stark 1965; Greil 1977), or because "respected leaders publicly abandon some part of past grounding assumptions, [weakening] their authority." The conversion process follows "a methodological application of common sense... a fairly simple set of procedures for assessing new claims in terms of past experience" (Heirich 1977: 676). It is similar to the adoption of new paradigms in science (cf. Kuhn 1970).

Summarizing: a religious quest, shaped by individual factors, forms the basis of conversion, followed by social networks. Heirich only looks at conversion as the expression of religious activity, and only at conversion among young adults, since university students make up the bulk of both samples. A highly relevant finding is that Heirich (1977: 658) suggests that converts tend to exaggerate their preconversion sinfulness to increase the power and value of their current conversions.

Bromley and Shupe: A Role Theory of Conversion and Commitment

The central idea in the role theory approach as developed by Bromley and Shupe (1979: 162) is that "an individual's needs are not merely met by a group but … may be shaped to the group's own purposes." Their model is based on a detailed case study of young adults in the Unification Church in Texas. The authors divide the "affiliative process" into five conceptual components (emphatically *not* stages): predisposing factors, attraction, incipient involvement, active involvement, and commitment (ibid.: 167).

Regarding predisposing factors, they find little evidence of stress or alienation in the age group of their sample, which is supposedly "characterized by considerable searching for meaning and direction" (ibid.: 170). The respondents were initially attracted to the Unification Church (UC) because of "the theology, the communal group, or a specific individual" (ibid.: 171). The initial involvement usually followed within a few weeks. If they decided to stay in the UC commune (active involvement), they would gradually learn the role of being a church member, that is, to go out into the streets for witnessing and fundraising for ten hours. They seemed to reserve the term "commitment" for the core members who were living in the commune fulltime, perfecting their knowledge of theology and fulfilling all the duties of membership. Bromley and Shupe (1979: 181) are among the first authors to recognize the importance of disaffiliation: members walking away "out of frustration with attempting to fulfill the church's goals in the face of rising public hostility."

The role theory approach offers a very fruitful synthesis of more active (seekers trying out various churches) and more passive (role learning shaped by the church's expectations of members) elements in the conversion process. Its five-component typology of religious activity is very refined. Bromley and Shupe also stress the high dropout rate, suggesting that recruitment and maintaining commitment among members may have quite different dynamics. Social networks or personality might come first as the main factor in conversion. They also indicate that recruitment usually precedes belief and is in turn followed (or not) by commitment. This is a clear break with the Lofland/Stark (1965) motivational model that assumes that conversion only follows after new beliefs have already been adopted.

Long and Hadden: Conversion and Commitment as
Specific Types of Socialization

Theodore Long and Jeffrey Hadden (1983: 2) note that all general conversion models "highlight two central aspects of socialization process: group efforts to *mold new members* (brainwashing model) and new members' *journey toward affiliation* with the group (drift model) ... each model has identified a central, but only partial, aspect of cult conversion processes." The authors define socialization as "the social process of creating and incorporating new members of a group from a pool of nonmembers, carried out by members and their allies" (ibid.: 5). This implies looking at the cultural and social organizational aspects of membership, acknowledging the fact that "members define who is a novice" (ibid.: 6), and analyzing the sorts of activities the participants carry out. *Incorporating activities* include recruiting novices, certification (monitoring of novices), and placing novices in certain church positions. *Creating activities* include "displaying the requisites of membership for novices" (ibid.: 7) and *shaping* novices by the application of sanctions ("shaping activities"). These three activities constitute the tools of the trade for religious organizations.

The Unification Church (UC) in the United States flourished in the 1970s. Many new members came in because recruitment focused on "available" young people. However, the dropout rate was also very high—presumably because commitment to the church was often low. Long and Hadden (1983: 10) conclude that

> the overwhelming attention to commitment displays for certification encourages novices to give a good show, which they do ... If commitment is not grounded in reflection, as seems to be the case with the Moonies, converts will eventually experience serious doubt about their membership. The power of doubt to generate disaffection is greatly increased by weak *cognitive socialization* to the UC worldview. When affective bonds become uncertain, converts' moral commitment to the group has no backing in cultural belief. The Moonie *placement system* encouraged quick but short-lived commitment.

So the same factors in the UC system of socialization that contributed to strong initial commitment also contributed to a very high dropout rate in the long term.

Like most authors, Long and Hadden focus again on young adults. Their typology includes affiliation, conversion, confession (that is, "commitment"), and even disaffiliation ("low retention," ibid.: 13). Although Long and Hadden do not analyze the origin of the need to join a religious group, their socialization approach allows for an integration of the more psychological brainwashing model and the more sociological motivational model (the "social drift" model going back to Lofland and Stark in 1965 and subsequent revisions). They manage to do this by distinguishing and analyzing various types of "creating and incorporating activities": novices following the requisites for membership as showed by members; core members shaping novices by applying sanctions; and the various forms of recruiting, certification (monitoring), and placing. Thus they accomplish an integration of more active and more passive elements in the conversion process. Like Greil (1977) and Bromley and Shupe (1979), they stress that recruitment precedes belief and commitment. However, by not addressing the original motivation for conversion, it is impossible to identify the factors that cause a change in religious affiliation.

Snow and Machalek: The Convert Role Within a Specific Universe of Discourse

Snow and Machalek (1984: 178–84) briefly assess six causes of conversion that are commonly mentioned in the literature. They reject "brainwashing" on grounds of lack of empirical evidence, the many documented cases of conversion without any coercion, and the fact that stories of apostates are almost always highly biased. They also find little empirical evidence for the notion that certain personality traits would make particular people "susceptible to cults." They point out that the term "religious seekers" does not explain much, because the question remains as to how these people become seekers (see Straus 1979 above). They reject "causal process models" (for example, Lofland and Stark 1965), because of a lack of empirical support, the fact that a certain sequence of events does not prove any causal relationship, and the obvious empirical problem that "the natural histories of conversion patterns vary from group to group" (Snow and Machalek 1984: 184). They acknowledge that situational factors that induce tension are important (see, however, Bromley and Shupe 1979; Heirich 1977; and Kox et al. 1991), but these are difficult to probe empirically. However, the social attributes that make people available for conversion are clear; that is, most converts in the United States are young (twenty to thirty), single, and middle class. The most important factor in conversion that they note are the social influences: social networks of family and friends (cf. Greil 1977), affective and intensive interaction (Lofland and Stark 1965), and role learning (cf. Bromley and Shupe 1979).

    In their 1983 article, Snow and Machalek aim to provide empirical indicators to help identity the convert as a specific social type. They reject common conceptions of conversion, especially "physical aberrations, demonstration events [like giving testimony], and group membership or participation." Although noting that group membership may include "varying degrees of commitment" (ibid.: 261), the authors do not develop a typology, but following Nock (1933) distinguish only between conversion and adhesion (*affiliation* in my terminology below). They never specify the stages of the life cycle of the convert(s) either. However, the members of the Japanese Buddhist cult Nichiren Shoshu of America (NSA), which they interviewed for their research and quote throughout their 1983 article, were all between sixteen and forty years old. So, in fact, they are primarily discussing conversion among young adults—as most informants are in their twenties—and conversion among married people.

The authors posit that conversion involves a "radical change," but they find this impossible to operationalize: "how much change is enough to constitute a conversion?" (ibid.: 264). Moreover, they wonder "exactly what is it that undergoes radical change? Is it beliefs and values, behavior and identities, or something even more fundamental?" (ibid.: 265). They conclude that it is the convert's "universe of discourse" (G. H. Mead 1934; see also Travisano 1970 and above) that changes radically: "the broad interpretive framework in terms of which people live and organize experience" (ibid.: 265). Snow and Machalek (1983: 266–78) discuss four key properties by which to identify a convert whose universe of discourse has changed: biographical reconstruction, adoption of a master attribution scheme, suspension of analogical reasoning, and embracement of a master role (which they change one year later into embracement of the convert role; Snow and Machalek 1984: 174).

They first selectively quote James (1958: 177; see also above) on conversion: "a complete division is established in the twinkling of an eye between the old life and the new." Noting that it does not always happen that quickly, they do agree with James in concluding: "Some aspects of the past are jettisoned, others are redefined, and some put together in ways previously inconceivable. One's biography is, in short, reconstructed" (Snow and Machalek 1983, 266). A consequence of this process is that "the convert's former understanding of self, past events, and others is now regarded as a misunderstanding" (ibid.: 267).

The second key property by which one can identify the convert is by the adoption of a master attribution scheme. "Feelings, behavior, and events that were previously inexplicable or accounted for by reference to a number of causal schemes are now interpreted from the standpoint of one pervasive scheme" (ibid.: 270). Since personal transformation is the goal of most religious groups, "effecting a shift from an external to an internal locus of control seems to be a necessary step in conversion to such groups" (Snow and Machalek 1984: 272).

The third characteristic of the convert as a social type is his/her tendency to avoid analogical metaphors. Instead, they prefer using iconic metaphors like "God is love" or describing themselves as "born again" (not *as if* they were born again). "Using iconic metaphors can establish the uniqueness of the group or its world view" (Snow and Machalek 1983: 273–74).

The fourth indicator of conversion is the embracement of a master (that is, convert) role, "discernable in both the behavior and the rhetoric of converts" (ibid.: 275). It involves "the generalization, rather than compartmentalization, of the convert role and its embracement by the convert" (ibid.: 276). There are various consequences of this. The convert role "governs their orientation in all situations" (ibid.: 277); in fact, converts "enthusiastically announce their identity in nearly all situations." "Finally, embracement of the convert role gives rise to what Travisano (1970: 605) calls the *ubiquitous utilization* of the identity associated with the convert role ... : all role identities are subordinate to the identity that flows from the master role of the convert" (Snow and Machalek 1983: 278).

The Snow and Machalek approach thus makes an important contribution to the role theory of conversion (see also Bromley and Shupe 1979 and above). However, their conceptualization of the individual is limited and voluntaristic: the active actor can choose his or her own religious group, his or her social networks.

In a methodologically sophisticated testing of Snow and Machalek's model, Staples and Mauss (1987: 137) similarly write that "Snow and Machalek's theory offers us a rather weak conceptualization of the *person* who experiences conversion. In their scheme, the person is replaced with the term 'consciousness,' and the concept is never well developed. In contrast, we see conversion as involving primarily a change in self-concept (Mead 1934) ... Thus, conversion is seen to involve a change in the way a person thinks and feels about his or her self." Snow and Machalek (1983: 279) assume that their analysis "provides the researcher with empirical guidelines for locating the convert."

However, Staples and Mauss (1987: 140) are correct when writing: "Unfortunately, Snow and Machalek (1983; 1984) do not provide any clues about how ... to operationalize the four rhetorical indicators in some explicit way." Staples and Mauss develop their own operationalizations of the four supposed key properties of converts and test these on samples of young (nineteen- to twenty-eight-year-old) active Christians at Washington State University. The results are very important (Staples and Mauss 1987: 143–44):

The fact that four "lifelong" Christians were equally likely as our 11 professed converts to suspend analogical reasoning, adopt a master attribution scheme, and embrace a master role, casts doubt, at least in our eyes, on Snow and Machalek's contention that these three rhetorical properties are unique to the convert.

If "conversion" involves the attempt to change, or create, the "real self," then it seems reasonable to view "commitment" as the attempt to maintain a consistency in the "real self." Where biographical reconstruction assists in the *creation* of a "real self," the embracing of a master role appears to assist in the *maintenance* of the "real self."

It seems reasonable to us that all three indicators (*other* than biographical reconstruction) are likely to be a product of religious *socialization*, and are also likely to play some role in the process of *maintaining* religious commitment.

Finally, Snow and Machalek (1983: 280) themselves note that "our observations raise serious questions about much of the research concerned with the causes of conversion ... Far from being trusted sources of information, converts are uniquely denied impartial knowledge about the factors that might have precipitated conversion." Staples and Mauss (1987: 138) are thus correct to conclude that "from Snow and Machalek's point of view, the researcher or analyst is better qualified to determine who is or is not a convert than are the subjects themselves." This is a pity, as it ultimately denies researchers the opportunity to probe the inside view on conversion by asking the subjects themselves about it. This is called the *emic* view in cultural anthropology.

Richardson: Paradigm Conflict between Active and Passive Conversion Approaches

James T. Richardson (1978, 1980) used the term *conversion career* to describe "multiple-event conversions" by people trying out a series of religious alternatives (Richardson and Stewart 1978: 31).[7] The adolescent converts to the Jesus Movement that they studied arrived there after prior involvement with, first, the drug scene and, then, the peace movement. Finding the Lofland/Stark (1965) model too static, Richardson and Stewart (1978: 33–34) propose a dynamic model of conversion with "three broad categories: prior socialization, contemporary experiences and circumstances, and the opportunity structure available for problem definition and resolution." They make a good summary of the existing conversion literature, which they put in a table (ibid.: 39). According to this literature, conversion will always occur when there are positive ties with members of the religious group, whether or not congruence of the group with the potential convert's predispositions is high, medium, or low (cells 1, 4, and 7 in Richardson's Table 1). However, if there are negative affective ties with group members, the potential convert will never convert (cells 3, 6, and 9 in Table 1). Thus they follow the conventional sociological models by stressing the importance of social networks (see above). Social factors come first, personality second, and contingency factors third.

In a later article, Richardson (1985: 164) presents a new way of looking at conversion models: "The old conversion paradigm, with its deprivation and strain assumptions about the passivity of human beings, and its over-emphasis on the individual, is giving way, at least partially, to another view of conversion. This new view stresses humans as volitional entities who assign meaning to their action and to the actions of others within a social context." The prototype of the old "passive" paradigm is the "sudden, dramatic, and emotional" conversion of Paul on the road to Damascus by "a powerful external agent" (ibid.: 165). Modern versions of the passive paradigm include the brainwashing or mind control models, for which there is little empirical evidence (ibid.: 166).[8]

The new and "active" conversion paradigm goes back to the definition of "volitional conversion" by William James (1958: 169; see also above), as opposed to conversion by self-surrender. The Lofland and Stark (1965) article was important in the rise of the active conversion model, which was later developed more fully—see above—by Straus (1976, 1979), Bromley and Shupe (1979), and Travisano's seminal (1970) work. "This view stresses an active subject seeking to develop their own 'personhood,' an emphasis that has caused something of a Kuhnian crisis because of the traditional paradigm's assumption of a passive subject" (Richardson 1985: 167). After 1965–1970, "several scholars have, in one way or another, recognized a more active subject 'working out' one's own conversion. They have noted that conversion to new religions often means a series of affiliative and disaffiliative acts that constitute a conversion career, and that individuals are often deciding to behave as a convert, playing the convert role, as they experiment with or reaffirm their personhood ... with affection and emotional ties playing key roles" (ibid.: 172). Following Long and Hadden (1983), socialization is seen as the key factor in bringing the needs of the individual and the needs of the religious group together.

Richardson gives a good overview of the conversion literature, and was the first to note the paradigm shift toward the new, "active" conversion approach. Especially in the psychology of religion, many authors, including the authors following a brainwashing model, had followed a more traditional "passive" conversion model. The influence of the Pauline conversion model is probably strongest within the Christian groups and churches themselves, but Richardson does not address this "institutional" factor, apart from his reference to socialization and role theory. However, his conceptualization of the dissatisfied individual undergoing conversion is again unconvincing, following a long tradition of sociological conversion research. It does not move much beyond voluntarism, limited only by socialization (but how, when, and for how long?), social networks, and contingency factors like coming into contact with representatives of certain religious groups. The rational choice models of conversion, which are dealt with subsequently below, provide a more detailed model of individual action—although they often ignore the social context or simply take it for granted.

Rational Choice Conversion Models: Gartrell and Shannon, Stark and Finke

The theory of Gartrell and Shannon (1985: 33) "views recruits to religious movements acting as if they weigh rewards and sanctions from affiliation with members and non-members in addition to weighing the attractiveness of movements' beliefs and ideas." The expected "rewards" constitute "social-emotional outcomes like ... approval, love, respect, and cognitive outcomes: ... individual beliefs about, for example, the nature of the world and one's place in it" (ibid.: 34). Based on their study of the Divine Light Mission, without specifying the age of the converts, Gartrell and Shannon (1985: 37) conclude that "prior to their involvement with the DLM, converts encountered a series of problems that could not be explained by conventional means ... perceived ineffectiveness of counseling and therapy is perfectly associated with conversion." From their data, the authors develop various axioms, of which 4 and 5 are particularly useful:

> *Axiom 4* (Cognitive Utility) The utility of a NRM's beliefs varies directly with (a) their ability to explain problematic features of individuals' stocks of knowledge and (b) the degree to which they are consistent with existing elements of individuals' belief systems. ...
> *Axiom 5* NRM's vary in the degree to which they supply cognitive rewards as part of a conversion strategy and also in the timing of the supply. (38)

They add that "groups such as the UC ... and Mormons ... downplay core beliefs initially to avoid alienating prospective converts" (ibid.: 39). Finally, Gartrell and Shannon (1985: 42) point out that "persons highly constrained by dense, strong contacts with foci outside of a New Religious Movement (for example, family, school, work) have few reserves of time, effort and emotion to invest in participation in the movement. On the other hand, those with little investment in outside foci are prime candidates for conversion." They conclude that conversion is "a linkage between individual attributes and dispositions and movement goals and ideologies" (ibid.: 45).

Gartrell and Shannon conceptualize the individual as a rational actor, experimenting with conversion to see if one gains more by changing religious affiliation than by not doing so. They do not distinguish between others levels of religious activity beside conversion. Socialization endows people with certain religious preferences. When they encounter new problems, which cannot be solved with conventional religious ideas, people will experiment with other religious groups and try out new religious ideas. If they like the social and cognitive rewards of these groups, they will stay and become members.

Stark and Finke's (2000) rational choice approach to religion has a much longer history, which I have analyzed elsewhere (for example, in Gooren 2006a: 43ff. and in Chapter 2). Stark and Finke (2000: 114) first of all distinguish between *conversion* ("shifts across religious traditions") and *reaffiliation* within the same religious tradition. They stress that "most people remain within the religious organization into which they were born, and most of those who do shift from one organization to another remain within the religious tradition into which they were born ... fewer than one percent of Americans convert" (ibid.: 115). They present no sources to corroborate these strong statements, but rely on GSS data.[9] Like Lofland and Stark (1965), they assume people converted because "interpersonal attachments to members overbalanced their attachments to nonmembers. In part this is because ... social networks make religious beliefs plausible and *new* social networks thereby make *new* religious beliefs plausible" (Stark and Finke 2000: 117).

The authors (ibid.: 119) propose that "marriage and migration are major factors tending to produce shifts in attachments ... Consequently, reaffiliation and conversion will be more prevalent among the geographically mobile, teenagers, and young adults, at marriage and following a divorce. Each of these generalizations is supported by a wealth of research." Stark and Finke (2000: 122) make the new claim that "converts very seldom are religious seekers, and conversion is seldom the culmination of a conscious search." Seeing themselves as seekers is something that is part of converts' "biographical reconstruction" (Snow and Machalek 1983, 1984; see above). Converts are attracted and recruited by churches, which are actively competing with each other on the religious market (see Chapter 2 for a critique). This is a surprisingly passive conceptualization of the individual—particularly in a self-proclaimed rational choice approach to religion.

But, somewhat contradictorily, Stark and Finke (2000: 123) also conceptualize individuals as active agents, rationally weighing the benefits of one religious group over another. If these individuals are not seekers, where does the need to change one's religion come from? Stark and Finke again follow Lofland and Stark (1965) in seeing tension and stress as the source for individual dissatisfaction, but they do not describe how this process works for rational actors. Nor do Stark and Finke address Heirich's (1977) detailed and methodological critique of the tension factor (see also Bromley and Shupe 1979 and Kox et al. 1991). Following Leatham (1997: 295), Stark and Finke (2000: 123 ff.) distinguish between conversion and recruitment, but again they do not specify how one would follow the other. Although their rational choice model of religion is highly controversial, many studies are being conducted to obtain empirical evidence to explore its assumptions and hypotheses (see Chapter 2 for an overview).

Rambo: A Holistic, Interdisciplinary, and Open Process Model of Conversion

Rambo (1993: 4; 1999) provides an interdisciplinary model of open-ended stages that combines insights from psychology, sociology, anthropology, and theology. He adds: "Each theory and model offered by these various disciplines should ideally take into account a religious system's own model of conversion, appreciate the metaphors and images of the anticipated transformation, and delineate the methods used by the given religious community to realize its goals ... Most studies of conversion to date have been too narrow in orientation." He therefore rejects universalistic approaches, because each conversion is a unique process through time, contextual, and influenced by "multiple, interactive, and cumulative factors" (ibid.: 5). Rambo's holistic approach identifies four components, "cultural, social, personal, and religious systems," which "are of varying weight in each particular conversion" (ibid.: 7).

Rambo's (ibid.: 13–14) broad typology of conversion stresses "how far someone has to go socially and culturally in order to be considered a convert":

(1) *Apostasy*/defection: the repudiation of a religious tradition ... by previous members.
(2) *Intensification*: the revitalized commitment to a faith with which the convert has had previous affiliation, formal or informal.
(3) *Affiliation*: the movement of an individual or group from no or minimal religious commitment to full involvement with an institution or community of faith.
(4) *Institutional transition* (or denominational switching): the change of an individual or group from one community to another within a major tradition [for example, Baptist to Presbyterian].

(5) *Tradition transition*: the movement of an individual or a group from one major religious tradition to another [for example, from Roman Catholicism to Islam, my explanation].

From all these components, Rambo (1993: 16–18, 165–70) develops a process-oriented, seven-stage model of conversion:

(1) **Context** is the dynamic force field in which conversion takes place … We forget that the political, religious, economic, social, and cultural worlds are shaped by people. Conversely, people are shaped by the socialization processes of the wider world.

Rambo (1993: 22) distinguishes the macrocontext of political and ecological systems from the microcontext of family, friends, and religious or ethnic community:

(2) **Crisis** forces individuals and groups to confront their limitations and can stimulate a quest to resolve conflict, fill a void, adjust to new circumstances, or find avenues of transformation.
(3) **Quest** is, to some degree, influenced by a person's emotional, intellectual, or religious availability … Most converts are actively engaged in seeking fulfillment.
(4) **Encounter** … brings people who are in crisis and searching for new options together with those who are seeking to provide the questors with a new orientation … Potential converts as active agents are skillful in seeking out what it is they want and rejecting what they do not desire.
(5) **Interaction**: Relationships are often the most potent avenues of connection to the new option. Important here are rituals, rhetoric, and role-learning and -playing.
(6) **Commitment** is the consummation of the conversion process. Central to the converting process is the convert's reconstruction of his or her biographical memory and deployment of a new system of attribution in various spheres of life.
(7) **Consequences**: a radically transformed life, … a sense of mission and purpose, … security and peace. [… But] One may find that the new orientation is not what one expected.

This seven-stage approach is systematic and very extensive, reviewing a huge amount of conversion literature involving cases from all over the world. No firsthand research was carried out, although various interviews with converted Christians are mentioned. Rambo's own involvement with conversion studies seems highly personal (1993: xi–xiv). Although he frequently mentions the possibility of negative influences of conversion, on the whole he seems to have a positive bias toward it. For example, his hypothesis 2.5 states that "the most talented, creative people will take the lead in conversion" (ibid.: 41).

Looking carefully, one can see that Rambo's open-ended process model synthesizes and weaves together in seven stages generations of conversion research—especially the Lofland and Stark (1965) model. Context was influenced by work on conversion in cultural anthropology; crisis owes a huge debt to both William James and Lofland and Stark; quest goes back to Lofland and Stark and especially Straus (1979); encounter comes again from Lofland and Stark (and mission studies); interaction is directly adapted from Lofland and Stark, while commitment is clearly based on Snow and Machalek (1983, 1984). The use of theology, however, seems rather limited and normative: "The central effect of theology on conversion is the creation of norms for what is expected in the conversion process and the shaping of expectations and experiences of converts" (Rambo 1993: 181).

The Rambo approach covers the full spectrum of religious activity and offers a very useful synthesis of many previous models, including their weaknesses. Rambo (1993: 13, 33, 53, 112, 136, 137) mentions disaffiliation various times, but does not analyze systematically why or when it happens. The concept of the individual is again that of an active agent (the "seeker"), but there is a keen sense of the constraints of culture, personality, society, and the religious group one is converting to. "The reality is that some people are passive and others are active, and many people are active at certain times and passive at other times" (Rambo 1993: 59). The power of religious organizations is explored by referring critically to the brainwashing model (ibid.: 158). That gender is important in conversion matters is mentioned once ("Do women experience conversion differently from men?"; ibid.: 174), but not elaborated in the approach. Another omission is the lack of reference to the age of the converting subject and so to the importance of distinguishing between conversions at various moments in the individual life cycle.

Rambo's approach to analyzing conversion is very useful for researchers, but it did not cause many follow-ups, and there was only one testing (Kahn and Greene 2004). Rambo's own (1999) follow-up mentions fifteen theoretical options on conversion, including globalization and feminist theory (1999: 263), narrative and identity theory (ibid.: 265), and even psychoanalytic theory (ibid.: 266). After reviewing literature on conversion and personality change, Paloutzian, Richardson, and Rambo (1999: 1073) conclude that "religious conversion influences people's goals, strivings, and identities, but seems to have little appreciable effect on basic personality structure. Inversely, certain types of personalities may be more prone to religious conversion than others."

Kahn and Greene (2004: 238) also note that "Rambo's model has been accorded little empirical attention." Their sample consisted of sixty-five female and forty-five male participants, ranging from twenty-five to eighty-four years, "who self-identified as having experienced religious conversion." However, there was no control group, as was deemed essential by Kox et al. (1991). Kahn and Greene (2004: 240, 256) conclude that the context stage was impossible to operationalize, and the encounter stage was probably "not a distinct dimension in religious conversion experience." They do, however, regard these results as an empirical validation of Rambo's seven-stage model and his fivefold typology of conversion.

A Critique of Conventional Conversion Approaches

After this extensive summary and assessment of thirteen conversion approaches, it is easy to see the overlap and repetition between them. On the other hand, there are also a number of biases, omissions, and unsubstantiated claims of being representative in these approaches. I will first present my criticisms and then use these as the basis for a new theoretical synthesis in Chapter 2.

First of all, the *conceptualization of the individual,* as it appears from most authors, is insufficient. It seems too voluntaristic for active conversions, suggesting that seekers are free to decide which group to join (for example, Lofland and Stark 1965; Straus 1979), and too deterministic for passive converts, suggesting that groups can control the minds of converts. Part of the voluntarism was corrected by a socialization approach (for example, Greil 1977; Richardson and Stewart 1978; Long and Hadden 1983). It is remarkable that the sociological approaches to conversion in the 1970s, starting with Travisano (1970), put much more emphasis on individual attributes (identity, socialization, seekership, networks), neglecting and almost downplaying the importance of the religious organization. A holistic conversion approach acknowledges that each conversion is the result of interaction between the individual and the religious organization and thus necessarily incorporates both active and passive elements as part of a continuum (Rambo 1993: 59).

Second, Greil (1977: 116) and Greil and Rudy (1984: 311) noted that some approaches confused *recruitment* by a church with conversion. Less attention was given to the worldview of the subject prior to conversion (that is, *preaffiliation*), or to members becoming regular visitors without ever reporting a conversion experience (*affiliation* in my typology: see Chapter 2). A change in religious activity always seemed to imply a conversion experience. It is true, however, that most authors did acknowledge the existence of other levels of religious activity. Lofland and Stark (1965) distinguished four levels: preconverts, verbal converts, total converts, and core members. In fact, six out of thirteen approaches used a four-tier typology of religious activity. Bromley and Shupe (1979) and Long and Hadden (1983) stressed the importance of disaffiliation by acknowledging the high dropout rates following conversion in many religious groups. However, none of the approaches systematically tried to explain both conversion and disaffiliation in one model.

Third, most conversion approaches (for example, James 1958; Lofland and Stark 1965; Snow and Machalek 1983, 1984; Rambo 1993) seem to include a certain determinism, implying that *crisis and tensions* are at the heart of conversion. However, many authors (for example, Bromley and Shupe 1979, Heirich 1977, and Kox et al. 1991) present highly convincing data questioning the importance of stress and crisis. There were often able to do so by using a control group of nonconverted adolescents that suffered from very similar stress and tension as the religious converts. The earlier studies had never used such control groups. Stress and tension may certainly contribute to people looking for a conversion experience, but they are not necessary conditions for a change in religious affiliation.

Fourth, the attempts to construct general and *universal conversion models* have failed. Lofland and Stark (1965) never pretended to do this, but many scholars took their model to be universal. Snow and Machalek (1984) and Rambo (1993), however, clearly established that it was not. Even the socialization and role-learning approaches to conversion, which obviously corrected many of the flaws and biases of the earlier models, cannot be assumed to be cross-culturally valid. Socialization and role learning are heavily influenced by cultural patterns and social control.

Fifth, then, an important empirical limitation is the fact that the thirteen approaches mentioned here were all based on research regarding *Christian churches or NRMs*. In fact, three used the Unification Church as a case and two studied the Divine Light Mission in detail. The scope of these studies is also severely limited by the fact that they were all conducted in the United States or in Europe. Unfortunately, there are almost no instances of these models being applied to the 85 percent of the world population living in the other continents. A systematic approach should be able to deal with conversion all over the globe, and should not be limited only to Third World countries, as was the case with some anthropological conversion approaches.

Sixth, the conversion approaches clearly suffered from *disciplinary biases*. Psychologists tend to focus on personality and crisis, sociologists stress social networks and institutional factors, and anthropologists explore social and cultural factors. Only rarely did authors attempt to synthesize approaches from various scientific disciplines, as for instance Rambo (1993) did and as the new conversion careers approach will attempt to do as well.

Seventh, with only a few exceptions, all of the approaches assessed here followed James (1902) in limiting themselves to study conversion among adolescents and young adults. Almost all authors based their approaches, models, and conclusions on research among people under thirty, students, or young couples. Strictly speaking, this *age bias* means that these approaches are therefore unable to shed any light on conversion in midlife or conversion at old age. A systematic approach should include older informants from all cycles of life.

Eighth, the young adult bias is further exacerbated by a *gender bias*. Although all researchers had female informants, hardly any attempt was made to explore possible differences in the conversion experience between men and women. This did not even happen among the scholars following a socialization approach, in which gender has an acknowledged impact. It should also be mentioned that, again with only a few exceptions, not much attention is given to the influence of social class on conversion. Most informants, in fact, seem to come from a middle-class background—just like the researchers who study them (cf. Kilbourne and Richardson 1988: 15; Richardson 1985: 175–76).

Finally, almost all of the conversion approaches mentioned here conform to the typical social science bias of tending to *reduce religion to social-economic or psychological factors*. James ([1902] 1958: 201, 366 ff.) concluded that the extreme religious experiences of his informants originated in their subconscious mind. Most approaches ignore what people believe in (that is, beliefs and doctrines), why this is so important to people, and how they express their religious feelings in rituals, emotions, or phenomena like speaking in tongues. Ironically, the rational choice models, which are often blamed for being highly reductionist, actually stress the importance of belief as a way for churches to compete (Gartrell and Shannon 1985; Stark and Finke 2000). The importance of rituals is also stressed in Bromley and Shupe (1979), Snow and Machalek (1984), and especially Rambo (1993). The social science approaches to conversion would benefit greatly from the input of theology and mission studies to balance their inherent tendency to reduce religion to societal, cultural, or individual factors.[10] Hence, it is now time to introduce the conversion career approach in more detail.

2

The Conversion Career

Turpin has a specific understanding of conversion in mind, namely the lifelong process of awakening, repentance, justification, and regeneration—the order of salvation as Wesley understood it ... the *via salutis*, a lifelong process of conversion and sanctification in the life of the believer.

(*Kenda Creasy Dean 2007: 405*)

The Need for a New Approach to Conversion

In Western Europe, most people live thoroughly secularized lives, without any participation in churches. In the United States, someone who was born as a member of the Presbyterian Church may remain active in that church until death (although the extent and intensity of actual church participation may, of course, vary greatly through time). Other people, who were also born as Presbyterians, however, might join a Pentecostal church group in their twenties and remain active in that new group—or not. Nominal Catholics in Latin America, people born into Catholicism without ever feeling committed to it, might convert to a Pentecostal group. In sub-Saharan Africa, people may grow up fulfilling the demands of traditional religion and witchcraft, until converting to Christianity or Islam. But following this religious conversion, will they reject witchcraft entirely or simply give a new meaning to it (demons and bad spirits)? Will they put it in another framework of meaning that will guarantee its continued importance in their lives?[1]

It is difficult to address these questions with the older models of religious conversion,[2] which were mostly based on research in the United States in the 1960s and 1970s and influenced by the situation of religious pluralism in that country. The older models were, moreover, mostly based on studies of conversion from one Christian church, sect, or movement to another. Another problem is that the classic process models of conversion from the scholarly literature of the 1960s and 1970s took a chronological rather than a phenomenological perspective on religious change. Converts were supposed to go through a fixed set of various stages, each stage bringing him or her closer to full participation in the new religious group.

However, the old models are difficult to use in the contemporary situation of growing religious pluralism in Latin America and other parts of the developing world. In process models of religious conversion, like the original one by Lofland and Stark (1965), converts of various world religions at different moments in time are supposed to go through similar stages, until finally reaching a full or spiritual conversion. It is clear from, for example, the literature on conversion to Protestantism in Latin America that such process models of conversion are no longer valid, because there seem to be no fixed stages and because the patterns of conversion are much more complex and heterogeneous.[3] Hence, a new model of religious conversion should also be connected, in the contemporary context of pluralism and/or globalization, to recent sociological theories on the importance of religious economies and the religious market.[4]

In my opinion, any new approach to conversion should define a limited set of parameters that can be empirically observed and investigated during fieldwork at different locations worldwide. These parameters would be needed to identify the factors in the conversion process, the indicators that show an actual conversion has taken place, and the indicators that demonstrate an ongoing church commitment after conversion. Hence, I use the more dynamic concept of the conversion career, which includes all periods of higher or lower participation in one or more religious groups during a person's life history. It has three important elements:

1. Factors in conversion.
   The main factors in conversion are contingency factors, individual factors, cultural factors, institutional factors (for example, the church position toward cultural practices, evangelization activities, the charisma of the leaders, the appeal of the church organization and doctrine), and social factors (especially the role of social networks).
2. The indicators to show that an actual conversion has taken place.
   The most promising indicator of conversion is related to changes in converts' speech and reasoning. Converts supposedly engage in "biographical reconstruction: reconstructing their past life in accordance with the new universe of discourse and its attendant grammar and vocabulary of motives."[5]
3. The indicators that demonstrate an ongoing church commitment after conversion.

Clifford Staples and Armand Mauss (1987) have shown that the three factors mentioned by Snow and Machalek[6] as conversion indicators are actually commitment indicators. These are: the adoption of a new master attribution scheme, the suspension of reasoning by analogy, and the embracement of the convert's role. These I use below, in my conversion career typology of religious activity, as indicators of *confession*: a theological term describing a new social identity following a successful conversion. But the definition of what constitutes a successful conversion is strongly influenced by the multiple scholarly disciplines that study it.

The Bias of Scholarly Discipline

Each scholarly discipline tends to emphasize certain sets of factors, often at the price of ignoring or slighting others, and this can be clearly discerned in a chronological look at the development of models of individual religious change since 1900 as was done in Chapter 1:

(1) The *psychology of religion*, following in the footsteps of early pioneer James, has obviously tended to focus on individual and contingency factors (especially stress), hence leaning to a more pathological treatment of conversion. This perspective was dominant until the 1960s and mostly studied adolescent subjects who converted to a more "emotional" form of Christian (evangelical) religion.

(2) *Sociologists of religion* became interested in studying conversion to deviant new religious movements (NRMs), often with an Eastern origin, like the Hare Krishna or Rev. Moon's Unification Church, which had arrived in Europe and the United States since the 1960s. The subjects were again mostly adolescents, often with a middle-class background, leading sociologists like pioneers Lofland and Stark (1965) to acknowledge the importance of social networks and the institutional attractions of these "cults." Moral panic in western society also led to the rise of a second, competing perspective: the brainwashing or mind control approach in psychology.

(3) The traditional perspective of *anthropologists of religion*, starting with Malinowski and continuing until the 1970s with Horton, was to focus on relatively isolated peoples in a colonial setting. These peoples often abandoned their traditional religious perspective in exchange for becoming a member of a world religion (usually Christianity, sometimes Islam). The interaction of the traditional and the world religion led to theorizing on, for example, syncretism or "popular religion." Hence the primary focus of anthropologists was on cultural factors, although social and institutional factors

also received considerable attention, especially when these were seen as interacting with culture.[7]

(4) *Theologians* and religious studies scholars generally looked at religious change in a long—stretching over 2,000 years—historical perspective, while stressing the importance of doctrine and belief, church forms, cultural context, and especially the lifelong process of searching for God (*metanoia, ephistrein*). The focus was mostly on institutional and cultural factors.

Snow and Machalek (1984: 178) identified three waves of modern research on religious conversion. First, from 1900 to roughly 1930 (I would say 1940), it came mostly from theology and psychology, with authors like James [1902] and Nock (1933). Second, from 1950 to 1960, they see the rise of the psychological brainwashing or "mind control" model after the Korean War (1950–1953), with authors like Sargant (1957) and Lifton (1961)—later followed by Singer and others. Third, after 1965, a huge wave of sociological conversion research was inspired by the arrival and increasing success of (usually Indian or Japanese) NRMs in the western countries, with authors like Lofland and Stark (1965), Bromley and Shupe (1979), and many others mentioned below. I think a modest fourth wave started in the 1990s and gained momentum especially after September 11, 2001: conversion to (and *from!*) Islam.[8]

Synthesizing Conventional Conversion Approaches

Chapter 1 analyzed thirteen approaches to conversion from various disciplines in the social sciences. What are the best elements of the approaches used by scholars of conversion in the past that should be integrated in a new approach to conversion? I mention the basics here:

First, following William James (1958 [1902]), the emphasis on subjective *religious experience* should be reestablished, since this tended to become neglected, especially in the process models inspired by Lofland and Stark (1965). This is connected to the necessity of developing a new conceptualization of the *individual* that is neither voluntaristic nor deterministic.

Second, conversion in the narrow sense should always involve a change in religious worldview and hence a change in *identity*. Travisano's (1970: 598, 605) empirical indicators of conversion as a "rupture with a former identity" and the "ubiquitous utilization of the convert identity in all areas of life" are still highly relevant in contemporary studies of religious conversion worldwide.

Third, in the concept of *spoiled identity* (Greil 1977; Goffman 1959, 1963) conceivably lies the basis of changes in levels of religious activity.

In the course of their life, individuals all over the world occasionally encounter new problems that make new solutions necessary (Greil 1977; Heirich 1977; Gartrell and Shannon 1985).

Fourth, spoiled identities may turn some people into religious *seekers* (Straus 1979). This seeking quest, however, will always be constrained by their prior cultural and religious *socialization* (Greil 1977). In turn, socialization is, of course, strongly gender-specific.

Fifth, as people consider the pros and cons of membership in a particular religious organization competing for members on the religious market (see below), they always make an implicit or explicit rationalistic cost-benefit analysis (Gartrell and Shannon 1985; Gooren 1999; Stark and Finke 2000).

Sixth, it is clear that religious commitment is built up through *role learning* and mastering (Bromley and Shupe 1979). Conversion is clearly shaped by prior (religious) socialization and subsequent role learning and mastering (Long and Hadden 1983). The influence of gender is equally important in both of these influences and should be further explored.

Seventh, it is fruitful to analyze the organizational side of the conversion process by using the concepts of *incorporating activities* (recruitment and monitoring of affiliates), *creating activities* (showing the requirements for membership in the religious group), and the *shaping* of the (pre-)affiliate's behavior with a religious code of conduct and the application of sanctions (Long and Hadden 1983).

Eighth, the empirical *indicators* of conversion as developed by Snow and Machalek (1983, 1984) should be carefully operationalized to analyze changes in religious activity levels. More research is necessary to test if biographical reconstruction is, indeed, the only true indicator of conversion (Staples and Mauss 1987). The development of a master attribution scheme, the tendency to prefer iconic over analogical reasoning, and the embracement of the convert's role must also be empirically observed in converts (cf. Rambo 1993), unless they are simply signs of a more general religious commitment (Staples and Mauss 1987).

Ninth, spoiled identity, seekership, and "conversion" are clearly influenced by significant others (relatives, friends, and acquaintances) through the *social networks* the individual belongs to (Lofland and Stark 1965). It is clear from the literature that almost all people (men *and* women) are recruited into religious organizations through social networks.

Tenth, recruitment by religious organizations is influenced heavily by the competition happening between various religious groups in most parts of the world (Gooren 2006a). Whether one likes the term or not, this religious competition means that, in fact, a *religious market* is already in operation. More research is needed in different cultural contexts to analyze how the religious market functions; it is clearly influenced by state regulation of religion (Chesnut 2003; Gill 1998; Stark and Finke 2000).

Eleventh, the methods by which religious organizations compete on the local (and perhaps national) religious market must be carefully described and analyzed. What *recruitment strategies and methods* do they use to attract people's interest? Do religious organizations employ *cultural politics* to attract members and compete?

Twelfth, the *cultural or societal factors* that influence differences in religious activity levels must be carefully described and explored. Rambo's (1993) seven-stage model will help to integrate these influences with other factors.

The Conversion Career

The *conversion career* is defined as "the member's passage, within his or her social and cultural context, through levels, types and phases of religious participation" (Droogers, Gooren, and Houtepen 2003: 4). It represents a systematic attempt to analyze shifts in levels of individual religious activity: preaffiliation, affiliation, conversion, confession, and disaffiliation. The key elements of this new approach are: a five-level typology of religious activity, the need for a life cycle approach, and a systematic analysis of the many factors influencing changes in individual religious activity (contingency, individual, cultural, institutional, and social factors).

A typology of religious activity

If conversion is to remain a useful concept for scholars, it has to be carefully distinguished from its original religious—Christian—context and meanings (see Introduction). In other words, conversion needs to be thoroughly reconceptualized to move it beyond the Pauline idea of a unique and once-in-a-lifetime experience. To be able to do this, it is necessary to develop a typology of religious activity that includes more dimensions than just disaffiliation and conversion. A review of the existing literature from psychology, social and cultural anthropology, sociology, and religious studies allows us to distill five primary levels of individual religious participation:[9]

Preaffiliation is the term used here to describe the worldview and social context of potential members of a religious group in their first contacts to assess whether they would like to affiliate themselves on a more formal basis.

Affiliation refers to being a formal member of a religious group. However, group membership does not form a central aspect of one's life or identity.

Conversion, used here in the limited sense, refers to a (radical) personal change of religious worldview and identity. It is based both on self-report and on attribution by others. These others can be people from the same religious group, but also outsiders.

Confession is a term from theology for a core member identity, describing a high level of participation inside the new religious group and a strong "missionary attitude" toward nonmembers outside the group. People thus use the testimony they have of their conversion experience to engage in evangelizing activities.[10]

Disaffiliation refers to a former involvement in an organized religious group. This category may include various relationships with institutionalized religion. It can refer to an idiosyncratic personal religiosity, for example, New Age. But it can also stand for an unchurched religious identity: either an apostate rejecting a former membership or an inactive member who still self-identifies as a believer. In the last case, the difference between affiliation and disaffiliation can be very small.

A prime factor for religious change should logically be some sort of *dissatisfaction* with current religious affiliation. This dissatisfaction may take three forms that can be operationalized in a fairly straightforward manner for the preaffiliation stage:

(1) People may go from disaffiliation to reaffiliation with their former (for example, childhood) religious tradition. This could be the same variant (for example, orthodox Roman Catholicism) or a special variation of this tradition (for example, the Catholic Charismatic Renewal movement). Rambo (1993: 13) calls this type of religious change *intensification*.

(2) People may go from disaffiliation to affiliation with a religious organization in the same religious tradition as their childhood religion. According to the literature, which admittedly deals mostly with the United States, this is the most frequent and usual form of religious change. It involves Roman Catholics becoming Presbyterians, Methodists joining a Pentecostal church. This common type of religious change is called *institutional transition* in the typology by Rambo (1993: 13).

(3) However, people may also go from their current state of disaffiliation to affiliation with an organization representing an entirely different religious tradition than their childhood religion. Christians may become Muslims, or vice versa. Hindu untouchables in India became Buddhists in large numbers in the 1950s and 1960s (Rambo 1993: 149). This most drastic and often dramatic type of religious change is called *tradition transition* by Rambo (1993: 13).

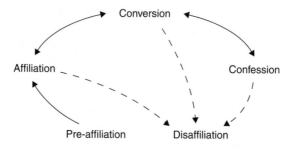

Figure 2.1   Movement between levels of religious activity in the conversion career approach

Affiliation, conversion, confession, and disaffiliation are the dynamic levels of individual religious activity, but they do not necessarily follow any chronological order during a person's conversion career (see Figure 2.1). A person may go from affiliation to conversion, which is how leaders of religious groups like to see it, or vice versa. Similarly, people may go from conversion to confession and vice versa. From the literature it is also clear that many go from affiliation, conversion, or even confession to disaffiliation. The many terms that are available for this—apostasy, backsliding, dropping out, church desertion, et cetera—and the severity of the punishments for apostasy in some traditions already attest to the frequency of its happening.

Individual levels of religious activity in the conversion career

1. *Preaffiliation:* life situation and worldview of person before affiliation or conversion.
   Church term: "visitor."

2. *Affiliation:* formal membership in a religious group, without change of identity.
   Church term: "member"; "baptized member."

3. *Conversion* (in the limited sense of the conversion career approach): a (radical) change of religious identity, followed by a commitment to a (new) religious group.
   Church term: "convert"; "full member"; "baptized member."

4. *Confession:* a core member identity with a high level of participation inside the (new) religious community and a strong evangelism on the outside.
   Church term: "leader"; "core member"; "deacon"; "missionary."

5. *Disaffiliation:* no church membership or visits.
   Church term: "inactive member"; "seeker"; "unchurched Christian."

A life cycle approach

Since changes in the level of religious activity may occur throughout the entire lifespan, a life cycle approach to conversion obviously becomes necessary. However, most of the literature on religious change[11] deals with conversion during adolescence. Hence it is imperative that a more systematic approach should distinguish the various levels of religious activity during the various phases of people's lives. At the very least, the different aspects and dynamics of five phases of the life cycle should be recognized: childhood, adolescence, marriage, midlife, and old age. These phases are operationalized both in terms of age and life phase (for example, a teen-aged couple with children would be in the "marriage" stage). The next step is to analyze the factors that influence a person's religious activity at a certain stage of his or her life.

Factors influencing religious activity

The many factors influencing religious participation and change must be identified, operationalized, weighed, and analyzed in the conversion career approach. I identify five main groups of factors influencing changes in the individual level of religious activity:

1. Social factors:
   - The influence of relatives, friends, and/or acquaintances on joining or leaving a religious group (social networks).
   - The influence of religious group members through socialization and role learning.
2. Institutional factors:
   - Dissatisfaction with current religious group or with religious inactivity.
   - Presence of different religious groups.
   - Recruitment methods of these religious groups (evangelization, TV/radio messages).
   - Appeal of their leaders, organization, practices, rituals, rules of conduct, ethics, values, and doctrine (cf. "interreligious competition").
3. Cultural and political factors:
   - Appeal of the culture politics of a religious group (its view on local culture and society; its view on local politics).
   - Tension between religious group and society and/or a specific ethnic group or country.

4. Individual factors:
- A religious worldview or need to become religiously involved (prior socialization).
- A personal need to give a concrete expression to feelings of meaning (or meaninglessness).
- A personal need to seek meaning and/or spirituality in a religious group.
- A personal need to change one's life situation.
- Certain character traits inducing religious participation (for example, insecurity; cf. the "convert personality").[12]
5. Contingency factors:
- An acutely felt crisis or turning point (for example, illness, alcohol problems, joblessness, marriage, divorce, migration).
- A religion-based or inspired solution to the crisis (for example, healing, finding a new job through a church member).
- A chance meeting with representatives of a religious group (for example, missionaries).

The Methodology of the Conversion Career Approach

To trace people's conversion career, a systematic combination of various methods (triangulation) is necessary. Our international Conversion Careers research program on global Pentecostalism,[13] for example, used the following methods: a survey of literature; open, topic list, and informal interviews; collecting life histories; and participant-observation in multiple religious groups. All research projects used standardized checklists for the interviews and participant observations. In all four continents, interviews were conducted with members corresponding to each of these five categories. Since each religious group has its own definitions of formal membership (affiliation) and conversion, our comparative and multisite research in four continents teased out both commonalities and differences.

The conversion careers approach does not attempt to locate the basis of conversion exclusively at the level of the individual, (religious) organization, or society—as so many approaches, for example, in sociology, have done in the past. Instead, it identifies the many factors operating at each of these three metalevels and pays special attention to their *interconnections*. Conversion can be viewed as a way to break out of old social roles and embrace new ones. As this never happens in a social or cultural vacuum, every individual conversion is unique. However, scholars must always attempt to identify both the patterns and the local variations, which are invariably influenced by the competition between different religious groups on the local religious market (see Chapter 3).

3

Conversion and the Religious Market

Do you really wonder why Catholics are leaving the Church? Look around you, Cardinal. People have lost respect. The rigors of faith are gone. The doctrine has become a buffet table. Abstinence, confession, communion, baptism, mass—take your pick—choose whatever combination pleases you and ignore the rest.

(*Opus Dei Bishop Aringarosa in Dan Brown,*
The Da Vinci Code, *2003, 545*)

Introduction

The aim of this chapter is to give a critical overview of the religious market model to assess its usefulness for analyzing religious conversion in local contexts characterized by increasing pluralism. The model's central idea is that religious organizations are competing for adherents who make (rational?) choices from the available options in a metaphorical "religious market."[1]

I first present the main tenets, contributions, and possible shortcomings of the religious market model at three different levels of analysis: micro, meso, and macro. Then I describe and analyze the approach to religious conversion that follows from the religious market model, as developed in Stark and Finke (2000: 114–38). I end with my own evaluation of the usefulness of the market model for empirical research in a situation of religious pluralism. The conclusion will sketch the connections between individual religious demand and the supply side of competing religious organizations.

In polemical style, Stark and Finke refer to secularization theory as the "old paradigm" and put it in the grave: "Secularization, R.I.P."[2] They note that the older religious monopolies are wearing down and that religious pluralism is increasing in most parts of the world. In apparent contradiction to secularization reasoning, however, this growing religious pluralism does not seem to undermine the *plausibility structure*[3] of monopolistic religions and hence does not lead to secularizing trends. In fact, quite the contrary seems to take place: religion is alive and well all over the world as a structure for meaning-making, as the basis for individual or group morality, and, of course, as the foundation for various "fundamentalist" political movements, especially in their Christian, Muslim, and Hindu variants.

In the religious market model, pluralism and religious freedom are the essential conditions that make religious competition between religious organizations possible. In turn, this religious competition is supposed to form the foundation of strong individual religious commitment and thus also of conversion to another faith.

Since the religious market model has caused some confusion and much controversy, I first present its main tenets, contributions, and possible shortcomings at three different levels of analysis: the micro, meso, and macro; the micro-level involves the supposed rational actor, the meso-level is concerned with the competitive religious organization, while the macro-level deals with the religious market as part of a greater religious economy. Then I describe and analyze the approach to religious conversion that follows from the religious market model, as developed in Stark and Finke.[4] I end with my own evaluation of the usefulness of the religious market model for empirical research in a situation of religious pluralism.

The Micro-Level: The Rationalist Actor

A first difficulty of Stark and Finke's religious market model concerns the very definition of rationality. The basic assumption of human rationality is formulated by Stark and Finke as follows: "Within the limits of their information and understanding, restricted by available options, guided by their preferences and tastes, humans attempt to make rational choices."[5] Bankston, however, points out:[6]

> Rationality consists of at least three major dimensions: teleology, systematization of ends, and consistency of goals. On all three dimensions, human actions can be interpreted in terms of degrees.

Spickard[7] equates goal-oriented teleological action with means-ends rationality, which in turn is based on Weber's *zweck-rationalität* or instrumental rationality. Spickard also mentions two other forms of rationality: value rationality (Weber's *wert-rationalität*, which is based on a higher value or ideal) and *cathekontic* rational action (which is based on the responsibilities following from an individual's social networks). The religious market model seems to be limited to teleological, goal-oriented rationality only. Because of this limitation, the other two kinds of rationality cannot be conceptualized or analyzed further.

Stark and Finke[8] (2000: 119) build on the human capital approach, as developed by Iannaccone.[9] This approach postulates that "in making religious choices, people will attempt to conserve their social and religious capital." Social capital refers to interpersonal attachments, religious capital to "the degree of mastery of and attachment to a particular religious culture" (ibid. 2000: 120). From this it follows that people are reluctant to change their religion and if they change at all they usually stay within the same religious tradition,[10] because it takes time and effort to learn new doctrines and about new people (for a further elaboration, see the section called "The Religious Market Model and Conversion" below).

A second important criticism of the religious market model is its failure to analyze the impact of various crucial influences on the actors: beliefs,[11] community,[12] the sociocultural and political context,[13] gender,[14] preferences (and its measurable form, choices),[15] and scarcity of resources.[16] All of these influences could be considered as constraints on the actors and should be included in some form or other in the religious market model (see below).

Although Stark and Finke (2000: 38) nowadays acknowledge that "people may differ in what they want and how much they want it" and that "culture ... and socialization ... will have a substantial impact on preferences and tastes," much of their model still depends on the old adage "There's no accounting for tastes." A great deal of the variation is so idiosyncratic that people have no idea how they came to like certain things.[17] The religious market model is thus, third, criticized on ideological grounds for being individualistic, since the frame of reference is always the individual rational actor. Social action is considered as the aggregate result of the decisions by individuals and groups to achieve certain religious goals.

A fourth main problem of the religious market model is its tendency to equate the aggregate of individual decisions with the formation of so-called social equilibria.[18] Spickard[19] correctly points out that both religious monopolies and religious free markets lead to growth instead of equilibrium. Moreover, "the rational choices of individuals do not necessarily result in the rational organization of groups or societies."[20] The aggregate totals of rational individual decisions can be highly irrational.

Fifth, the religious market model in its current form is basically a supply-side model. Religious demand is considered as a constant and hardly explored further, as was done in the "old paradigm": secularization. Furthermore, Robbins[21] correctly points out that "supply-side and demand-side factors promoting change are often subtly intertwined and may sometimes even be difficult to distinguish." Many authors[22] have shown that religious demand is obviously not stable across individuals, countries, and time. Bankston also correctly notes that a model that looks only at religious supply

> tends to present a top-down perspective, in which individuals are chiefly passive recipients of collectively created goods ... Choice in religious activity and expression is widely acknowledged to be affected by social class ... social mobility ... racial or ethnic minority status ... socialization by family and peers ... and individual life events ... None of these influences are distributed in a constant fashion across history or geography.[23]

However, according to Stark and Finke,[24]

> When people change churches or even religions, it is usually not because their preferences have changed, but because the new church or faith more effectively appeals to preferences they have always had.

For Stark and Finke, the main proponents of the religious market model, the only variation in demand consists of people looking for religious organizations in either high or low tension with society. This forms the basis of a limited group of identifiable religious market *niches* that can be exploited by competitive religious organizations on the religious market. I get back to this issue in the next section.

The Meso-Level: The Competitive Religious Organization

Ironically, religious market theory was originally tied in with Peter Berger's perception that "secularization brings about a demonopolization of religious traditions and thus, *ipso facto*, leads to a pluralistic situation."[25] A crucial quote soon followed:

> The key characteristic of all pluralistic situations, whatever the details of their historical background, is that the religious ex-monopolies can no longer take for granted the allegiance of their client populations. Allegiance is voluntary and thus, by definition, less than certain. As a result, the religious tradition, which previously could be authoritatively imposed, now has to be *marketed*. It must be "sold" to a clientele that is no longer constrained to "buy." The pluralistic situation is, above all, a *market situation*.

In it, the religious institutions become marketing agencies and the religious traditions become consumer commodities. And at any rate a good deal of religious activity in this situation comes to be dominated by the logic of market economics.[26]

In recent years, of course, Berger has publicly deconverted from his ideas on secularization;[27] he never systematically worked out the concept of the religious market in his work. This was done by Stark and Bainbridge since the early 1980s, culminating in *A Theory of Religion*,[28] and later by Iannaccone,[29] and especially Stark and Finke.[30] These three authors are consistently working on a growing body of literature, refining their formal models of religious markets, human capital, and rational choice. They refer to this as a "new paradigm," although others are careful to distinguish a religious markets approach from a rational choice approach.[31]

The functioning of competitive religious organizations—Stark and Finke's focus on Christianity is revealed in their preference for words like *church* and *sect*—is rather straightforward. According to Stark and Finke,[32] churches are "in relatively lower tension with their surroundings," whereas sects are in relatively higher tension and often tend to reject the existing social order. A central tenet of religious market theory is that "the higher a group's level of tension with its surroundings, the higher its average level of commitment."[33] Integrating the religious market model with the church-sect typology, Stark and Finke assume that successful sects will gradually lower their tension with society, causing first schisms and later decreased growth and stagnation. In a relatively unregulated religious economy, new religious organizations will then appear, entertaining higher levels of tension with society, thus generating higher commitment, and, presumably, higher growth.[34]

An important commitment variable is congregation size. "Congregational size is inversely related to the average level of member commitment ... The larger the congregation, the less dense the social networks within the group."[35] Large congregations supposedly lead to less dense social networks (or bigger *external* networks), lower church commitment, and "less efficient monitoring of member behavior." This will allow for the presence of more *free-riders*, who use the networks of the religious group without committing themselves to it. Moreover:

> the more prevalent member ties to external networks, the greater the pressure on the group to reduce tension ... As religious organizations grow, their administrative sector grows more rapidly ... As the administrative sector expands, authority will become more centralized and policies will be standardized.[36]

When this happens, the formation of new congregations of the same church group is often made more difficult:

> By contrast, most growing religious movements place few restrictions on the formation of new congregations. From the Pentecostal sects to the growing segment of independent churches, new congregations are the work of religious entrepreneurs—volunteers who felt called to begin a new church.[37]

Stark and Finke point out that churches trying to limit religious competition with other churches often become complacent.[38]

The fundamental question for Stark and Finke thus becomes: *why do religious organizations change so that they no longer enjoy mass appeal?* Their own answer is:

> It is not church-switching that is the primary dynamic in religious economies. Rather, it is *the shifting of religious firms from niche to niche* that has the greatest impact on the overall religious economy.[39]

Here we get to an interesting paradox, because religious organizations would seem to be limited in their options to attract adherents. After all, doctrine, beliefs, and organizational forms cannot be changed so easily. Thus, the competitive performance of a religious organization depends mostly on how it positions itself on the local religious market, which in turn is part of a larger religious economy. "All religious economies include a set of relatively stable [aggregated] market niches ... Niches are market segments of potential adherents sharing particular religious preferences (needs, tastes, and expectations)."[40] Shared preferences are usually based on shared social characteristics such as social class, socialization effects, gender, ethnicity, and particular life events.[41]

According to Stark and Finke,[42] the overall result is a religious economy that is made up of six religious niches: ultraliberal (for example, New Age groups, liberal Episcopalians); liberal (Presbyterians, Methodists, Episcopalians); moderate (Lutherans, Baptists); conservative (Southern Baptists, Adventists); strict (Mormons, Jehovah's Witnesses, and almost all Pentecostal groups); and ultrastrict. Members of religious organizations in the ultrastrict niche even employ outwardly visible markers in their clothing—for example, Benedictine monks, Hare Krishna members, and orthodox Jews. I doubt, however, whether Muslim women wearing headscarves in western societies would always belong to the ultrastrict niche.

A very obvious way for churches to compete among each other, although this is not mentioned by Stark and Finke, is by exploiting their particular level of tension with the surrounding society through a so-called culture politics, which refers to the position taken and strategy adopted with regard to the local social and cultural environment, in this case based on religious views.[43] This perspective often forms the basis of a church policy, which in turn may be used to compete for members with other churches.[44]

Summarizing: in a situation of religious pluralism, competing religious organizations find and cultivate their own religious market niches. This allows them to cater to the needs of social groups sharing certain characteristics (for example, social class, gender, or an ethnic identity). Religious organizations should maintain a moderate to high tension with society, use this tension through a culture politics to compete with other religious organizations, and make high demands on their own adherents. All of this will, in turn, raise their members' commitment. They should also rely on voluntary leaders, because pastors who receive fixed salaries have no incentive to compete for members. After all, more members simply mean more work against equal wages in this situation.

Stark and Finke's strong emphasis on a high/low tension typology in religious competition seems rather limited. It is true that they also mention six other methods for religious organizations to compete among each other; these are all aimed at reducing the risk of supernatural rewards for their members: ritual, prayer, miracle, mystic experience, a committed leadership setting a fine example, and testimony.[45] However, Stark and Finke only mention these as methods to reduce risk; they do not operationalize these to explore the ways in which religious organizations actually use them to compete for members. As I mentioned earlier, religious organizations are constrained in their freedom to change their forms of ritual or prayer for improving their competitive advantage on the religious market.

The whole concept of religious competition, so essential to the religious market model, remains curiously vague and unelaborated.[46] It seems to me that religious organizations also compete with the attraction of their doctrine, their rules of conduct, their particular use of missionaries, their general evangelizing efforts, and the strength of their organization.[47] But again, these are not elements that religious organizations can manipulate at will. One could think of it as a continuum, in which changes in doctrine are hard to achieve and relatively rare (as they might damage the group's credibility), changes in rules of conduct are somewhat easier to accomplish over time, missionary efforts are even easier to adjust, and the typical organizational forms are likely to mutate constantly under changing societal and economic influences.

The Macro-Level: The Religious Economy and the Religious Market

A religious economy consists of all the religious activity going on in any society: a "market" of current and potential adherents, a set of one or more religious organizations seeking to attract or maintain adherents, and the religious culture offered by the organization(s).[48]

This quote clearly suggests that "market" is used as a metaphor. The formulation "in any society" seems to indicate that the religious economy is a *national* phenomenon, suggesting that the religious market on which churches are supposedly competing must be a *local* one. However, nowhere in their book do Stark and Finke define the religious market—or their crucial concept of religious competition.[49]

Instead, Stark and Finke choose to work out the implications of religious pluralism:

> Pluralism arises in unregulated markets because of the inability of a single religious firm to be at once worldly and otherworldly, strict and permissive, exclusive and inclusive, expressive and reserved, ... while market niches will exist with strong preferences on each of these aspects of religion. Thus, no single religious organization can achieve monopoly through voluntary assent—religious monopolies rest upon coercion. By the same logic, it becomes clear that religious monopolies can never be fully monopolized.[50]

They continue, however, by noting:

> Our model of religious economies holds that the demise of religious monopolies and the deregulation of religious economies will result in a general increase in individual religious commitment as more firms (and more motivated firms) gain free access to the market. Many factors can slow the development of vigorous pluralism ... Deregulation of a religious economy often is more apparent than real. The government may announce a policy of religious freedom, or at least of religious toleration, but continue to grant special privileges and financial aid to the traditional monopoly firm.[51]

Thus it becomes clear that the religious market model of Stark and Finke is actually a full-fledged supply side model of religious change. They suggest that the old secularization paradigm focused on the matter of religious demand. A crucial quote soon follows:

> Why did people's religious preferences change? Do people suddenly develop new, unmet religious needs? Not only do we think this is the wrong answer, we think it answers the wrong question. We shall suggest that religious demand is very stable over time and that religious change is largely the product of supply-side transformations.[52]

By taking this polemical stand against researching religious demand, and by attributing religious change largely to changes in supply-side processes,

Stark and Finke are guilty of the same one-sidedness that they reject in the secularization paradigm. The available evidence overwhelmingly shows that religious demand *does* vary according to historical, social, and cultural influences. Lower religious demand in Western Europe, for example, certainly affects the functioning of the religious economies, because this makes it more worthwhile (that is, goal-oriented and rational) for many Christian churches there to cooperate rather than to compete with each other. This might explain why Western Europe was such a favorable environment for the development of the ecumenical movement.

Besides, the religious market model allows only one criterion for success: membership growth. Implicit is the bias that if a religious organization and its leaders really stand for something, they have to be able to convince others to join them and thus build up a strong church with highly committed members. But it is quite possible that other religious organizations will have very different criteria for success: perhaps the correct performance of elaborate rituals, obtaining a moral influence on politics and society, or pursuing ethical ideals such as the fight against poverty.

These differing criteria for church success touch upon a central issue: *how, exactly, do religious organizations compete?* Obviously, their freedom to change their religious products is rather limited: religious organizations cannot change their doctrines, organizational forms, or beliefs that easily—but they can certainly downplay them.[53] Moreover, religious organizations do not compete in the national religious economy, but on the local religious market. How does this religious market actually function? To explore this question, I turn to Olson, because Stark and Finke do not really address it.

Olson[54] suggests using the concept *religious opposition*, since Stark and Finke nowhere define their crucial concept of religious competition. After reviewing the literature, Olson finally concludes that religious competition and religious conflict operate through different causal mechanisms:

> Where religious opposition (either competition or conflict) is weak, particular religious groups can grow more easily and rapidly. Where religious opposition is greater, the growth of any particular group is more difficult and slow and the loss of adherents is more likely.[55]

Adding the concepts of *substitutability* and *diversity* to the religious market model is another refinement achieved by Olson:

> [T]he competition facing any religious group should be defined as the number of nearby *substitutes* for that religious group. Thus, if congregation B is the only other nearby congregation that people attending congregation A would want or be able to attend, then congregation A faces less competition than another congregation, call it C, for which there are four nearby

congregations ... But is there only one religious market in which all religious groups compete as potential substitutes? ... [O]ne might reasonably ask whether a local mosque should be considered a substitute for a nearby Lutheran church.[56]

Olson then succinctly points out:

> Stark et al.'s claim that small market share reflects higher competition rests on the assumption that the competing groups are denominations rather than congregations. It is not entirely clear whether Stark et al. see religious diversity and the choices it implies as an element of competition (Stark and Finke 2000, 201) or if they view religious diversity as a separate variable that is the *result* of competition ... These two implicit meanings of religious competition (substitutability and diversity) may actually be contradictory ... Substitutability implies similarity, diversity implies difference.[57]

It is useful to end with Olson's final conclusion:

> [I]f government regulation is a form of religious conflict and the invigorating effects of conflict operate primarily through conscious demand-side, rather than supply-side, processes, then it may be that demand-side, rather than supply-side, processes dominate most of the world's religious economies.[58]

I think that religious market theory has two *implicit* presuppositions that are rarely mentioned or systematically addressed. First, religious market theory tends to identify (perhaps even equate) religiosity with church membership, although especially outside of the United States there seem to be large segments of the population who consider themselves religious without belonging to a religious organization.[59] Second, active church membership is seen as the prime indicator of religious commitment, although there are many religious traditions (Roman Catholicism is an obvious example) that seem to foster a more passive church membership, stressing, for example, the importance of ritual behavior. This is one reason why Stark and Finke always have to control for Catholics in their multilevel analyses (they may have to do the same for Buddhists if this group continues to grow strongly). It also explains why the highly demanding Mormon Church, with its strict code of conduct and its emphasis on missionary work, always forms such a perfect illustration of their theory.[60]

Stark and Finke cannot adequately analyze the mechanisms behind the huge numbers of inactive members that Christian churches all over the world have. Even the Mormon Church, Stark's favorite case,[61] which seems to embody all the elements that the religious market model considers important in religious organizations, suffers from levels of inactivity that lie between 45 and 75 percent.[62] This shows the need to develop a *typology* of religious activity that includes more dimensions than just disaffiliation and conversion, which I do in the conversion career approach.

Summarizing: although supply-side processes can explain much of the behavior by religious organizations, a model that neglects religious demand can never tell the whole story. Rather than focusing only on supply (as in Stark and Finke's religious market model) or only on demand (as in the traditional secularization model), an approach is needed to systematically explore and analyze the *connections between the individual demand of religious believers and the supply of competing religious firms.*

The Religious Market Model and Conversion

Stark and Finke[63] distinguish between *conversion* ("shifts across religious traditions") and *reaffiliation* within the same religious tradition. However, they conveniently ignore the practical problems of *defining* a religious tradition. Do Protestants and Catholics really belong to the same Christian tradition? If so, do Mormons and Jehovah's Witnesses as well? Are Sunni and Shia Muslims really part of the same tradition: Islam? Nowhere do Stark and Finke even begin to explain or specify their criteria for defining a "religious tradition."

Unbothered by these considerations, Stark and Finke stress that:

> most people remain within the religious organization into which they were born, and most of those who do shift from one organization to another remain within the religious tradition into which they were born ... fewer than one percent of Americans convert.[64]

Stark and Finke present no sources to corroborate these strong statements, but rely on General Social Survey data.[65] However, putting all shifts *within* Christianity in the same category of reaffiliation makes it hard to explore and analyze the often quite dramatic nature of these shifts. If the members of your family are all Presbyterians, then being the first to become a Pentecostal might lead to your being cut off from your relatives. Why are people willing to pay such a high price? Moreover, conversion to another religious tradition or to another world religion might be rare, but it *does* happen—and its consequences can be even more dramatic. How do Stark and Finke explain this?

Stark and Finke (2000) follow the classic Lofland and Stark (1965) conversion model here, which stresses the importance of social networks (see Chapter 1). People converted whose interpersonal attachments to members overbalanced their attachments to nonmembers. In part this is because ... social networks make religious beliefs plausible and *new* social networks thereby make *new* religious beliefs plausible.[66]

Social networks also constitute the reward for conforming and converting. A crucial quote soon follows:

In effect, conversion is seldom about seeking or embracing an ideology; it is about bringing one's religious behavior into alignment with that of one's friends and family members.[67]

Stark and Finke cite evidence supporting this explanation, but they never deal with the obvious critiques. First, how many families anywhere in the world can boast of such religious unity and harmony? Multiple religious affiliations are increasingly common in the United States, Latin America, and even Western Europe.[68] Second, why do so many people convert to a religion that is not shared (and is often, in fact, rejected) by their friends and family members? This frequently happens on the basis of only a few contacts with members from this new religion. How could this conversion be based solely on the *hope* of building up a new social network, even to the point of paying such a high price: losing an already existing social network?

Another conventional wisdom of the conversion literature, converts as seekers (see Chapter 1), is plainly rejected by Stark and Finke:

Converts very seldom are religious seekers, and conversion is seldom the culmination of a conscious search ... Many studies of conversion have noted that one of its primary aspects is the "reconstruction" of the convert's "biography" to show how conversion was the end result of a self-conscious search for truth. This is neither duplicitous nor irrational. Rather, having embraced a new faith, people look back over their prior lives and reinterpret various past events and thoughts in the light of the present (Beckford 1978; Snow and Phillips 1980; Snow and Machalek 1983; Greil and Rudy 1984; Staples and Mauss 1987; Machalek and Snow 1993).[69]

Stark and Finke neglect to mention, however, that autobiographical reconstruction is a highly controversial issue among scholars: see Chapter 1.

The factors underlying conversion are quite basic and very sociological, according to Stark and Finke:

Marriage and migration are major factors tending to produce shifts in attachments ... Consequently, reaffiliation and conversion will be more prevalent among the geographically mobile, teenagers and young adults, at marriage and following a divorce. Each of these generalizations is supported by a wealth of research (Beit-Hallahmi and Argyle 1997; Wuthnow 1978; Tamney and Condran 1980; Iannaccone 1990; Stark and Bainbridge 1985, 1997).[70]

Marriages are supposed to be more stable if both partners share the same faith, the same religious tradition, or if one or both lack religious capital:

> When mixed religious marriages occur, the couple maximize their religious capital when the partner with the lower level of commitment reaffiliates or converts to the religion of the more committed partner.[71]

The importance of belief is thus recognized in a rather limited sense in the concept of *religious capital*, which is defined as "the degree of mastery of and attachment to a particular religious culture."[72] This leads to two propositions:

> In making religious choices, people will attempt to conserve their religious capital ... The greater their religious capital, the less likely people are either to reaffiliate or convert ... Research confirms that converts are overwhelmingly recruited from the ranks of those lacking a prior religious commitment or having only a nominal connection to a religious group.[73]

Another proposition states: "When people reaffiliate or convert, they will tend to select an option that maximizes their conservation of religious capital."[74] That is why Stark and Finke write that most people with a Christian background will prefer to join the Mormons and not Hare Krishna.

But I am left with two questions. First, why do people with a Christian background opt to become Mormons, instead of becoming Pentecostals? Second, why don't many people from India join Hare Krishna, since this would certainly conserve their religious capital? The Hare Krishna movement is not at all popular in India,[75] suggesting, again, the importance of context, culture, and history—in short, the importance of religious demand.

Conclusion: Connecting Religious Demand and Supply

I think that scholars need not choose between paradigms that limit their explanations of religious activity to either religious supply or religious demand, but they should instead strive to describe and analyze the connections between demand and supply in each local context. I will sketch a few possible outlines of such an alternative religious market approach here.

Some of my criticisms are also expressed by Steve Bruce, a vigorous critic of the religious market model.[76] Although Bruce believes that "most behavior is rational," he categorically rejects "the very specific claim that economic (as distinct from social, legal, or political) rationality provides a useful model for understanding religious belief and behavior."[77] Bruce's main criticism is that rational choice supposes utility:

> as we have no way of knowing the best balance of costs and rewards, and hence cannot say where utility lies, what appears to be an explanation is reduced to tautology ... Another religion is not an alternative to a religion in the sense that a Ford is an alternative to a Chrysler.[78]

Bruce prefers alternative sociological explanations for pluralism, secularization, and religious vitality in the United States. He quotes the conclusion of Chaves and Gorski (2001) after an evaluation of twenty-six articles: "The empirical evidence contradicts the claim that religious pluralism is positively associated with religious participation in any general sense."[79]

However, many authors have shown that churches do compete for members in certain local contexts, even on simple matters like geographical location.[80] It is also clear that successful churches can force formerly dominant, yet currently unsuccessful, churches to adopt some of their methods. This has happened, for instance, with the Roman Catholic Church in response to Pentecostal growth in Latin America.[81]

The acceptance of the religious market model has been hindered by Stark's tendency to engage in fierce polemics, and also by the confusion caused by Stark and Finke themselves in *Acts of Faith*. Sometimes they seem to imply that the religious market is a *metaphor*[82] for a pluralist situation of competing religious groups trying to win new members by selling their "product" called conversion. However, at other times the religious marketplace is a *literal* description of certain churches merchandising religious products (videos, cassettes, books, etc.) and using marketing strategies to identify, approach, and recruit new members. Many of the opponents of the religious market model direct their criticisms at the second usage, while ignoring or neglecting the first.[83] I have shown in this chapter that many elements in Stark and Finke's model can be criticized. However, I think that a careful application of the religious market model as a metaphor is useful to analyze religious actors and organizations in the new situation of pluralism that is developing in many parts of the world.

Some researchers simply seem to find the central idea of the religious market model degrading. They resent the notion that religious organizations are competing among each other in a manner similar to commercial enterprises. They abhor the implicit idea of religion as a commodity. However, competition between theories, models, and ideas—or paradigms—is considered to be the essential element in the historic development of science, at least since Popper and Kuhn. The idea of competition between religious ideas and the organizations that sponsor them could be seen as similar.

An alternative use of religious market theory should certainly take into consideration Olson's criticisms, which I discussed above. The concept of religious competition needs more refinement and has to be operationalized. Religious organizations cannot easily change their basic doctrines. This would obviously undermine their credibility. However, the religious organizations' practical rules of conduct and organizational structures can change over time and improve their competitive advantages on the religious market. What religious organizations can also do is to stress certain elements of their doctrine and rules of conduct and use these to develop a *culture politics*. This might include a critique on certain local customs—like *machismo* in Latin America—or on the dominant religion.[84]

Another adaptation should address and remedy the way belief is left out almost entirely in the religious market model as developed by Stark and Finke—except as *religious capital* and as a way to reduce supernatural risks (see above). Here, the conversion career approach will depend on conceptualizations of conversion and belief from theology.[85] What exactly do people believe? How does this belief shape their conversion(s)? And how does their belief in turn influence the organization and concrete forms of the churches they belong to?

A final adaptation involves adding the element of religious demand to the religious market model, which we do in the conversion career approach. The *conversion career* is defined as the member's passage, within her/his social and cultural context, through various levels of religious activity. This can happen in the same religious organization or in a new one. Conversion is only part of the story of people's varying levels of religious activity during their entire lifetime. The conversion career approach thus synthesizes approaches to conversion in psychology, sociology, anthropology, and theology to address the above criticisms. Hence, the conversion career approach aims to connect the religious demand of individual actors with the religious supply of competing religious organizations on the religious market.

I concluded in Chapter 1 that people always make a cost-benefit analysis when considering the pros and cons of membership in a certain religious organization. I would prefer to speak of *rationalist* actors, instead of rational actors.[86] People are not trying to maximize the utility of membership in a religion, but they tend to make certain cost-benefit analyses. People are not engaged in goal-oriented action, but rather strive for Weber's value rationality and especially in Spickard's *cathekontic* rationalist action that is based on the responsibilities following from one's social networks. This ties in nicely with the supreme importance of social networks in conversion, as mentioned in Chapter 1.

Stark and Finke (2000) basically developed a supply-side model of religious change that focuses on religious competition. But they never define or operationalize this concept. Olson concludes: "Where religious opposition (either competition or conflict) is weak, particular religious groups can grow more easily and rapidly."[87] Local religious competition depends on the number of nearby substitutes for a particular religious organization.

Some of Stark and Finke's conclusions are relevant for the conversion career approach and open for empirical verification. Is it always true that the higher a religious group's tension with society is, the higher will be its average level of commitment? Is congregation size inversely related to the average level of member commitment? How do religious groups find and occupy their market niche? Is a religious group's capacity for competition with others dependent on its leadership and hence on its power structure?

The religious market model identifies many different ways for religious organizations to compete with each other: ritual, prayer, miracle, mystic experience, a committed leadership setting the example, and testimony.[88] Based on my own research, I added doctrine, rules of conduct, the use of missionaries, evangelizing efforts, and the attraction of its organization.[89] The religious market model is biased in its indicator of success: membership growth. Religiosity is simply equated with church membership. Active church membership is the prime indicator of religious commitment; the religious market model cannot deal adequately with dropouts and apostasy.

Stark and Finke conclude that social networks are the motor behind conversion and also constitute its most important reward. Hence, religious organizations are also competing with the strength of their social networks and the access that they allow their members to these. The religious market model is thus very useful for analyzing certain elements within the conversion careers approach, more specifically the importance of institutional and social factors and their interconnections.

It is now time to insert a healthy dose of empirical data into the discussion, which has been rather abstract until now, by taking a closer look at concrete stories of conversion and disaffiliation in Chapter 4 (Europe and the United States) and Chapter 5 (Latin America).

4

Stories of Conversion
and Disaffiliation

I began to see that the fundamentalist "born-again" mentality was not all
it was cracked up to be. The born-again gospel promises joy and peace
of mind, but it does so by prolonging childhood ... Fundamentalism fills
you with answers before you even think to ask the questions.

(*Robert Price, 1997, a theologian involved in "Heretics Anonymous"*)

Introduction

This chapter elaborates the conversion careers approach in detail, stressing particularly the interconnections between the various types of factors.
This is done by a careful analysis of the five typical conversion careers
that can be distinguished from the general literature on Christianity in
the United States and Western Europe.[1] These five conversion careers are
entitled: parental religion, religious seekers and shoppers, committed converts, confessing leaders, and disillusioned disaffiliates.

A few things stand out in the general literature on conversion:

First, more conversion stories can be found among psychologists
than among sociologists, with the anthropologists located somewhere
in between. Hardly any of the many authors dealt with in Chapter 1, for
example, included actual conversion stories in their publications.

Second, the available scholarly literature is biased in concentrating
heavily on—in the conversion career terminology—committed converts
and confessing leaders. Chapter 5 shows that a similar bias exists in the
literature on Latin America.

Third, it is not easy to find detailed disaffiliation stories in the literature.
In the end, I had to resort to the Internet to find some additional stories

of disaffiliation. In the process, I also discovered some interesting conversion stories floating about in cyberspace. My sources, then, are varied, but always contemporary. Almost all stories originate in the United States, but there are a few from (Western) Europe as well. No (de)conversion story presented here goes back more than forty years.

Parental Religion

I take as my starting point the limited conversion career of people who remain active in their parental religion, whether they "convert" or not. The lack of literature on the spiritual biographies of these people is puzzling. Do scholars consider them less interesting perhaps? Or do they assume that only a *change* of religion merits scholarly attention? Is it conceivable that secularization theory biased many scholars in Western Europe into believing that people continuing their parental religion will eventually—automatically, as it were[2]—drop out altogether and become disaffiliated to any religion?[3] The disaffiliation category is dealt with in the last section of this chapter and does include these cases.

Kristen: Teenage religion and family trauma

One interesting story of ongoing successful socialization—up until the point of research, at least—involves Kristen, a sixteen-year-old Southern Baptist in a "southwestern state" (Arizona or New Mexico), whose case is described extensively in Christian Smith's brilliant study of religious teenagers in the United States, *Soul Searching* (2005: 17–25): "When Kristen was six years old and living in California, I learned, her father separated from her mother and shortly thereafter committed suicide. Not only that, but it was Kristen and her mother and four brothers and sisters who were the ones who found him dead on a bed with a self-inflicted gunshot wound to the head." Although Kristen's family had been Christian all her life, this event seems to have been a religious turning point:

> It was something tragic … But you know, God used it in a great way and to shape my mom … My mom then just really trusted in God and went to the Word [the Bible] and then two years later she took us out of school and home-schooled us for three years and we did some really great curriculum that was just all focused around the Bible. She taught us, you know, God is the father to the fatherless and she didn't let us become depressed and clinging on to what had happened.
>
> (Smith 2005: 18)

Since the suicide, Kristen's family has been deeply involved in church, Sunday school, Wednesday-night children's church activities, vacation Bible school, and more. Kristen says she definitely feels close to God:

> It's kind of, you know he's just there, you know he's watching over you, it's great but you [also] know that there are going to be hard times and that he's still there then ... I grew up in a Christian home and my parents, they taught me this, they live it out every day to me in their lives. And watching how God has worked in other people's lives and how he got my mom through stuff. And church and Sunday school and seeing other people there, listening to the pastor's message. And reading his Word, being in it daily and finding out stuff.
>
> (Smith 2005: 19–20)

Kristen seems to love her church youth group, led by a volunteer youth pastor, for its fellowship, sharing, encouragement, and teaching from the Bible. Kristen believes in divine miracles, the supernatural, angels, and demons, although she has never had a direct experience with any of them. Smith asked whether she ever has doubts about her faith:

> I have. I have wondered if I'm really saved and if I died would I go to heaven and is there really a God. But even if there's not, I don't think there's anything else better to believe 'cause then you've lost hope. Sometimes I wonder, there's so many other religions and they all claim to be true and I claim mine to be true and so, you know, what's right? And then I think, whatever it is, [Christianity] is the best that I've heard.
>
> (Smith 2005: 20)

At sixteen, Kristen is among the youngest informants whose stories are quoted extensively here. Her story perfectly illustrates the enormous impact religious upbringing and religious socialization have on people's lives. In her case, this is emphasized by the fact that her mother provided Kristen with three years of primary schooling at home "that was just all focused on the Bible." With such intense socialization, combined with her father's suicide when she was only six, it is perhaps no great surprise that she turned out to become a committed believer of her mother's religion.

When stories of successful socialization into the parental religion appear, they are typically framed as "revitalization" or reawakening stories. Lewis Rambo (1993: 13) calls this type of conversion *intensification*: "the revitalized commitment to a faith with which the convert has had previous affiliation, formal or informal." However, he does not pursue this category any further.[4]

From reviewing the literature it appears that intensification almost always follows a certain pattern. Through a friend or a relative, people come into contact with another denomination or another current within the religious tradition people grew up with. They like the people in this group and over time learn more about its distinguishing features. Through various mechanisms, similar to Long and Hadden's (1983) *shaping activities* analyzed in Chapter 1, their religious commitment is gradually enhanced. Three typical examples are discussed below. One is from Sweden and takes the form of conversion from mainstream Protestantism to Pentecostalism, the second involves an Episcopalian Church in California, and the third takes the form of conversion from mainstream Catholicism to the Catholic Charismatic Renewal in the United States.[5]

Betty: Spiritual rebirth through the television

In her landmark study *Charisma and Community* (1987), Mary Jo Neitz analyzes the "conversion experience"—the term some of her informants used and she adopted as well—of mainstream Catholics joining a suburban Charismatic Renewal prayer group called Precious Blood. Based on her informants' reports, Neitz (1987: 63) does not hesitate to apply the term *conversion* to the Catholic Charismatic Renewal (CCR), because she "constantly heard participants claim 'it changed my life.'" Here I discuss one conversion story and one story on the importance of speaking in tongues for the new members of the prayer group.

The following conversion story, for which Neitz (1987: 76) first provides the background information, is told by Betty Zelezak:

> On August 22, 1972 at 2:30 in the afternoon something happened that changed her life. She regards that date as her birth date—her spiritual birth date. She claims that she became alive on that date.
>
> At the time she was in her early thirties and had five children in grade school and one at home. She describes herself as being isolated in her home. Her husband, a policeman, neither shared her experiences nor felt she could share in his; there was little communication between them. She said that her only contact with the outside world was the "Mike Douglas Show," which she watched every day on television. One day Pat and Shirley Boone were featured on the [talk] show. They spoke about the problems they had had in their marriage and how those problems had been resolved when Shirley was born again, and Pat noticed the change in her and wanted what she had. Betty identified with the Boones; she felt their problems were identical to hers and she wanted what had happened with them to happen to her.

Betty Zelezak said:

"It took about a minute from the time I shut off the television to get to the bedroom. And I went in there and I got down on my knees and I threw myself across the bed and I said to the Lord, 'God, I know what I heard and I just want to thank you. I just want to receive what you have got for me. I want you to come and live in me like that.' I remember putting up my hands and all of the sudden the tears started coming and I didn't even understand why I was crying ... I could really feel a sense of warmth coming down into my chest and just building up until I felt like my chest was going to explode. And I knew at the moment that the Lord was really present within me."

It is not difficult to recognize all the factors identified in the conventional approaches to conversion, as presented in Chapter 1: remembering the exact date and time of the conversion experience, a situation of crisis, loneliness, an unhappy marriage (with six children), and the sense of isolation from the outside world.

Noteworthy is the somewhat late conversion age, early thirties, and the fact that the catalyst was a television talk show—not even a religious program. But the subsequent events are typical: the plea to God for an intervention and a change in her life, the raising of her hands, the spontaneous flooding of tears, and the sense of warmth inside. Since Neitz did not provide basic data on Betty's background and how the informant ended up in the Precious Blood prayer group, no further analysis is possible.[6]

Sara: Seeker returns to renewed parental church

A different kind of reactivation, "recovery of tradition," can be found in Roof (1999: 26). Sara Caughman is a forty-four-year-old, married graphic designer:

Though raised as a Christian, she was not active in any church for many years. Like so many in her generation she dropped out in her twenties, disillusioned with organized religion. But to hear her tell it, there was a "great turnaround" in her life. She dates her religious rebirth in her early forties to the time her older brother died from cancer at 46—a sobering moment that led her to think through again what her own life was about.

This was aided by a change in her Episcopalian congregation in southern California:

"We're no longer squabbling about what it means to be the church. There is a new mood. You know when you walk into the place it's now an inclusive church, open and ministering to people of all kinds and lifestyles. It's alive spiritually. It's been a great turnaround from the old place it used to be."

"You like it a lot better, I can tell."

"You bet. We're serving people, representing Christ to the needy and not just to the comfortable middle-class people. People are genuinely excited about what we are doing. The place had become dry and empty. It was death to the spirit. Rote religion."

(Roof 1999: 27)

Roof presents this explanation of the changes in St. Michael's Episcopalian Church:

The turnaround in the congregation came several years ago when a young group of members, with the leadership of the new rector, organized a study group to explore new methods of ministry. "It was a small group when we started," she says, "but we had great enthusiasm and a sense that we would not stop until we felt marked by the Spirit and bound to our mission." Almost all in this group were [Baby] Boomers and many of them—as with Sara—had read books on improving the self, dealing with stress and feeling good about themselves, and enhancing their lifestyles ...

Then came the creation of a base community of six to eight people, meeting weekly to read the Bible and study liberation and feminist theologies and varying styles of Christian spirituality ...

A middle-class Boomer culture pervades the congregation with its sensitivities to women, child care, single parents, singles and divorced, gays and straight. The congregation's spiritual style is shaped by its celebration of openness and diversity; its members will tell you that here, unlike many other churches in their experience they feel accepted ...

Sara describes her own turnaround as "a journey in faith toward greater understanding of the meaning of life" ... Her spiritual style reflects an accommodation to the larger seeker themes in today's culture but without sacrificing historic religious language or religious self-understanding ... "Many people," she says, "start out walking it as if they are alone but discover fellow travelers along the way." At St. Michael's, such people are welcomed in their spiritual pursuits.

(Roof 1999: 28–29)

Here we have an example of a seeker (the topic of the next section below) who returned to her parental religion after a spiritual quest, which Roof considers to be typical of the baby boomer generation in the United States. After reading very different books on subjects ranging from feeling good about oneself to liberation theology, middle-class boomers started a small base community and social projects for the homeless. In the process, they changed their congregation into a seeker church (see below; cf. Sargeant 2000). This parental church renewal ended their religious seeker-ship almost before it began.

Continuous conversion in Pentecostalism

Another good example of "a revitalized form of Christianity gone stale" is offered by Simon Coleman (2003: 19) in an article on a Swedish Pentecostal "Faith" ministry called Word of Life. He notes that the great majority of its Uppsala members were already active Christians before they joined, most of them coming from other Pentecostal churches or from the Lutheran state church.

Coleman (2003: 17) makes a plea for a broader definition of conversion that he names *continuous conversion*:

> It can imply that movement of the self toward charismatic conviction is an ongoing process ... it indicates a blurring of the boundaries of identity between religious affiliations; and it suggests that analysis of conversion practices should focus not only on the potential neophyte, but also on broader sets of social relations and ideological representations that include and influence the evangelizing believer.

In the end, Coleman (ibid.: 18) sees conversion as:

> a set of ritualized practices that are key to Swedish charismatic identity on personal and collective levels ... My argument is that conversion as a mul-tivalent idea and as a quality of action permeates the charismatic life, and under the right conditions it can help sustain that life, whether outsiders are persuaded to enter the body of Christ or not.

Through participation in the group, members are involved in a huge number of "conversionist" activities: evangelization, rituals, Bible courses, excursions, et cetera. Hence, Coleman (2003: 22) concludes:

> The personal revitalization that is a feature of Word of Life participation is intimately linked to practices that appear to orient the self beyond parochial and physical limits ... The Faith rhetoric of outreach can be read as denying the possibility of limiting ambition in cultural, economic, or even political terms, or of submitting to Swedish state bureaucracy. More broadly still, it implies the possibility of feeling part of a global Christian movement whose scope and significance are not confined to one country alone.

In sum, Coleman makes an interesting link between local conversion and feeling part of a global Christian movement. He sees the conversion discourse and its associated practices in the worldwide Faith ministries as a revitalization mechanism in Pentecostalism and mainstream Protestantism in general. Coleman's analysis is related to the idea of the "circulation of the saints," which supposes that a good deal of church growth is caused by religious seekers and shoppers circulating from one church to another.[7] This usually takes place within the religious tradition most people grew up with, whether Catholic or Protestant. But the key question is: does this revitalization mechanism really work? Or is it merely a temporary solution, until people become restless again and seek out another, more interesting religious option? In the last case, these people will turn into seekers and shoppers (see next section).

*   *   *

I conclude that for people to continue following the religion of their parents—or alternatively to experience a reawakening of their parental religion—various factors must come together and interconnect. First, naturally enough, people have to be exposed to an intensive and often lengthy primary socialization in their parental religion. The standard elements are frequent church attendance, religious education, active participation in church groups (youth, evangelization)—all elements related to the institutional factor. Kristen is the typical case here.

Second, for those people who temporarily drifted away from their parental religion—typically during adolescence—a catalyst is needed to bring them back. This reaffiliation is often triggered by a relative or a close friend, the typical social factor, but sometimes also by a contingency television program (as in the case of Betty). A sudden urge to reach out to the world—the globalization factor—may also contribute to this, as the Swedish case shows.

Third, reaffiliation is stimulated when people encounter a subgroup in their parental religion that caters better to their specific needs and demands, for example, the Charismatic Renewal in the case of Catholics (like Betty) or a new, more seeker-sensitive church form in the Californian Episcopalian Church (as in the case of Sara). Thus, the institutional factor comes in again, which is greatly strengthened when combined with a fourth element.

Fourth, a direct confrontation with the death of a close relative may trigger a turning-point experience in people leading to acute fear of death and spiritual confusion. Sara went through this when her brother unexpectedly died at forty-six of cancer. This event is a combination of a contingency event (a sudden death), the social factor (the deceased is a near relative), and an individual factor (acute fear). When combined with changes in her local Episcopalian Church—the institutional factor—all of these factors combined to bring Sara back to her parental religion. If the institutional factor had been weaker, or if no new Episcopalian subgroup had appeared in her congregation, she would have become a religious seeker.

Seekers and Shoppers

Roof (1999: 9) posits that religious seekers have become the norm in contemporary U.S. society, because of "the sheer numbers of people involved." The main thesis of his fine book *Spiritual Marketplace* (1999: 10) is that "the boundaries of popular religious communities are now being redrawn, encouraged by the quests of the large, post–World War II generations, and facilitated by the rise of an expanded spiritual marketplace."[8] The book relies on survey data, in-depth interviews, and field observations. Roof (1999: 230) finds that "disproportionately, metaphysical believers and seekers appear to have grown up in families that lacked warmth, were highly controlled and demanding, and did not communicate easily." Lack of family warmth surely made it easier to abandon the parental religion. I will briefly present two of Roof's seeker stories.

Sam: Back to church through a computer bulletin board

Sam Wong (37) is "a second-generation Chinese-American, married with a young child, employed as a software programmer. His parents were not very religious, nor was he at the time he was growing up. It was not until he went to California State University at Long Beach that he confronted and engaged Christianity for the first time. There he met his wife, and both were introduced to Evangelical Christianity. They were in and out of churches, never really all that active, until they moved to San Jose six years ago when he got a better job as a computer programmer. . . Sam belongs to a Vineyard Fellowship congregation organized only a few years ago, one he describes as a "seeker church.". . . Seeker churches organize activities and programs with the expectation that people have questions, maybe even doubts. . . The music, the preaching, the programs are oriented to contemporary life and relating faith to spiritual seeking. . . Sam conceives of faith especially as a growth experience, a process of learning and exploring its meanings for moral and spiritual life. . . [T]he profile of an "Evangelical seeker" is particularly evident in the way that Sam came to join his church, in his religious style, and the manner in which he witnesses to his faith:

> "How did you get involved in this particular church?"
> "David, my friend from college," he said, "told me about this bulletin board on the Internet where Christians talk to each other. We talk to one another about what it means to be a Christian and what Jesus would do in a particular situation. We share our experiences and pray for one another." Further in the conversation he mentioned that he and his friends were extending the network all across the country (the "Jesus Network," as he

called it). It was clear that they saw the Internet as an opportunity to create chat rooms for people around the world who were searching for the Lord. "Our church has a computer club and we plan how to reach people and to answer their questions about our faith. That's why I like this church."

(Roof 1999: 24–26)

Vicki: From Scientology to Buddhism to Star Trek

Vicki Feinstein (35) represents perhaps the quintessential Generation X religious shopper (Roof 1999: 29–33). "Born in 1964 ... Never married, she works as a physical therapist in a veterans hospital and lives in a Maryland suburb outside Washington, D.C. ... Her parents were divorced when she was six. She has two older sisters, both of them now divorced ... She expresses many of the cynical attitudes of Generation Xers: skepticism about the future, doubts about marriages succeeding, and uncertainty about any religious or metaphysical claims as 'objectively true.' As she sees it, the world is not only a place of many differing religious beliefs, it is hostile and unpredictable, somewhat like in a video game. 'Sometimes you win, sometimes you lose,' she says, 'but you are always calling the shots and trying to figure out what's happening.'"

Asked about her parents' religious affiliation, she replies: "My father was Jewish but not religious. We never went to a synagogue ... I don't know what my mother is. Nothing really. Catholic, I suppose ... I'm a secular Jew." She says she cannot imagine herself belonging to any religious organization (Roof 1999: 29–30).

As a teenager growing up in Massachusetts, Vicki read about Dianetics and was drawn to the philosophical teachings of Scientology. She liked the idea that human beings are basically good but in need of greater self-knowledge for expressing goodness and escaping from painful past experiences. She and some friends got involved in the religious movement. Suffering at the time from anorexia and low self esteem, she was drawn toward, as she says, "motorcycles, drugs, and Scientology." The latter offered what she felt at the time she most needed, a practical means of improving her life. Scientology promised hope and survival. "I liked what Scientology taught about how my mind was shaped, and how I could know myself better."

"What about any other religions? Did you check any others out?" I inquired.

"Oh yes," she said. "I read all the books I could on Buddhism."

"What about this religion did you like?"

"I like the fact that it encouraged me to focus upon myself. To look within my self and to find out what was right and true for me. I also like *Star Trek*—is that a religion? I don't know."

"Why *Star Trek*?" I asked curiously.

"I like the fact that people all work together, to explore and expand the world we live in. It doesn't matter who you are, what race, sex, religion, whatever planet you come from, all get along well and look to a future together. It's promising. If we lived that way we would have a better world."

(Roof 1999: 31–32)

One does not easily put a religious label upon her. Very much an independent thinker, she is on a spiritual quest characterized largely by pragmatism, self-reliance, and hope for a happier life than she knew as a child. There are themes of science fiction and utopianism, bound up with her search for deliverance from a world that seems chaotic, violent, and at times hopeless. She wants very much to live in an ordered world and to feel that her life fits into some larger narrative. Even if she cannot articulate very well that larger story, she senses that it exists, that there is a story for her. Asked if she believes in God, she says, "Yes, in my own way."

Of all the people we meet, Vicki comes closest to being a "tourist" of religion. One religion is as true as another from her vantage point, and shopping around is appropriate. For any religion to "work" for her, it has to grab her and deliver on its promise—in effect, it must break through her cynicism and convince her of its hold on mystery and meaning. One is struck by the eclectic—at times seemingly contradictory—mix of symbols, teachings, beliefs experiences, and practices she claims as her own. What is lacking is any fixed, neatly ordered religious system we can identify as hers. She points us to what one commentator calls a "problem of boundaries" in the contemporary study of religion (Roof 1999: 21–33).

Roof characterizes Vicki as an "eclectic seeker." Her childhood and her subsequent relationships were unhappy. She does not believe in organized religion, but wants to believe in a larger narrative. However, since she does not recognize the authority of any one tradition, she ends up experimenting with a contradictory variety of religious options. First contact with these options is provided through friends (Scientology), books (Buddhism and New Age), and even television series (*Star Trek*). Since any religion must "grab her and deliver on its promise," she is more likely to be involved in low-commitment religions than in high-commitment ones.

The literature abounds with the many different seeker stories of ex-Catholics. Dean R. Hoge's book title *Converts, Dropouts, Returnees* (1981) neatly summarizes the three main categories of young Catholics under twenty-two. These Catholic dropouts come in five sorts: family-tension dropouts (about half of the sample), weary dropouts (bored with the church: 31 percent), life-style dropouts (23 percent), spiritual-need dropouts (7 percent), and antichange (pre-Vatican II: also 7 percent) dropouts (Hoge 1981: 96).

Ron: "Checking into different sources"

Hoge's fine study includes an example of a typical spiritual seeker drop-out of Catholicism, Ron (23), who had a devoutly Catholic grandmother he felt close to. He spent his first two college years "goofing off and partying" (Hoge 1981: 119). Ron was troubled by the clash between his Catholic training and the "humanistic" psychology espoused by some of the teachers:

> I cried out to God. I believed firmly there was a God—since I was raised a Catholic—there was never any doubt in my mind. There had to be a creator ... So I just said, "God, you're out there. You show yourself to me. You make yourself real to me. I want to know!" So I began checking into different sources. I began reading the Bible, I got into Buddhism fairly heavily, a couple of Eastern religions, meditation, and thought of being a vegetarian, and (laugh) ran the gamut. But God's voice rang the loudest and the clearest. ...
>
> Several months after this interview we talked with Ron again, and he told us he was getting married soon to a girl he met when he started going to the [Pentecostal] New Prophecy Church. She is very active in the church too. Ron has had no more contact with the Catholic Church or even with members of the Catholic charismatic renewal.
>
> (Hoge 1981: 119–24)

Hoge (1981: 131, back cover) concluded that the majority of people who drop out of Catholicism as teenagers or young adults return to active church life later in their thirties and forties.

Bonnie: "Dear God, I don't know if you're out there"

Another interesting story of a religious shopper that may illustrate this trend concerns the conversion experience of Bonnie B. Hays (2005), who went from Catholicism through Neopaganism and New Age to finally "meet God in Florida":

> When I was 14, I renounced my childhood faith in Roman Catholicism. It started when I became involved with a charismatic, non-denominational group ... My involvement in this group was a whirlwind of bible study, praise songs, and door-to-door evangelization ... A few months I was gung-ho, but then I became disillusioned by all the hypocrisy ... That was when my older sister, Jen, introduced me to Wicca, Neopaganism, and the New Age Movement ... So from the age of 14 to twenty-two, I became completely absorbed in all things related to the occult ... I soaked every lesson

up like a sponge, all the while hiding it from my Baptist father and devout Catholic mother ...

It didn't take long for me to become anti-Christian in sentiment ... Despite my feelings, I fell in love with a Christian, Bill ... He was definitely a factor in my conversion ... I suffered from long bouts of depression and spiritual confusion ... The mood-swings were so bad that Bill dumped me ... Bill came back on the condition that I work on my behavior ...

I worked as a nursing assistant while taking courses in massage therapy for the following two years ... In my second year, Bill proposed to me ... About a week later we were on our way to Florida ... The Internet opened up so much for my spiritual beliefs ... It's not like Christian church shopping, for Neopagans it's more like a covert operation trying to find others like you ... Eventually I created a cyber coven community ... I became somewhat of a New Age guru and counselor and Reiki Practitioner to my members ... I loved offering advice and training when it came to the occult ... I was also out to convert Christians, I wanted to show them the error of their ways! ...

After the initial invigorating months of shepherding my own flock (so to speak) I began to see problems with my belief system. The main thing was that there was no system ... Everyone had different gods/goddesses or just believed in their own divinity, they had different rituals and spells, they had different morals and politics. [However,] They had no common ground ... I really doubted that whatever was divine depended on my subjective beliefs ...

Nothing, not even nightmares and anxiety attacks, could compare to the spiritual desert I found myself wandering lost in ... In my utter confusion, I began to read about any and every religion or cult I could think of ... It was the prayer of an almost-atheist:

"Dear God, I don't know if you're out there and I don't know your name ... I can't go on like this. I'm so lost I don't know which way is up or down. Please show me who you are, show me the truth ... If I don't find you soon, I'm gonna have to give up. Please, show me soon!"

Well, He showed me. I suppose some might think I "found God" out of desperation alone, but after that prayer my desperation ended ... When I would go to the bible I started to see scriptures in a new light. I would see verses I had read before but this time they seemed to hold different meaning ...

The next big question was which church is the right church? ... I had been raised Catholic and even went to a Catholic school for five years, though I'll admit that my childhood faith was pure faith with precious little understanding ... So, my next step was to compare the various Protestant teachings to the Catholic ones. I still held to not believing in eternal security and plain old logic told me that sola fide and sola scriptura were not enough ...

With wonder and joy, my mind, my heart, and my soul found the answers they sought in the Roman Catholic Church. All of my issues with

Church teaching have been resolved ... I am grateful for moving to Florida that year. I truly needed to go into that darkness far away from all family influence to learn the truth for myself.

Strictly speaking, Bonnie Hays should perhaps be included in the section on parental religion, but doing that would imply that her lengthy conversion career was not being taken seriously. After a deconversion experience with Roman Catholicism at 14, she ended up in a charismatic youth group, where she left because of its hypocrisy. Through her sister's influence, she was immersed in New Age and Neopaganism and even became a "New Age guru" on the Internet, following her marriage. But ultimately she missed a coherent belief system, so she fell back into "darkness and spiritual confusion." After a desperate prayer, God was suddenly there. The final step was almost a cost-benefit analysis of different Christian churches. In the end, her childhood church won. Bonnie eventually went back to the Mother Church—*her* mother's church. I find the interaction between individual and social factors in her case striking. Even more remarkable is the new possibility of becoming a self-proclaimed New Age pastor through the Internet.

Bilqis: From New Age spirituality to Sufi Islam

Bilqis was a fifty-four-year-old white woman with a middle class background, who was married to a husband from a similar background. This is how she described their conversion career into Sufi Islam in Colorado:

> [Before conversion] my husband and I were reading a lot and tracing the footnotes in books such as *Be Here Now*.[9] We saw the connection of the teachings we liked to people of the past who had been practicing Muslims. My husband and I lived in a small town but we drove to Boulder to try and connect with Muslims in mosques ... We wanted the spirituality. I attended a woman's Sufi retreat and encountered the *salat* [Islamic prayer]. I came back and said: "This is what we want." We found Islam at that time to be something that could be woven into the fabric of our lives. It was more accommodating to children than many other spiritual paths we were encountering. Also it did not require spending large sums of money for classes and seminars. In Santa Fe we connected with a number of families who were followers of the Naqshbandi shaykh Nazim. We started fasting Ramadan and making the *dikr* with them. We wanted to make allegiance (*bay'a*) to the shaykh and were told *shahada*[10] came first and we were ready for that.[11]

Note how quickly Bilqis and her husband moved from the New Age–inspired *Be Here Now* to an intellectual quest for knowledge on Islam. They kept looking until they found the type of Islam and the community of believers they wanted. A cost-benefit analysis[12] of the more practical aspects of the new religion was obviously included: it was "more accommodating to children than many other spiritual paths" and it did not require spending lots of money on classes. They soon found a Sufi leader and liked the Sufi Muslim rituals and were ready for the declaration of faith.[13]

Ben: From Catholicism to EST[14] to Baha'i

The final seeker and shopper case is from Ullman's psychological study of conversion, *The Transformed Self* (1989: 147–51), which contains various detailed conversion stories: "Ben, a 26-year-old Baha'i believer who holds a PhD degree, converted twice. His first religious conversion, which he considers the most significant one, was a conversion to Christianity. The second, a year prior to my interview with him, was a conversion to the Baha'i faith.

Ben is the middle child in a Jewish middle-class family. His childhood was a lonely and agonizing time. He describes a withdrawn father, who would disappear for long stretches of time, and an anxious, overprotective mother. Ben's parents did not practice their Jewish religion but they sent him to Hebrew school, which he remembers with distaste. Ben describes his adolescence, his high school years, and his early years in college as extremely unhappy. During his later years in graduate school, Ben became interested in religion through the influence of a friend, his current object of admiration. This friend had been "experimenting" with religion and then left for California and wrote to inform Ben that he had become a Catholic convert and a monk. It was his friend's conversion that gave the main impetus to Ben's own conversion to Christianity:

> I thought, well I'm going to investigate this and I'm going to find out what this is all about because, when I go visit him then I'll be up on it, so I did it, investigating on my own and I knew that if he was so strongly committed to it that there was something in it because he would not commit himself to anything, being a very rational and intelligent person that I admired ... So I started reading the Bible, et cetera and not long after that, say a couple of weeks, I knew that I would be strongly attached to that.
>
> (Ullman 1989: 149)

Ben's own account of his growing "attachment" to Christianity is a blatant statement of his need for an undemanding, totally protective object:

> [What attracted me] was the fact that Christ was so forgiving that all of the things that I felt were wrong with me and everything all of a sudden could

be erased and that I could live a whole new life, could start a relationship with someone [Christ] who would never cause me any pain and that this relationship was something that I always knew I wanted all along.

(Ullman 1989: 149)

Two weeks after he had learned of his friend's conversion, Ben commenced instructions to become a Catholic. The day prior to his scheduled baptism, he decided, however, not to go through with the formal conversion. His mother and other family members had been taking EST at the time, and in an attempt to prevent his conversion, they persuaded Ben to do the same:

Everybody was smiling and they were happy and had a lot of Christian spirit in them, even though they did not know it was Christian. It was nice. I learned an awful lot. I realized that I was creating everything that was happening to me including the religious thing and I did not go through with the baptism although I remained a Christian. I still consider myself Christian.

(Ullman 1989: 150)

Ben's account of his more recent conversion to the Baha'i faith was strikingly casual. He told me that last spring he had met a Baha'i and had gone to fireside talks with him, and two months later he had declared himself a Baha'i:

It seems a good religion and it does a lot to me. It seemed too easy to do that I just did it. But there was always this sneaking suspicion in my mind that I am more Christian than Bahai.

(Ullman 1989: 150)

Ben believes that after his second conversion he developed a better understanding of other people. But he experiences frequent relapses. Last summer, for example, during a vacation in Europe, he felt that:

My conversion was tested, my religion was tested. I would revert back to selfishness and antagonism and sometimes very bad feelings toward my parents. The whole embrace of religion was very weak. I did not have a job, I had no stability, I did not have a good time in Europe, and I felt mean, very mean.

(Ullman 1989: 151)

Ben's account of his preconversion life portrays the recurring disappointments in previous relationships and his relief at discovering one that was "easy to get." His story is remarkably self-centered. He perceives others only in terms of their ability to satisfy his own wishes" (Ullman 1989: 151).

In Ullman's depiction of Ben's conversion story, individual factors were the drive behind his quest for religious meaning at the preaffiliation level. The first contact with Catholicism was established through a good friend, whom he admired very much. When this friend moved to California to become a monk, Ben was strongly impressed and wanted to become a Christian—a Catholic. But when his mother and other relatives took him to EST, he was equally impressed by their friendliness and Christian spirit (although the EST people themselves deny this) and he felt right at home. When a casual acquaintance took him to a Baha'i fireside, Ben just as casually declared himself a convert to the Baha'i faith within a month. The narcissistic motive is convincing, but the contacts with the religious groups were always established through Ben's social networks. Ullman's case again makes clear how social and individual factors are strongly intertwined and can reinforce each other in certain people. This is how commitment is built up. However, I would say that—in the terminology of the conversion career approach—Ben is not a convert, but only an affiliate.

Various common factors are visible in the conversion careers of the religious seekers and shoppers presented in this section. First, with only one exception (Bonnie), all came from families with a low or nonexistent religious commitment. Hence, they received no or very little religious socialization. Second, people had to be structurally available for seekership, and there had to be an easily accessible supply of competing religions options to shop around for through books, the Internet, friends, and relatives. Third, the trigger experiences that made them start their conversion career as a seeker were different combinations of factors. The five cases mentioned here were teenage existential confusion (Vicki), the influence of relatives and friends (Bilqis, Ben, and Bonnie), a dissatisfaction with parental religion (Bonnie and Bilqis), a clash between Catholic upbringing and humanistic psychology in college (Ron), or finding the right seeker church after a move (Sam). In general, people who start seeking as teenagers seem to be more influenced by a combination of individual and social factors, whereas people who become seekers later in life are more affected by individual and institutional factors. No pattern seems to be dominant on its own, although it is remarkable that all the five seekers described here belong to Generation X:[15] they were all born between 1958 (Ron) and 1964 (Vicki). Among the six cases described here, I would characterize four as examples of *affiliation* (Bilqis, Ron, Vicki, and Ben) and only two as showing a change in identity and religious worldview, that is, a "genuine" *conversion* according to the typology of religious activity in the conversion career (Sam and Bonnie).

Committed Converts

In the conversion careers typology, all converts experience a change of worldview and identity, whether radical or gradual. I concluded in Chapter 1 that all of these genuine converts engage in biographical reconstruction through the use of distinct narratives and discourses.[16] Stromberg (1993: xi) is a fine study of the importance of language in the conversion process: "I will argue that it is through the use of language in the conversion narrative that the processes of increased commitment and self-transformation take place." Stromberg (1993: 3) acknowledged the "remarkably high level of cooperation" he received with evangelical Christians: they were all happy to tell him their conversion story. He remarked: "The conversion narrative offered an opportunity to celebrate and reaffirm the dual effect of the conversion, the strengthening of their faith and the transformation of their lives."

George: "I really know hell on earth"

Stromberg (1990: 48–51; 1993: 112–18) presents a highly detailed interview with George, who was sixty-seven at that time:

> George's father, who died when George was 26 years old, was a committed Christian and a firm person. By this I mean he had strong opinions on things and shared them with his son. George emphasizes that he and his father had many disagreements, but insists they did not fight with one another. Rather, for the most part George tried to bow to his father's wishes, for he admired the older man tremendously ...
>
> After college, George married his high school sweetheart, but after three children and seven years of marriage he struck up an affair with a coworker. He eventually left home and decided to divorce his wife. The relationship with the coworker also broke up, and thereafter George embarked upon a period in which he dated many different women. However, on a visit to his family, George was shocked when the youngest of his children did not recognize him. He was troubled, and seeing this, his ex-wife recommended he go and speak to a minister.
>
> George did so, and the minister asked him "where he stood with God." George answered that he did not believe in God, to which the minister responded that perhaps he should give that position some thought. George left the pastor's office with a Christian book and, after some days of debating with himself the existence of God, decided to pray to God and ask his forgiveness. Upon doing so he was flooded with a profound feeling of forgiveness; he refers to this as a "road-to-Damascus type of experience" (comparing his conversion to the Biblical description of the conversion of

Saul of Tarsus). Having thus been converted to Christianity, George decided that he should put his life in order.

(Stromberg 1990: 48–49)

This is a part of George's conversion story:

> Oh. I really … I mean I know hell on earth. I *really* know hell on earth. Two things especially stand out in my mind. One time I came home and our daughter didn't know me. I was just a stranger … Oh I tell you, boy, that *really* shook me up …
>
> And then another time or maybe the same visit—I don't know—my son said … who was five, six said: "Daddy aren't you ever coming home?" … Talk about a shake up. Oh brother …
>
> And finally on noon on the third day I was … thinking about it and then all of a sudden I just felt I should pray. And I … My prayer went like this: "Dear God, if you exist, let me know that you exist and that you can forgive me."

(Stromberg 1993: 114–15)[17]

This is an example of how informants themselves use the Pauline conversion experience from the Bible as a model of—but also as a model *for*[18]—their own conversion experience. For George, "hell on earth" was represented by feeling alienated from his children. Hence, George's conversion story again confirms the importance of social factors in the conversion process.

Peter: "I was overwhelmed with evil"

Ullman's (1989: 133–39) psychological conversion study was already mentioned above. Here I quote extensively from her extended case study of Peter (32):

> Although he had been brought up in a clan of Evangelical, born-again Christians and had "turned onto the Lord" himself when seven years old, Peter pulled away from religion early in adolescence. He then felt reborn through his discovery of a life without God:
> "I went to church because it was expected of me. I came out of that [religious life] and felt like a snake shedding its skin or a butterfly coming out of a cocoon. I felt that God and my new understanding of the richness and joy of life were antithetical."

(Ullman 1989: 133–34)

Throughout his adolescence Peter describes feeling lonely and lost, confused about his goals, and isolated from his parents as well as peers.

During his first year in college, his confusion had intensified, culminating in visions that were terrifying and deeply unsettling for him:

> I was lying in bed in the early hours of the morning and was fully rationally awake and could see everything … and all of a sudden when the tower clock struck a certain hour I had a vision, in my mind's eye. I saw a figure of Christ standing before me in silence … I saw it, I felt no emotion, I could not speak to him, I felt myself totally an observer.
>
> Two weeks later I had fallen into a deep sleep and awoke at the last stroke of the clock in the tower, again at the very same hour, but as I came into consciousness I realized with the same kind of mind's-eye vision that lying next to me in bed was a charred corpse. And as I came awake this charred corpse lightly and airily rolled off the bed and bounced on the floor and disintegrated into ashes, and immediately the whole room seemed to be filled with the presence of evil.
>
> Just as I beheld the reality of Christ as calm and peaceful, I felt that far from a take-it-or-leave-it situation, I was overwhelmed with evil and again the room was filled from floor to ceiling with snakes writhing. I was so petrified that all I could do was lie there and repeat over and over again things I learned from childhood, like the Lord's Prayer and 23rd Psalm, and so forth.
>
> (Ullman 1989: 134)

During the following two years Peter became increasingly withdrawn and desperate, obsessed with fears and ideas he could not control, tormented by indecisiveness and emptiness. After moving to another [college], he met a former drug dealer who had become a follower of Meher Baba. He converted to Meher Baba's cult overnight, rented a house with other devotees of the loving and silent guru, and immersed himself in the occult, astrology, and Eastern religions. At present, Peter views his involvement in the cult as a "psychological trip," a way of avoiding responsibility:

> I felt I found reality in the context of people who were happy and loving. I did not see I was fulfilling a psychological need, I had gone into debased Christianity in oriental dress … Here I was believing in Karma, and no responsibility, there was always another trip around it.
>
> (Ullman 1989: 135)

As a faithful Baba follower, he patiently awaited the promised reward of ultimate realization, of a transformation that would set him free of all desires and all painful strivings. But the more he searched for the promised metamorphosis, the more fearful he became of being deceived. He began to harbor growing doubts in the powers of his master. On his way home from a rare visit with his parents, he asked God for a sign that would resolve his doubts, that would prove to him whether or not he had been deceived. This became the occasion of his second conversion—back to the Evangelical Christianity of his childhood. This second conversion was the outcome of a prearranged meeting with a "hard-shell" Baptist minister, a friend of his parents. Peter had anticipated that he would be able to convince the minister about Baba's divine powers. Instead he was himself persuaded that he had been deceived, that he had been "working with the forces of evil," and that Jesus Christ alone is the real God. The meeting with the minister, Peter decided, was the unequivocal divine sign he had been praying for. As in his conversion to Meher Baba's cult, he again felt instantly converted.

Peter's second religious conversion did not immediately produce a sense of peace and joy. For several months following his dinner with the Baptist minister, he was still plagued with doubts and depression. Convinced that he had not yet fully accepted Christ, he was sure that he was in constant danger:

> The man I had dinner with told me, "Peter, if you ever try to break away from the forces of evil that you are working with it might kill you," and I thought, "How romantic," but that's exactly what happened. I had some narrow scrapes with near accidents, people phoning me and attempting to lay a curse on me. One person tried to attack me physically.
>
> (Ullman 1989: 137)

Peter interpreted these events as indications that he had been "keeping God out and just hurting myself." Once again, he accepted God in prayer, subsequently experiencing profound peace, a sense of certainty and release. He knew that God had taken his hand:

> God had just in huge leaps lifted me out of one problem after another. I'd had incipient colitis and ulcers and asthma and migraine headaches … I'd been tempted with thoughts of suicide. God pulled me out from under the worst of it in an astoundingly short time.
>
> (Ullman 1989: 137)

Peter believes that God's miraculous guidance also inspired his vocation in the Evangelical Christian community where he now resides and works as a motivational consultant for Christian corporations. Peter describes his childhood as lacking in parental love and protection. His mother was unavailable, his father was dead, and he hated and feared his stepfather.

Peter's eloquent description of his life is replete with imagery and ideas that reveal a fragile self. He experiences himself as powerless in the midst of a struggle of giants—the forces of good and the forces of evil. In the midst of this struggle he is tossed about like an insignificant chip (Ullman 1989: 138–39).

Psychological motives dominate Ullman's analysis; hence, personality seems to be the driving factor of the two conversions described by her. Evangelical Protestantism was the parental religion and source of prime socialization. The first contact with the Baha'i religion was made through an acquaintance. Peter was instantly convinced by the powerful testimonial of a former drug dealer, who had changed his life entirely. The first contact with the second religious group, which represents a reconversion to his parental religion, was established through a friend of Peter's parents, the Baptist minister. Again, he converted instantaneously. Seeing the confirmation of his second choice in personal miracles—for example, concerning his health and how he found his new job—was a recurring theme. It illustrates how the convert's role dominates his life.[19]

Ken: "When you become a believer you get the whole package"

The final conversion story from Ullman (1989: 153–58) involves Ken, "a 24-year-old member of a charismatic church who considers himself a Jew for Jesus. The eldest of three in an upper-middle-class Jewish family, he was raised by a mother who was a Hebrew teacher and by Jewish Orthodox grandparents. He describes both his parents as overprotective, constantly worrying and fretting over him and his younger siblings. Ken's fears of dangerous, uncontrollable powers worsened during his adolescence. Around the age of fourteen, he stopped believing in God but continued to pray "just in case": "I was preoccupied with what happens to a person after death, what part of the person was real, was the real self" (Ullman 1989: 154).

Ken's fears and his uncertainty of a "real self" fostered a defensive aloofness and an increased withdrawal from family and peers:

> I was depressed about everything. I did not know who I was, where I was, what I was supposed to be. All in knew was that I had not done well in school and that was why people did not like me.
>
> (Ullman 1989: 154)

Ken describes the following six years of his life as desperate. He had managed to graduate from high school and then tried college but soon dropped out. Experimenting with drugs during his short stay at college further debilitated him. He spent a year at home doing nothing. He lived for a while with a group of young Jewish Zionists who were preaching a form of Orthodox Judaism diluted with radical politics.

Leaving home and receiving psychiatric help for three years helped Ken survive the emotional upheaval of his adolescence, but it did not transform him. The only happy times were on camping trips, in nature, away from the company of people. On one of these trips, Ken was introduced to Christianity. He was told of a Jewish friend who had become a Christian after several "incredible" events.

Ken decided he would try to test God for himself. Walking alone one night he requested a first "miracle"—to see a girl he had been working with and whom he had not seen at work for a while: "I went to the second floor to get some paper towels and just there at the desk was the girl I had asked to see. She was sitting and I went over and talked to her" (Ullman 1989: 155).

A month went by and Ken received another sign. Walking alone, contemplating the uniqueness and importance of individuals and thinking that "life is a drag," he recalls crying out loud, "What's the answer?" and at that moment a car drove by and a bumper sticker on its back windows read "Jesus Saves." Ken was astounded by the "perfect timing." He became convinced that somebody was listening.

A new excitement had taken over Ken's life. To his mother's astonishment and at first with her ardent blessing, he began to frantically read the Bible, looking for the prophecies that indicated Jesus was the new Messiah, as his friends had suggested.

A charismatic Catholic meeting marked another turning point in Ken's conversion:

> When I went to the prayer meeting, listening to people praying really loudly it was making me uneasy. I was thinking this is crazy, but all of a sudden I hear people speaking languages and I recognized, it sounded like Hebrew, like a synagogue, it was amazing, I was freaking out, these people were Catholic. How come they can speak Hebrew? My friends were telling me those are the gifts of the spirit: When you become a believer you get the whole package.
>
> (Ullman 1989: 157)

While praying and praising God with two other former Jews who had become followers of Christ, Ken had another mystical experience. Already veterans in the new faith, his friends had been guiding Ken in their version of Christian doctrine and had told him about the baptism of the Holy Spirit. They then laid their hands over his head, praying that he would receive it. Ken felt flooded with joy, which he describes as a blissful feeling of being drunk, of being fed. That night, lying in bed, he experienced again, with even greater intensity, the divine power his friends had promised him:

> I said, "OK, God, if you want to do it, you can do it now." Just as I was starting to fall asleep, all this intensity started hitting me from above, like intense

warmth, like a blanket of love. ... All I felt was this warm love, I could not really describe it ... I just started saying, "God, I love you." ... I never experienced that before and I was trying to find ways to express it, something said to me, telling me to speak and I opened my mouth and all of a sudden this foreign language was coming out.

(Ullman 1989: 157)

In his religious conversion, Ken entered a safe, protective reality populated only by the chosen of his peers. Most striking in Ken's story is the series of "miracles" that guaranteed his rebirth as a Christian. These miracles are miraculous only in Ken's eyes. Ken's religious conversion provided him with the protection of a "blanket of love," annulling the pain and dangers he had known throughout his preconversion life. There is no evidence that Ken was "brainwashed" by peer pressures as his parents contend; his peers' expectations had fallen on fertile ground. They resonated with Ken's lifelong resort to magical rituals to avert real and imagined dangers (Ullman 1989: 158).

Ken stopped believing in God at fourteen, but also suffered from anxiety over what happens after death (not uncommon for that age; see also Chapter 5 on Latin America). He was depressed, experimented with drugs, and did not know what to do with his life. Through a Jewish friend in his social network, he was introduced to Christianity. Ken experienced various "personalized miracles" that confirmed to him that God cared about him and that he should commit himself to Christianity. His friends laid their hands on him, which led to strong mystical experiences for Ken. In the Charismatic Catholic group, he heard people speaking in tongues—in Hebrew. This confirmed to him that God was present there. Ullman consistently stresses the individual factors in conversion, showing how these interact with social factors: the influence of his Jewish friends who also converted to Christianity. The institutional factors, however, are neglected: Ullman provides no detailed information on the religious group. Information is also lacking about the time after the conversion. One wonders whether or not Ken stayed active in the group, but there is no way of knowing.

Esther: "Wanting to be a Catholic scared the hell out of me" (A family collision cause)

One of the most detailed conversion stories from the literature, based both on interviews and on written self-reports, involves Esther (34)—another informant with a PhD. Esther was "the only child of a mixed marriage. Her father was a non-observant Jew who died when she was 16; her mother, a lapsed Catholic who did not remarry" (Rambo 1992: 229). The death of Esther's father proved to be a crucial experience:

> In Esther's home life, religion was a subject of derision, when it was mentioned at all. She recalls her parents as distant—they were older than is common when she was born, her father 52, her mother 35 ... Esther "hung around" her father a lot but never felt truly comfortable with him ...
>
> "I didn't grow up with the sense that the world was a safe or fair place ... I actually tried to bargain with God at the time [when her father died] ... I got my first dose of unconditional love from Sophia, my mother's best friend ... Unconsciously I must have been very angry at my parents ...
>
> [On moving for graduate school . . .] It was the first time in my life I had ever lived away from home. That took me out of the family orbit, and I think that was crucial. I also made a friend, an intellectual Christian, the first one I'd ever known.
>
> There was lots of evangelizing going on at the campus, and there were these people I considered rather ridiculous who would do their hell-fire and brimstone teaching ... I realized that I was in this prayer business because of very self-interested motives. I realized I needed a teacher ...
>
> I started getting more and more anxious because Christianity just started to look like a burr under the saddle ... If you want to be a Christian, then you have a lot to be anxious about. You're getting into hot water with your family, it's going to involve serious commitments, your life's not going to be the same ... I hadn't yet faced the fact that I wanted to be a Catholic, and a week later I realized that's what I wanted to be. That really scared the hell out of me, because I knew that was going to put me on a collision course [with my family], and I also wasn't terribly crazy about some of the things the Vatican does ...
>
> When you convert, there's a kind of enthusiasm. You set for yourself very high standards. A part of you really believes you can be living like that. Then after you fall on your face five or six times, you begin to think either I'm not a Christian or something else is going on that I need to address. What you go through is called a second conversion: I can fail, I can be narcissistic, I can be selfish, I can be less than I want to be and still be a Christian because I have some apprehension of God's love and forgiveness ...
>
> It makes living a lot different when you see each day as an opportunity to go out on a detective hunt and at least try to look for some signs of grace here and there. I think a very big part of Christianity is trying to make a commitment ... This is a world that would, in its distorted way, distract us from God ... I think a very big part of being a Christian is resisting that gravitation. In some ways being a Christian can actually expose you to stress rather than alleviate it, because you have to take evil seriously, deal with the brute reality of death, face your own human finitude ... Being Christian means living in tension, because you're simultaneously given a vision of just how wonderful a thing a God-saturated world really can be, and made brutally aware of the fact that it hasn't happened yet."
>
> (Rambo 1992: 233–43)

Esther did not receive a primary religious socialization from her parents, but at the age of sixteen, she was thrown into an existential crisis when her father suddenly died. Moving to graduate school took away her mother's influence, and Esther became friends with an intellectual Christian. She started praying and looking for a teacher. When she "found out" that she wanted to be a Catholic, she knew she would collide strongly with her mother. In her "second conversion," she accepted that she did not have to be perfect as a Christian or as a person. Being a committed Christian was a constant struggle, but she always found a few "signs of grace" that made it all worthwhile.

Cecilia: From party girl to devout Muslim

Starting with Hassan Butt, who returns in the next section, I use the conversion stories of Muslims living in the West as interesting comparisons to the majority of informants with Christian conversion careers. This is the story of Cecilia (35), who is Swedish and grew up in a very Catholic family but had problems with major ideas like the Trinity ("God is three and then suddenly one") and original sin: "How can someone invent such a hopeless idea that a baby is born with sin?" In two years, Cecilia went from being a secular party girl to a modestly dressed Muslim who always used the veil:

> It took a pretty long time for me ... this process of becoming Muslim myself. I couldn't call myself a Muslim until two years ago ... I also felt it was of totally vital importance ... The logic is very simple. There is only one God; there is nobody besides God. There are no priests who stand between God and me but I have straight communication with God by myself.[20]

Cecilia explained that she resented being viewed as a "sex object" when walking in town, which is why she was happy to use the veil every day after her conversion to Islam:

> I have a rather feminist view on things. I refuse to see the woman as a second-class citizen. I refuse to see why a woman should be worth less than a man. I like Islam's emphasis on the rights and obligations the woman and the man have. This is very, very important ... I really dislike a religion which says that the woman should keep quiet within the church ... I have always had a remarkably good-looking body. And that has been a basis for many people in forming a judgment of me. I was only a walking body ... It is not nice when people forget that you actually can have an IQ of 120. Because, in their eyes, if you are sexy you are also stupid ... With the veil and so-called decent clothes I get judged in a whole different way ... I have nineteen veils at home in different colors and patterns. I don't think there is an excuse to

look silly just because one is Muslim. I believe one should look neat and rather well dressed anyway.[21]

Soon after Cecilia's official conversion, she met and married a Muslim man from the Middle East. Cecilia criticized him for never really reading the Quran and for having "ideas based more on traditional customs than religious teaching."[22] She had a strong character, but her conversion to Islam gave her the tools for autonomy in marriage. But the main factors mentioned in her conversion career to Islam were a cultural critique of secular Swedish society with its messages to girls to be beautiful in contrast to the traditional gender patterns in Islam, which apparently were attractive after a life of partying and dating. However, no religious attractions of Islam are mentioned and one wonders about Cecilia's long-term commitment to Islam.

*   *   *

It is a challenge to identify and analyze the common factors in the conversion careers of the five committed converts presented in the preceding section. First, with only one exception (Esther), all the informants came from families with a high religious commitment. Hence, they received a strong religious socialization. Second, most of the conversions presented could be called predominantly *social conversions*, because the primary factor influencing the conversions was social. George's conversion was triggered by alienation from his children after divorce, Peter's by having dinner with a friend who was a Baptist minister, Ken's by his introduction to Christianity by Jewish Christian friends, Cecilia's by Muslim friends, and Esther's by a spiritual teacher. Third, with only two exceptions (Cecilia and Esther again), all cases involved deeply moving mystical experiences: prayer and forgiveness (George), speaking in tongues (Ken), or receiving terrifying visions (Peter). Fourth, all the informants experienced a lonely childhood and adolescence, making identity questions all the more poignant. Fifth, two people (Ken and Esther) mentioned a close confrontation with mortality as the trigger for their conversion career. Sixth, two of the informants reported experiencing a "second conversion," although the meanings differ. Peter first converted to Meher Baba's cult "overnight" and "immersed himself in the occult, astrology, and Eastern religions" (Ullman 1989: 135). Peter's second conversion was to (Baptist) Christianity. For Esther, her "second conversion" was the important insight that she could be selfish and still be a good Christian. In general, people's conversion careers were not very varied in the sense that they experimented with many different religions. In fact, the continuity was remarkable—sometimes people returned to a faith that was similar to their parental religion. However, none of the committed converts mentioned here became a leader or even a core member of their religious group. Hence, none of them reached the *confession* level of religious participation. The next section explores what it takes to bring somebody to that level.

Confessing Leaders

Detailed conversion stories of confessing leaders are not easy to find in the literature on the United States—and almost impossible to find in the European literature. One excellent example is provided by Susan Harding (1987), who like Stromberg (1990, 1993) also stresses the importance of language in the conversion process: "at the center of the language of fundamentalism is a bundle of strategies—symbolic, narrative, poetic, and rhetorical—for confronting individuals, singly and in groups" (Harding 1987: 167).

The Reverend Cantrell (1): Emptiness replaced by meaning and purpose

Harding presents the detailed conversion story of the Baptist Reverend Melvin Cantrell (46), including his calling to the pastoral office:

I was saved when I was 15 years old. I was a member of a Methodist church all of my life as a child. At the age of 15 I still had not heard the gospel story of Jesus Christ and how that he died for our sins. I was instructed as a child coming up in the Methodist movement just to live a good life, to be morally good, and to maintain all of those particular statuses, and I would be okay. Now I was invited by a friend to visit a Baptist church ...

And of course they had one of those hell-fire-and-damnation preachers in there, and he got down on my case that night. And I began to look at things and I realized there was something missing in my life ... And even though I wasn't saved I knew there was something bombarding my life that was beyond my power to see or really understand at the time ...

So after attending about three or four of their services—and incidentally they were in revival that week—then the spirit of God began to convict me about my place in life, ... so I was saved that week, I went forward and gave my heart to Christ. Now this is a process that some folks misconstrue along the highways of life. They think, you know, perhaps that because I joined the church, and I'm a good member, faithful, I tithe, I put all the nine yards in that really belongs there ... they think often that this is all that's necessary. But I realized that night that there was a need in my life and that need was met, and so much the spirit of God came to live in my heart. Now this is God's gift to every person that receives Christ.

So I joined that particular church after about a month of visiting there. But I was first saved and then I followed Christ to baptism, which I hadn't been baptized before. Of course the Methodist Church, they sprinkle, and I don't have any argument with them there, other than the fact that I believe the Bible teaches immersion. And then after this my life began to grow and materialize into something that was real, something that I could really identify with. The emptiness that was there before was now being replaced by something that had meaning and purpose in it. And I began to sense the need of telling others about what had happened to me.

And basically I think perhaps the change could be detected in my life, as the Bible declares, that when a person is saved, the old man, the old person, or the character that they were passes away, and then they become a new creation in Christ Jesus. That is to say, they might be a character that may be drinking and cutting up and carrying on and a variety of other things that are ill toward God. All of these things began to dissolve away. I found that I had no desire for these things, but I began to abhor them. I actually began to hate them. And this was in accordance with the Scriptures as I found out later. And then as my life began to mature in Christ I found that I too could win other to Christ the same way I was won: by simply telling them that there's a heaven to gain and a hell to shun ...

Now when I had my calling at age 29, I was operating a service station. And I was in the station one afternoon, working on a car. And God did not speak to me with an audible voice, but he spoke to my heart. And there was a conversation going on much like the one that's here. I'm doing the talking and you're listening. And God was doing the talking and I was listening.

I was down under the car, changing the oil, and ... God was just dealing with me about doing this. And I said, "I can't do that." And much like Moses when the Word called him to do something, he said, "I can't even talk." And God said, "Well, I'll send your brother Aaron to help you." So every excuse I would come up with, he would head me off by instructing me that he would do something to meet my shortcomings. So I finally surrendered in the sense of the word that afternoon ...

Now I realize many times when I preach, the Bible says preaching is as of foolishness. But there is another agent working while I'm preaching. And he's the Holy Spirit. And he's the one that grips the heart ... Now until we're saved, he lives without us, but when you're saved, he comes to live within us ... And he is not a figment of the imagination. But the Bible says, he's a real personality, a real person. And actually he can catch your next word and stop it, if you're sensitive to him ... If you let him, he becomes the tutor of your life, the instructor, the guide, the teacher ... this is the way the Holy Spirit works with me. He impresses me. He moves upon my heart to do certain things ... In reality, it's God living within us.

(Harding 1987: 171–74)

Many familiar elements are visible in the Reverend Cantrell's conversion story: the importance of primary religious socialization (Methodism), the typical early conversion age of fifteen, the friend who invited him to another church, the realization that something was missing in his life, and the quick acceptance of the need to repent (one month, four visits). Important additions are the equally quick change of his life following his conversion and the urgent need to give testimony of this—this is typical of the confession level. The hate expressed for drinking and other things of his former sinful lifestyle is also highly symbolic. The Biblical expression "new creation in Christ Jesus" (2 Corinthians 5: 17) again shows up in Chapter 5 on Nicaragua. Cantrell was an independent small entrepreneur, conducting repairs on a car, when he received his calling from God to become a pastor. He did not want to do it. He felt insecure. He compared himself to Moses, who was also called by God against his will. It was his divine destiny, but he could only fulfill it with the active support of the Holy Spirit.

The Reverend Cantrell (2): "I accidentally killed my son that morning"

The Reverend Cantrell's conversion story did not end there. Harding (1987: 177; 1992: 60, 72–74) describes how he continues trying to convert her, the researcher, by telling the following "unforgettable story" (Harding 1992: 60):[23]

> Now if in this life, the Bible says, only we have hope, then we of all men are most miserable. But you see my life, my hope, is in the life to come, and I realized this life is a passing thing. Jeremiah says it's like a vapor. It appears but for a little while and then vanishes. We know how uncertain life is. We're just not sure how long things are going to go.
>
> I went to work one morning. I had some work to do on a Saturday morning. And one of my sons was 14 years old. And the other was 15 years old. And we got up that morning. And I went in, and I rassled [sic] with my son and rassled [sic] him out of bed, the one that was 14. And we got up that morning and ate breakfast. We opened the Word of God. We read and we prayed together as a family, my wife, my two sons, and I. And I went on to do that work that morning. It was a Saturday. And I had something I wanted to move. And I was operating a crane. And I accidentally killed him that morning.
>
> And I looked at God. And I said, "Lord, you told me in your Word that all things work together for good to those that love you, especially those that are called according to your purpose." And I said, "I've served you faithfully. And I've loved you. And I've given you my heart, my life, my soul, given you everything about me. And now I can't understand this, why you've taken my son."

And God didn't speak with a voice that I heard with my ear, but he spoke to my heart. He said, "Milton, you know maybe you don't understand what I've done at this particular time, but can you accept it?" And I said, "Yes, sir, I can accept it." And Susan, when I made that statement, and I settled that in my own heart, and I said, "Lord, I accept it though I don't understand it." I don't know where to say it came from other than that God gave it to me, but he gave me a peace in my soul. And I have not questioned it since …

And we watched them close the casket on that little fellow and my, he was just super. I mean, he was almost my heartthrob, you know, that was my baby. And yet he died in my arms. And yet I looked at God and I said, "Lord, I'm going to love you if you take my other son. I'm going to love you if you take my wife. I'm going to love you if you take my health, if you strip me of everything I've got, I'm going to love you."

Now I'm saying that because, Susan, he is real. This is not mythology. I'm forty-six years old, and I'm no fool. God is alive. And his son lives in my heart.

Of all that I could give you or think of ever giving over to you, I hope that what we've talked about here today will help you make that decision, to let him come into your heart, and then he will be your tutor. And he'll instruct you in things that perhaps I've stumbled over today. Sometimes the vocabulary may not be appropriate to really describe the depth and the detail of the things that need to be said. But this is where the Holy Spirit can make intercession for us.

(Harding 1992: 60–61)

The Reverend Cantrell not only makes his conversion a central element of his identity (see Chapter 1), but he even "uses" a shattering personal experience—the accidental death of his son by his own hands—as an illustration of our need to accept Jesus Christ as our personal savior. He shows supreme spiritual strength by accepting that God is responsible for his boy's death. Harding's (1992) article is an excellent narrative analysis of one extended conversion story and it is useful to quote from her conclusions:

Hard to grasp, it is simply put: you convert to born-again belief the moment you *know* that someone infinitely superior to you gave his life, or his son's life, to save your lowly life … It is the *knowledge* of ultimate, inexplicable, transcendent compassion that "saves" the unwashed, that ushers them into the born-again kingdom, not only licensing them to speak and according them the enabling point of view but also instilling in them a desire to repay the debt, to come to know and to obey and to become one with the one who gave them so much … The Reverend Cantrell hoped that the storied gifts he offered his listener that afternoon in his study would engender in her the same poetic of desire, the same knowledge of divine love, that Christ's sacrifice evoked in him.

(Harding 1992: 74; emphases in original)

Wilfried: "I was spiritually kidnapped into a weird sect"

For a very different perspective of a confessing church leader, I turn to a self-report by Wilfried Decoo (1996), who converted to the Mormon Church in Belgium, aged around twenty. At twenty-two, he was called to preside over a small church unit in Flemish Belgium in June 1969. He was shocked to find that only about 10 percent of the Mormon members on record showed up regularly on Sunday, and his article is a frank attempt at analysis of the question why this was—and *is*—the case:[24]

> In the European setting, whether or not a family is "religious," it is almost always regarded as a tragedy for a family member to join the LDS church.[25] My own case is typical. I was (in the eyes of my parents) spiritually kidnapped into a weird sect by two foreigners who had dropped by uninvited and unwanted. In a matter of days their son had simply abandoned the faith and traditions of his ancestors. They felt bewildered, betrayed, and destitute of hope. In the intervening years they have come to accept the inevitability of my remaining a Latter-day Saint, but they never understood how a sound-minded European could join such a blasphemous American sect. Something broke in our relationship and has never been fully restored.
>
> This breach between converts and their families is not limited to the moment of conversion but continues to plague family relationships. In the event of a temple marriage the non-Mormon parents and relatives cannot attend; when a child is born, there will be no christening from them to attend, and none of them will be selected as godparents; there is no sharing of religious commemorations at Christmas or Easter; if the LDS member attends a Catholic funeral for another member of the family, he or she will be conspicuous by declining to take communion; and so on.
>
> (Decoo 1996: 102)

Several elements are notable in Decoo's story, however different it may be from the Reverend Cantrell's. First, Decoo was also called at a young age, as a recent convert to Mormonism with little experience, to perform in a leadership position. The Mormon conversion stories in Chapter 5 show that the Mormon Church continues to put recent converts relatively quickly in important leadership positions, thus hoping to increase their commitment (or, in terms of the conversion career, to bring them quickly up to the confession level). Second, there is again a sacrifice: not the death of a child, but the severing of important social relationships with parents and relatives.

Hassan: From radical to moderate Muslim convert

I started this book with the life story of Hassan Butt, a hothead in a disordered world. Butt is a British citizen of Pakistani origin who converted to radical Islam at the age of seventeen in 1997. Aged twenty, Butt became a recruiter for the Taliban and claimed that he had sent 200 British Muslims to fight in the Jihad in Afghanistan. This is how he described his profound conversion-like experience earlier:

> I would agree to being called a radical and one day may even be called to be a terrorist, if Allah permits me. That is something it would be an honor to be called …
>
> Every Muslim must work for the Shari'a to be implemented as a political way of life. They can do that physically, by involving themselves in revolutionary coups, or through political means. As long as they don't attack or compromise other Muslims who are doing something different from them, I have no problem with any of these ways of establishing the Shari'a …
>
> Islam is a way of life, a way of life superior to communism and capitalism. Christianity is a mere religion and can't cater for people's way of life, but Islam can. With the fall of the Soviet Union, people started turning to Islam as a way of life, whereas America wanted to spread capitalism across the world. That's why Islam became the enemy.[26]

However, Hassan Butt started to develop serious doubts about radical Islam after the July 2005 London bombings, questioning whether these were justified in Islam. The leaders from Hiz ut-Tahrir summoned him to a meeting in the Middle East, but they did not give any answers, only new orders:

> They were trying to force me into Iraq to fight basically … The actual word they used was that I needed "reprogramming." And Iraq would give me the opportunity to basically be reprogrammed for what I needed. I mean, I was quite shocked at the analogy. To think that … Well, firstly, I'm neither a computer nor a robot. And I don't know on your say so, I do on God's say so. And if you can't justify to me or prove to me that this is what God wants, then I'm gonna have to go my separate ways. What I've come to realize is that killing for the sake of killing, and killing in the name of Islam for the sake of killing, is completely and utterly prohibited. And there's a big disease, a big problem and a cancer in the Muslim world. And it's a very dangerous cancer, and it needs to be dealt with.[27]

In 2006–2007, Hassan Butt completed his second 180 degree turn. In a 2007 newspaper article, he argued that:

> The fact is that Muslims in Britain are citizens of this country. We are no longer migrants in a Land of Unbelief. For my generation, we were born here, raised here, schooled here, we work here and we'll stay here. But more than that, on a historically unprecedented scale, Muslims in Britain have

been allowed to assert their religious identity through clothing, the construction of mosques, the building of cemeteries and equal rights in law.

If our country is going to take on radicals and violent extremists, Muslim scholars must go back to the books and come forward with a refashioned set of rules and a revised understanding of the rights and responsibilities of Muslims whose homes and souls are firmly planted in what I'd like to term the Land of Co-existence. And when this new theological territory is opened up, Western Muslims will be able to liberate themselves from defunct models of the world, rewrite the rules of interaction and perhaps we will discover that the concept of killing in the name of Islam is no more than an anachronism.[28]

Hassan Butt is still a committed Muslim convert, who went through a profound intensification of his parental religion during his adolescence. But the same radical Islam he espoused as a seventeen-year-old provoked serious doubts when he was ordered to carry out a suicide mission in Iraq at age the age of twenty-six. He made another 180 degree turn and now argues for an open theological debate on the permitted use of violence in Islam among all Muslims. Butt is still acting like a committed Muslim leader, offering his testimony and urging people to action. As a direct result of his life story, however, the contents of his message have changed radically.

In conclusion: individual factors seemed to be decisive in shaping confessing leaders, in combination with social and institutional factors. Confession always followed conversion—not the other way around. Converts who put their own personal sacrifices into a conversion perspective, thus making it part of their own testimony like the Reverend Cantrell did, strongly increased their church commitment. After converts experienced a life-shaking event—for example, the death of a child, a suicide attempt, receiving orders to commit a suicide attack, or isolation from parents and relatives—and were able to put this event into a meaningful perspective as part of their life story as a convert, their religious commitment increased and they reached the confession level in the conversion career typology of religious involvement. Reaching this level, however, was no guarantee that they were able to *maintain* it. Especially in Western Europe and the United States, many people shifted from the levels of affiliation, conversion, or even confession toward religious disaffiliation in the course of their conversion career.

Disillusioned Disaffiliates

Chapter 1 mentioned that the disaffiliation level includes different categories: apostates, secular "nones," and even religious "nones."[29] This section presents stories from all of these different categories here, starting with the case of a world-famous apostate from Islam.

Ayaan: From tribal Islam to missionary atheist

Somalia-born Dutch intellectual and former parliament member Ayaan Hirsi Ali was identified by the weekly *Time* as one of the 100 Most Influential People of 2005. Her books *The Caged Virgin* (2006) and *Infidel* (2007)[30] tell the story of a free-spirited Muslim immigrant girl travelling from Somalia to Saudi Arabia, Kenya, and Germany, and finally seeking and finding asylum in the Netherlands. She studied political science and worked for the research institute of the Dutch Labor Party, where she ran increasingly into conflict because of her critiques of Islam, singling out the religion's treatment of women and its poor record in both human rights and socioeconomic development.

Ayaan grew up as an innocent girl in Somalia, who was soon hardened by dire circumstances. She was socialized into the tribal version of Islam as a member of one of Somalia's important clans and was forced to undergo genital mutilation at the age of five (Hirsi Ali 2007: 31–34). Her family had to flee from Somalia as political refugees and went to Saudi Arabia before settling in Kenya. Aged twenty-two, Ayaan fled to Frankfurt, Germany, to escape from an arranged marriage with a cousin and arrived by train in the Netherlands in 1992.

I would argue that the deconversion experience from Islam to missionary atheism is the central chapter of Ayaan Hirsi Ali's life story.[31] Her conversion career went from tribal Islam in Somalia to a moderate form of "generic" Islamic thought in her teens and twenties to her disaffiliation experience in the Netherlands, which happened right after the attacks on the Twin Towers on September 11, 2001:

> I knew that a vast mass of Muslims would see the attacks as justified retaliation against the infidel enemies of Islam. War had been declared in the name of Islam, my religion, and now I had to make a choice. Which side was I on? I found I couldn't avoid the question. Was this really Islam? Did Islam permit, even call for, this kind of slaughter? Did I, as a Muslim, approve of the attack? And if I didn't, where did I stand on Islam?[32]

Ayaan reports that she became "fixated"[33] on the 9/11 attacks. She concludes that the main cause was "not frustration, poverty, colonialism, or Israel: it was about religious belief, a one-way ticket to Heaven."[34] She studied old interviews with and new videos from Osama Bin Laden and looked up all his quotes from the Quran. "I didn't want to do it, but I had to ... I needed to ask: Did the 9/11 attacks stem from true belief in true Islam? And if so, what did *I* think about Islam?"[35] This intellectual quest finally led to these inexorable conclusions on Islam:[36]

> By declaring our Prophet infallible and not permitting ourselves to question him, we Muslims had set up a static tyranny. The Prophet Muhammad attempted to legislate every aspect of life. By adhering to his rules of what is permitted and what is forbidden, we Muslims suppressed the freedom to think for ourselves and to act as we chose. We froze the moral outlook of billions of people into the mind-set of the Arab desert in the seventh century. We were not just servants of Allah, we were slaves ... I found myself thinking that the Quran is not a holy document. It is a historical record, written by humans ... It spreads a culture that is brutal, bigoted, fixated on controlling women, and harsh in war ...
>
> It didn't have to be this way ... We Muslims could shed our attachment to those dogmas that clearly lead to ignorance and oppression. In fact, I thought, we were lucky: there were now so many books that Muslims could read them and leapfrog the Enlightenment, just as the Japanese have done. We could hold our dogmas up to the light, scrutinize them, and then infuse traditions that are rigid and inhumane with the values of progress and modernity ...
>
> For me to think this way, of course, I had to make the leap to believing that the Quran was relative—not absolute, not the literal syllables pronounced by God, but just another book. I also had to reject the idea of Hell, whose looming prospect had always frightened me from making any criticism of Islam. I found myself thinking one night: But if that is so, then what do I believe, truly, about God?[37]

The turning point came in May 2002, when Ayaan read *The Atheist Manifesto* by the Leiden University philosophy professor Herman Philipse during a holiday in Corfu, Greece:

> I read the book, marveling at the clarity and naughtiness of its author. But I really didn't have to. Just looking at it, just wanting to read it—that already meant that I doubted, and I knew that. Before I'd read four pages I already knew my answer. I had left God behind years ago. I was an atheist.
>
> I had no one to talk to about this. One night in that Greek hotel I looked in the mirror and said out loud, "I don't believe in God." I said it slowly, enunciating it carefully, in Somali. And I felt relief.[38]

Ayaan vividly describes the sense of liberation that she felt after thus deciding to believe that God and Hell did not exist:

> It felt right. There was no pain, but a real clarity. The long process of seeing the flaws in my belief structure and carefully tiptoeing around the frayed

edges as parts of it were torn out, piece by piece—that was all over. The angels, watching from my shoulders; the mental tension about having sex without marriage, and drinking alcohol, and not observing any religious obligations—they were gone. The ever-present prospect of hellfire lifted, and my horizon seemed broader. God, Satan, angels: these were all figments of human imagination. From now on I could step firmly on the ground that was under my feet and navigate based on my own reason and self-respect. My moral compass was within myself, not in the pages of a sacred book.[39]

Ayaan's story shows that a profound deconversion experience mirrors the conversion story in all of its aspects. Disaffiliation is also a long process and it is influenced by individual factors like education, social factors like having many atheist friends,[40] and institutional factors having to do with how Ayaan perceived Islam after the attacks of 9/11. The last quote clearly describes how she already led a Western intellectual lifestyle as a student in Leiden before her actual deconversion experience on the island of Corfu. Ayaan's feelings of guilt on failing to follow Islam's rules were effectively neutralized by her increasing *intellectual* doubts about Islam, leading to the final profession of her faith in reason: the basis of her atheism. From that moment on, her new prophets would be Spinoza and Popper, and she wanted all Muslims to follow her conversion career toward secular disaffiliation and share in the same sense of relief and liberation.[41] This probably explains her strong attitude of "missionary atheism," which she shares with people like Richard Dawkins (*The God Delusion*) and Christopher Hutchinson (*God Is Not Great*). They are all located at the *confession* level of atheism.

John: From religious affiliation to spiritual disaffiliation

Roof (1999: 17–20) provides an excellent example of the category of people reporting that they are religious but do not belong to any church: the so-called religious none. John McRae (41) had a college degree in engineering and worked as an architect. He grew up in a Presbyterian family but had not been active in any church for many years. He had been married for five years, had divorced, and had recently become engaged for a second time. John stopped going to the Presbyterian Church when he left home at twenty-one (Roof 1999: 17–19):

> It's not that I'm opposed to church or anything like that, it's just that I got out of the habit of going and never got back ... Becky's been a big influence on me, I'd have to admit. Becky is my fiancée. She's Catholic. We're planning to get married ... She's been a part of a group here in Cleveland ... —most

of them Catholics, who read books and discuss them, sing with guitars, sort of like what they used to do back at the university ... I've learned a lot about Thomas Merton, the Berrigans, and Mother Teresa—people I really admire ... Their conviction and compassion.

I have nothing to add to the conclusion of Roof (1999: 19–20):

> John doesn't know if he is religious but he is experiencing a spiritual reawakening of sorts in this informal Eucharistic community of dissident Catholics and their spouses ... To think of him as a "None" (or a nonaffiliate) overlooks the fact that something profoundly moving is happening within him. Doubt and a lack of a clear conviction about what to believe do not here translate into a secular outlook; rather they appear to signify just the opposite—a more open, questing posture born in no small way out of disenchantment with secular alternatives to faith ... [H]e questions the secular and material values that have dominated his adulthood.

Significantly, I have to turn again to the Internet to find stories of dropouts who remained firmly disaffiliated from organized religious groups afterward. I quote from two of these: Luis and Robert.

Luis: From adolescent seekership to secular disaffiliation

Luis Jeremias (26) grew up in a Catholic family in a rural town of Portugal and learned about Pentecostalism from a school colleague:

> When I was 17, I began to be very interested in knowing if there was a "Truth" in religion, so I looked for it in books and other people. One of my colleagues at high school is an evangelical xtian [Christian] and often preached (literally) to the rest of us. So, obviously, I came to him, and he led me to his beliefs and later to his church—Assembly of God, as it's called here (it's a Pentecostal denomination).
>
> Soon I became a fervorous [sic] adept of the religion. It mattered everything to me; I placed school, my parents, my friends, my future in second place; first of all was Jesus, my savior ... My parents got worried about me—they are catholic by tradition, as the majority of Portuguese, but don't attend church—but never tried to stop me (they didn't know how to). I broke with all secular friends because they wouldn't understand me and didn't follow my way ...
>
> Pentecostal churches preach "baptism in the holy spirit." I wanted that more than anything in life, and so I tried it on every gathering and every prayer. I saw people screaming around me, falling on the ground in hysteria, speaking in tongues, getting (supposedly) cured from their diseases,

et cetera ... After the cult, I saw the same people fighting, lying, getting drunk, beating the spouses ... if God Himself touched those people, how could they do such things? ...

But I always felt a deep feeling of guilt, as if everything I did was unperfect and unsuitable to the holiness of the Lord ... I tried to live life as Jesus wanted, but I never could do it completely, and the moments of joy in the cult and prayer were overshadowed by a constant feeling of guilt and fear. I became a fanatic in everything I did ... I prayed at least twice a day, an hour each time ...

Being the musician, I started testing the congregation. They got so carried away when I played, but not when other people played ... So I found out how to play to get those results. In the beginning of the cult, I played lightly; they sang normally. When the "adoration" part came, I played in a way (louder, with high pitch chords, selecting "celestial" sounds on the organ) that made them shout and cry ... I tried this many times, and began to like it. It's like a rock concert, where you get carried away with the music and the beat, your adrenaline level rises, you go with the crowd dancing and waving your arms ...

Meanwhile, my girlfriend left me (of course) for being immature and ruining our relation with my fanatism [sic]; when I told her about my doubts she got angry and scared—she was not going to marry a heretic! ... After drying my tears out, I began to face that maybe—just maybe— something is very wrong with all this. I was very afraid to lose my faith, so in a desperate attempt to get "healed" I attended many "faith" reunions, where the big guys would blow—yes, blow—into the crowd and everyone would get healed and get the baptism of the holy spirit. I attended such an event with thousands of people (*EuroFire* in Lisbon, 1990) when he did that, he started blowing from one corner of the room to the other, and people fell like dominoes—all of them! "This is the time I was waiting for!" I cried and closed my eyes. When I opened them, everyone around me was on the floor looking stupid and crying and I was the only one standing up. I left much more convinced of the lie in all that ...

I started missing some services and getting back to the things I liked to do before going into church ... I was 20 when I quitted. Today I'm 26 ... and I'm a happy person, with my wounds—most of them—healed. I got back to my former friends and kept some "church" ones—but they are not fanatic like I was ... I surely won't get into another crap like that. There is no doctrine that can make me return to religious thinking now, and I'm fine that way; I remember vividly looking at the mirror one day and saying to myself "welcome back!!!" It was one of the happiest days of my life.

(Jeremias 2006)

Luis's case is an example of religious seekership leading to a Pentecostal church affiliation (although I would not call it a conversion experience), but ending in complete religious disaffiliation. At seventeen, that typical adolescent seeker age, Luis started looking for religious truth and found it through a fellow student in high school, who took him to the Pentecostal Assemblies of God. Significantly, he does not describe a conversion experience, but only a very high commitment that he labels fanaticism. He desperately wanted the baptism in the Holy Spirit, but never received it. He felt "unperfect" and guilty (shadows of Catholicism?). As the church musician, he discovered how easily he could manipulate the church members into frenzy. At a Pentecostal mass rally in Lisbon, everyone around him "falls in the spirit," but he could not. Hence, he saw the people lying on the floor as "stupid and crying." He gradually decreased his commitment by going less to church. Now he is free again to lead the life he had before. He gives testimony of the fact that he is happy now—in words mirroring almost literally the conversion stories of committed Christians.

Robert: From confession to secular humanism

Robert Price (1997) provided no information on his religious upbringing—his parents are never even mentioned—or on his age. He was probably in his early forties when he wrote *From Fundamentalist to Humanist*:

> At the ripe old age of ten (adolescence being the most common time of life for conversion, psychologists tell us), I began to fear the prospect of everlasting hell-fire and heeded the urging of the preacher at a local Baptist church to receive Jesus Christ as my personal savior ... It was not long before I broke open the Bible and began studying it, "witnessing" to friends and neighbors about my new-found faith, praying, and attending church at least three times a week. I loved the camaraderie of "Christian fellowship." ...
>
> Being intellectually inclined ... eventually my interest in the Bible and in evangelism began to converge ... So I began studying up on the "apologetics." This is the art of defending the faith ... But a funny thing happened on the way to the debating forum ... I went from believing the Bible because it was the Bible to believing the Bible because I thought the facts backed it up, to finally not believing the Bible once more evidence convinced me I'd been seeing only what I wanted to see ...
>
> At the same time, I began to see that the fundamentalist "born-again" mentality was not all it was cracked up to be. The born-again gospel promises joy and peace of mind, but it does so by prolonging childhood ... Fundamentalism fills you with answers before you even think to ask the questions. It discourages self-discovery and urges you to conform to a supposedly "Christ-like" stereotype ... Every minor disappointment and major disaster are messages from God to teach you some lesson ... All this pretty much crystallized for me, ironically, during seminary, while I was studying the New Testament for a Master of Theological Studies degree ... But I did

find Liberal theology to be quite helpful. Paul Tillich especially answered my questions ... One could be genuinely open to the evidence since "faith," Tillich argued, was not "belief," but rather "Ultimate Concern." ...

I finished my Ph.D. in Theology at Drew University in 1981. The same year I discovered an unusual Baptist church which combined serious discipleship with open-minded theology. It felt great to be back in a spiritual community ... I started attending the Episcopal Church and came to love the liturgical life ...

I taught for four years until my Baptist church back in New Jersey called me as its new pastor ... About this time I also began to read extensively in radical postmodern philosophy. Unfortunately for me, my congregation had been getting more traditional while I was getting more radical! ...

I had come to view religion simply as a matter of spiritual experience ... It was really a kind of esthetic experience. Worship was something akin to the awe we feel at great art or at beholding the starry sky ... But this meant that religion is nothing more than a creation of human imagination ... Religion now seems to me a kind of nursery school version of philosophy ...

I have abandoned the ministry, though I have not abandoned my friends who left the church with me. We still meet often and call ourselves "Heretics Anonymous." We discuss ideas.

(Price 1997)

The case of Robert Price began with a childhood conversion experience at age ten, followed by intense participation in and outside the evangelism of a Baptist congregation. With more theological schooling, his intellectual doubts regarding Christianity also increased. As a liberal Christian, he no longer felt at home in his Baptist congregation. He stopped being a minister when he concluded that religion was merely "nursery philosophy"—a creation of the human imagination. But he never stopped belonging to his social network of religious disaffiliates. Even in this case of religious disaffiliation, the social factor turned out to be the strongest.

It is useful to quote from the conclusions of Roof (1999: 226–27, 236):

Secularists growing up experienced a combination of influences shaping their worldviews: weak childhood socialization, intensive exposure to the counterculture, and often bad experiences with organized religion ... The family types currently growing—singles, divorced and separated, and the so-called nonfamily households—show lower levels of involvement in, and support of, organized religion, though by no means less personal faith or spiritual well-being. People in these family situations are more likely to hold privatized or family-based religious views largely unrelated to congregations, or to identify themselves simply as religious "Nones."

What are the common factors in the conversion careers of the people who ended up disaffiliated from organized religion at the moment of being researched? First of all, their religious socialization was typically weak: John's parents were Presbyterian and Luis's Catholic, but neither was active. Second, both Luis and John were influenced by their girlfriends or fiancées (the social factor again). Ayaan was influenced by her Dutch boyfriend and secular student friends. Robert was also profoundly influenced by his friends, the "Heretics Anonymous" support group, all of whom were also leaving their parental religion around the same time as Robert was. Third, the trigger experiences directly causing disaffiliation varied from the loss of the habit of going to church (John), being unable to participate fully in music and "falling in the Spirit" (Luis), and developing increasingly serious intellectual doubts (Ayaan and Robert). Finally, all had received higher education around the time of their religious disaffiliation. However, the same was true of many of the seekers, converts, and confessional leaders mentioned above.

Conclusion

This chapter distinguished and analyzed five typical conversion careers in the United States and Europe to put some meat on the bare bones of the conversion career approach. Based on the literature from the last forty years, I analyzed parental religion, religious seekers and shoppers, committed converts, confessing leaders, and disillusioned disaffiliates (spiritual as well as secular ones).

Religious upbringing emerges as the essential factor influencing individual religious activity later in life.[42] People who were exposed to intensive and lengthy primary socialization in their *parental religion* were most likely to develop a thoroughly religious outlook on life, if this was supported by their personality. Some of these people disaffiliated from their parental religion during childhood and adolescence, only to reaffiliate or reconvert under the influence of a loved relative or a close friend. Reaffiliation to parental religion was also stimulated by contingency contact with the mass media—usually television or the Internet. The trigger event was often a close and sudden confrontation with death, represented by a loved one. A sudden urge to reach out to the world—the globalization factor—could also contribute to a reaffiliation (the Swedish case). Among the five cases there were three I would characterize as affiliation (Ron, Vicki, and Ben) and only two that involved a change in identity and worldview, that is a "genuine" conversion in the conversion career typology (Sam and Bonnie).

A minority of people with a religious upbringing did not return to organized religion after they dropped out, thus remaining at the *disaffiliation* level. People with negative feelings toward their parents or negative experiences with organized religion (like abuse and hypocrisy) usually became atheists or nonreligious "nones." However, there was also a group of people with a weak primary religious socialization. They would typically opt for a personal type of religion, which is nowadays often called "spirituality."[43] Finally, all disaffiliation informants had higher education. However, the same applied to most of the seekers, converts, and confessional leaders mentioned earlier. The typical informant in the literature seemed to have a higher education and a middle-class mentality—making them very similar to the researcher.[44]

The majority of the people with a weak primary religious socialization will become religious *seekers and shoppers.* Seeking and shopping were stimulated by intellectual curiosity—voracious reading of all sorts of literature on religion and spirituality—and by having much spare time (structural availability). Another important structural factor was access to an extensive supply of religious options on the religious market. This was the typical situation of representatives of Generation X, who were born roughly between 1960 and 1980.[45] These many religious options could be contacted through the mass media—mostly television, the Internet, and radio—or through contacts with missionaries or members of various religious groups (the social factor). In many cases, people entered religious groups through existing social networks; seekers and shoppers tended to have more varied and perhaps more fluid networks. The trigger events in the case of seekers and shoppers were highly varied: teenage existential confusion, the influence of peers and relatives, dissatisfaction with parental religion, or finding the right seeker church catering to people's idiosyncratic religious needs.

Some seekers and shoppers eventually encountered a religious group that catered to their specific needs for a longer time—or perhaps their life entered a period of greater stability. The institutional factor is highly important for the religious *affiliation* level. Many childhood Catholics reaffiliated with the Catholic Charismatic Renewal, while some Episcopalians might find a more "seeker-sensitive" version of their church. A direct confrontation with the death of a close relative could trigger a turning-point experience in people, leading to acute fear of death and spiritual confusion—this event was a combination of a contingency event (a sudden death), the social factor (the deceased is a near relative), and a personality factor (acute fear).

It is harder to identify and analyze the common factors in the conversion careers of the *committed converts.* With only one exception, all came from families with a high religious commitment. Hence, they all received a strong primary religious socialization. Most of these conversions could be called predominantly *social conversions,* because they were above all influenced by social factors. George's conversion was triggered by alienation from his children after divorce, Peter's by having dinner with a friend who was a Baptist minister, Ken's by his introduction to Christianity by Jewish Christian friends, and Esther's by a spiritual teacher. Third, with only two exceptions, all cases involved deeply moving mystical experiences: prayer and forgiveness, speaking in tongues, or receiving visions. Fourth, all committed converts had experienced a lonely childhood and adolescence, making identity questions all the more poignant. In general, people's conversion careers were not very long in the sense that they experimented with many different religions. None of the converts mentioned here became a leader or even a core member—the confession level of religious participation.

Individual factors seemed to be decisive in shaping *confessing leaders*, although always in combination with social and institutional factors. Confession always followed conversion—never the other way around. If converts managed to put their sacrifice into a conversion perspective, thus making it part of their own testimony like the Reverend Cantrell did, it strongly increased their church commitment. After converts experienced a life-shaking event—for example, the death of a child, a suicide attempt, receiving orders to commit a suicide attack, or isolation from parents and relatives—and managed to put this event into a meaningful perspective as part of their life story as a convert, their religious commitment grew until they reached the confession level in their conversion career.

*   *   *

A few general conclusions can now be drawn, which apply to all five levels of religious activity that the conversion career approach distinguishes:

First, similar factors are involved in changes between religious activity levels: whether from affiliation to conversion, preaffiliation to conversion, or conversion to disaffiliation, et cetera. The interconnectedness between personality and social factors is particularly striking. I also find it remarkable how often contingency factors crop up. Of course, what I call contingency will surely be called providence by believers.

Second, childhood and adolescence are the important life stages for influencing religious activity later in life. This could be called the vindication of William James.[46] And perhaps even of Sigmund Freud?

Third, religious seeking and shopping seems to be connected to the privatization of religion, the increased availability of options in the religious market, and the increased accessibility of these options through the modern mass media (especially radio, television, and the Internet). First contact with new religious groups is nowadays probably more often established through the modern mass media than through personal agents.[47] Although seekers and shoppers may be the most visible category, they do not necessarily form a majority among all active believers. After all, most people stick to their parental religion.[48] Some of these people may (re)affiliate or (re)convert, but others always remain active in the faith of their parents.

An interesting question is whether these three general conclusions are also confirmed in the literature on religious affiliation and conversion in Latin America, which is the subject of Chapter 5.

5

Conversion Careers in Latin America

I went with long hair and a ring in my ear … but something stronger than myself touched my heart, it lifted me up and I walked to the platform … I threw myself down on the floor and I started to cry. I started to see my life one by one, step by step, everything that was my earlier life.

(Manuela Cantón Delgado, "Carlos," 1998: 195)

Introduction

This chapter applies the conversion career approach to Latin America by analyzing how people's involvement in religious organizations there is likely to evolve in the course of their lifetime. The conversion career includes all episodes of higher or lower participation in one or more religious organizations during a person's life. The posited levels of religious participation include preaffiliation, affiliation, conversion, confession, and disaffiliation. The central question in this chapter is: *what are the crucial factors that may cause people in Latin America to become religiously active or inactive at a certain stage of their lives?*

During each individual's life, differing levels of religious participation are influenced by social, cultural, institutional, individual, and contingency factors. At the same time, careful attention must be paid to the five main phases of a person's life cycle: childhood, adolescence, marriage, midlife, and old age. This chapter attempts to provide a systematic schema for understanding the conversion narratives of Pentecostals, Catholics, and Mormons that were collected by multiple researchers in various Latin American countries. In particular, I focus on the varying levels of religious involvement of each of these individuals over time. This is an exploratory approach to be confirmed by larger and controlled samples.

The chapter begins with an analysis of Pentecostal, Mormon, and Catholic conversion careers in the selected Latin American cases. The studies I quote from are excellent ethnographies, mostly collected by anthropologists, featuring rich conversion stories from randomly selected informants. A final section comparing Catholic, Mormon, and Pentecostal disaffiliation addresses a major gap in the literature on conversion: the issue of backsliding or leaving a given affiliation. The conclusion weighs the importance of the types of factors mentioned above by relating the case studies to the different levels of the conversion career: preaffiliation, affiliation, conversion, confession, and disaffiliation.

Pentecostal Conversion Careers in Latin America

Based on an analysis of many of the conversion stories contained in the literature on Latin America and my own fieldwork in Nicaragua, I argue that many informants did not really *convert* to a Pentecostal church in the strict sense of having a change of worldview and identity. Most people only *joined* the Pentecostal church for a while (that is, affiliation in the conversion career typology). Making this distinction between conversion and affiliation makes it easier to analyze the significant desertion rates in Pentecostal churches all over Latin America. It also helps explain the high mobility of some believers, who move easily from one church to another.

Few authors actually write out the conversion stories of their informants.[1] Others report that they collected conversion stories, but they do not actually write them out or they use only tiny fragments of them.[2] This is regrettable if one wants to identify the degrees of religious participation—in short, the person's conversion career.

The very first book on Pentecostalism in Latin America contains excerpts from thirty-four conversion stories from Brazil and Chile.[3] Willems skillfully combined secondary materials, ethnographic methods (participant observation and interviews), and surveys in three states of Brazil and three provinces of Chile. He interviewed many leaders and collected thirty-four life histories from random members of many different churches. In all cases, the informant's initials, age, occupation, marital status, and religious background are mentioned.[4] The only missing information is the age at which the conversion took place. Forty years later, this material is still very rich and the parallels with conversion stories that were collected decades later are very strong. In fact, many of the stories—right down to the phrasings—are identical to the more recent conversion accounts.

Take, for instance, the conversion story of "E. C. G.," an eighteen-year-old single woman:[5]

> Grandmother used to take me to a Pentecostal temple, but I had no energy to resist temptations. Afterwards I returned to church to repent but I always fell back into sin. One day I heard the voice of the Lord who told me that all my sins had been forgiven. My heart filled with *gozo* and I was seized by the Holy Spirit. I danced and heard soft voices singing exquisite melodies. I felt carried away to another place of wondrous beauty. When I recovered I found myself kneeling and praying in front of the altar. Immediately all temptations and anxieties ceased. I gave up painting my lips and curling my hair ... When I was 14 years old I had ear surgery and became almost deaf. After my conversion I took part in a *cadena de oración* (continuous prayer meeting for seven days). During one of these meetings an *hermano* laid hands on my head and gradually my hearing went back to normal.

Willems[6] concluded in this early study that all who joined a Pentecostal church shared a strong desire to change their lives. If a conversion took place, it was often connected to miraculous healings. This has proven to be a recurring theme in studies of Pentecostalism in Latin America.

The Argentine anthropologist Daniel Míguez analyzed Pentecostal identity in a Buenos Aires suburb. He collected many rich conversion stories, like this one by Víctor: "I was a true Catholic ... There were neighbors who were Evangelicals and [my grandmother] sent me there ... So I already had some respect for Evangelicals, a certain appreciation of them."[7] Víctor had already been attracted to evangelical television programs before his conversion, which happened after a dream:

> I was always looking for God, and ... I had a very real dream ... I kept getting smaller. And I knew I was going to disappear, I felt I was disappearing ... The only thing I could think of ... was to say: Lord, take care of me ... The desire to find God was so great that I read all the Bible ... Now the Church holds these house meetings ... Once there was a meeting near my home and a neighbor ... invited me ... Seven years ago I went forward here at church and I made my vow of faith ... I received Christ in my heart, that's where all our life starts ... I studied, if there was a need to visit people I visited, then I was designated as leader ... First I was Visitor ... I traveled on my bicycle ... Then I was made Area Leader.

Víctor's conversion career can be sketched chronologically. As a child, he respected his evangelical neighbors. During his adolescence, he liked to watch evangelical television programs, because he was "always looking for God." This is the preaffiliation stage. Then he had a supernatural experience in a dream, which seems to have confronted him with his mortality and insignificance. A neighbor invited him to a house meeting of a local Pentecostal church (a clear institutional factor), where he "received Christ in his heart." He became very active in the church, first as a visitor, then as an area leader. To utilize the terminology of the conversion career: he went from affiliation to conversion to confession in a relatively short time.

Míguez also describes the conversion experience of a married couple, Horacio and Elba García, who were around fifty. The Garcías converted in 1987 after experiencing economic hardship for some time. They were suffering from "extreme anxiety and consequent family disruption." Their son Mario said: "We first went to a *curandero* [shaman healer]. But the *curandero* offered us no solution ... Then some family problems started and we resorted to Umbanda[8] ... I never believed in them [Catholic priests]."

Elba, who was living separately from Horacio at that time, said: "Everything happened through television ... It was the program of pastor Gimenez, and through that message God touched my heart; things started to change. I had the desire to return home."

After this experience, Elba and Horacio gradually became reunited. At a certain stage, about a month and a half after her conversion, Elba decided to "hand in all the medicines to the pastor" and to trust God for her cure: "It wasn't easy, it was not from one day to the other."[9] Shortly after they reentered church life, Elba and Horacio were appointed as Area Leaders.

The conversion careers of Horacio and Elba are quite similar. In their preaffiliation situation, they suffered economic hardship, anxiety, and a separation (contingency factors). They experimented with a *curandero* (shaman healer), Umbanda, and a Catholic priest—showing they had a religious problem-solving perspective. Elba was touched by Christ through an evangelical television program (institutional factor). She went to church and Horacio started going with her. Their conversions contributed to their reconciliation; religion turned out to be part of the solution. Their son Mario converted at a later age, after finding a job through a church member (social networks). He was less active for some time, but he became more involved in church life when he was made an Area Leader. The same happened with his parents. As with Victor, Horacio and Elba went quickly from affiliation to conversion to confession.

The Spanish anthropologist Manuela Cantón[10] notes that conversion stories are more or less standardized and fulfill three different functions. According to her, the conversion testimonies are socializing, didactic, and proselytizing at the same time. The narratives then form the basis of the informant's "new spirituality." It thus comes as no surprise that Cantón's book also contains rich and detailed conversion stories.

The book also gives due attention to the time before conversion—preaffiliation in the five-tier typology described above. Cantón's informants mention the importance of their strong dissatisfaction with Catholicism, their extreme suffering, family and alcohol problems, illness, and a general dissatisfaction with their lives.[11] Over half of the informants report that the first contact with the church happened through a spouse, relative, friend, neighbor, or acquaintance.[12] Cantón's study thus confirms the importance of institutional, contingency, and social factors in recruitment.

The following conversion story is told by Carlos, who was forty-six at that time.[13] He became an alcoholic at fourteen or fifteen and started using marijuana after he joined the army at eighteen. When he had no money to buy drugs, he engaged in armed robbery on the streets of Antigua Guatemala and Guatemala City. He said that he had been imprisoned forty times and that his resentment against society had grown stronger each time he was there. He went to a Catholic church in Antigua Guatemala and said:

> Lord, I believe that you are the son of God; if you exist, change my life; take away this burden from my soul. Lord, I can't take it anymore! ... And you know what happened? Nothing happened, absolutely nothing happened! Witchcraft couldn't change my life; human science couldn't change my life; strong literature like Lenin and Marx couldn't change my life. Something was happening in my life; I didn't understand all of it ... For the first time I went to an evangelical congregation ... I went with long hair and a ring in my ear ... but something stronger than myself touched my heart, it lifted me up and I walked to the platform ... I threw myself down on the floor and I started to cry. I started to see my life one by one, step by step, everything that was my earlier life (he is crying). And I told Him: "Lord, forgive me, if you are more powerful, if you are stronger than the drugs, change me please, take away what I'm feeling in my heart." ... [N]obody could change my life, only His holy and powerful gospel.

Carlos's dramatic conversion career went from adolescent alcoholism and drug use to crime and a long prison life—a contingency crisis brought on by a combination of social and individual factors. Carlos was violent and full of resentment against society. He looked for solutions in various places—not all religious. Ultimately, his conversion experience took place in a Pentecostal church, although we are unable to gauge his subsequent level of commitment because the author does not provide us with the data.

These studies show how most authors have focused on conversion to Pentecostalism among adolescents and married people in the major urban centers of Latin America. The main factors reported in conversion were social (networks), institutional (evangelization methods), and contingency events. Unfortunately, the authors do not provide an overview of the entire life history of their informants, making it impossible to trace their complete conversion careers.

Charismatic Catholic Conversion Careers in Latin America

Focusing only on Pentecostal conversion careers in Latin America implies the risk that certain elements might be considered unique to Pentecostalism, whereas they may also be a part of conversion careers in other religious groups. By way of comparison, this section and the following one will look at Catholic and Mormon conversion careers, based on the available literature. Again, I should note that the literature is extremely scarce. Researchers rarely collect complete conversion narratives in general and hardly ever from Catholics or Mormons, even though the evidence suggests that the concept of conversion is also important in these religions.[14]

The Dutch anthropologist Janneke Brouwer concludes that there are many similarities between the conversion narratives she collected from (Protestant) Pentecostals and Charismatic Catholics in Masaya, Nicaragua.[15] For both of them, the conversion process was very emotional and happened at a crucial moment in their life. Both considered their "old" life to be meaningless, without purpose, empty, and often downright sinful. Both used the concept of "being reborn" to express the personal transformation they experienced. After conversion, life acquired a new meaning and a new purpose. Finally, both her Pentecostal and Charismatic Catholic informants said that they prayed often and that they have remained highly active in their respective churches by taking on various assignments. That is, her informants are located at the *confession* level of the typology of religious activity.

According to Brouwer,[16] the main difference between Pentecostal and Catholic converts in Nicaragua could be found in their conceptualization of the precise moment at which they converted. For the Pentecostals, conversion happened the moment they accepted Jesus Christ as their personal savior, usually by coming forward toward the pulpit during a church service. This moment in time was later ritualized by their baptism and their acceptance as a full member in the Pentecostal church. For the Charismatic Catholics, the conversion moment is equated with the moment at which they became fully aware of God's love for them. Since they were already baptized as infants, no second baptism could be performed. However, they were very much aware that their life had to be transformed after they dedicated themselves to Christ.

Another difference is that the Catholic informants in Nicaragua were converted to the Charismatic Renewal at a much later moment in their lives than the Pentecostals were. The average age for the Catholic converts was twenty-nine, against twenty for the Pentecostals.[17] Almost all of them were nominal Catholics, who became active under the influence of certain events in their lives.

Miguel (36) was an ex-Sandinista fighter against the dictator Somoza, who became disillusioned and later joined the Contras to attack the Sandinista army in the 1980s. In combat, he started to drink heavily and use marijuana. He beat up his wife and his mother. This made him cry when he was sober again, and he wanted to go to church. At a meeting of the Charismatic Renewal, he recognized the songs from afar and was greeted at the door by ex-friends from his Sandinista days. When the speaker invited people to accept Christ in their lives as the solution for their personal problems, he came forward. Miguel said: "Without realizing it, I had knelt down and I was crying ... Suddenly I longed for mass and the Eucharist. That week my happiness started." His drinking mates thought he would only last for a week without alcohol, but he never returned to his old ways. Church people took him to a prayer group to receive the Holy Spirit. He lost consciousness and had a vision of a man walking in the desert. He said: "Everybody started praying and crying. Then I was embraced by everyone. We went home and testified to all people of what had happened." He soon became an active leader and a preacher at Charismatic Renewal meetings.[18]

The conversion stories of the couple Isabel and José were very similar. Both had a conversion experience during a *retiro* (spiritual retreat) of the Catholic Church, but not at the same time. A close (lady) friend invited Isabel (40) to come with her to the retreat: "That last Sunday the Holy Spirit descended upon me ... I felt how something filled me up, for I realized there was an emptiness inside me ... I felt loved by the people who were there."

Isabel's husband José (39) said:[19]

On the last day of the retreat, the Holy Spirit descended [upon me]. I told the Lord: "If anything is going to happen here, I'm prepared to receive it. Lord, here I am." When the Holy Spirit descended, the speaker gave indications of things we might experience ... I felt a warmth deep inside me ... As of that moment, I no longer was the same. I felt differently, I began to look at things differently, and I began to do things differently. I now read the Bible, I pray, I go to mass, something I never did before.

All four Charismatic Catholics became very active in the church after their conversion experience. Two occasionally pray and sing in tongues. All four also report that they have a very intense personal spiritual life, full of prayer and Bible study.

Brouwer concludes that the Charismatic Catholic informants tended to emphasize the practical changes in their social lives after conversion.[20] Most reported that they used to have an impatient character, easily provoked to anger. After conversion, they said that they were more calm and at peace with themselves and other people. Collecting extensive life histories, Brouwer shows similarities between the conversion experiences of Charismatic Catholics and Pentecostals in Masaya, Nicaragua. The link between conversion and confession is again confirmed. But since almost all of her informants are leaders, located at the confession level of our typology, her findings cannot simply be generalized to all of Latin America.

Mormon Conversion Careers in Latin America

The detailed conversion stories of Mormon microentrepreneurs in Guatemala City shed interesting light on the conversion careers in this particular offspring of Christianity.[21] The average age for conversion among my twelve key Mormon informants in Guatemala was twenty-five, but almost all had gone through (long) periods of inactivity (see also the section below on disaffiliation).

In my study of Mormons in La Florida, a typical low-income *barrio* of Guatemala City, I found three primary groups of informants who had converted. First, there are adolescent religious seekers, who had visited various churches to see where they felt most comfortable (Mario, Patricio, and Ana). Second, I found informants who had joined a new church or reactivated a prior church membership after going through a turning point in their lives such as facing up to their problems with alcohol or becoming parents (nine informants). Third, I interviewed informants who had switched to another church under the influence of spouses or children (Raúl, Beatriz, and Miguel).[22] I will briefly analyze one conversion story of the seekers and the turning point groups.

Almost all (male) Mormon informants reported having a turning point experience in their lives; in all cases this was connected to alcohol problems. When Guillermo (29) was only thirteen, his father kicked him out of the family home and he was forced to live on the street. In 1984, at eighteen, he first learned about the Mormon Church:[23]

> I wanted to change my life, because I used a lot of alcohol, drugs; I hung out with youth gangs ... Some missionaries [Sisters] came here and talked to me about the gospel and I liked it ... They presented a Christ of love, someone who had mercy and that He could save my life. And at other times people had told me that I was a son of the devil, that I was possessed by Satan and that I'd go to hell with him. I got baptized, but I didn't have the strength—or the

support, I think—to stay in church. After two months ... I backslided ...
I started drinking again ... and I didn't have anything to do with the church
for seven years.

Alcoholics Anonymous helped Guillermo to overcome his alcohol
problem, but he still needed marijuana to make it through the day:

I was fed up with the life I had and there were only two solutions for me:
either I changed my life, or I would kill myself. That night I went to bed ...
and I awoke around five in the morning ... I saw all the scenes from my life:
the bad things I had done, what I was doing to my body, the suffering and
pain I was causing in my family ... I knelt on the bed and asked God for
forgiveness. And I said: God, if you really exist, if you have a purpose for my
life, manifest yourself. I put my life into your hands and do what you want
with me because *I* could never do anything with it. Take me to a place where
I will stop using drugs, where I can change my life, where I can be happy and
make my family happy ...
    So I got up, bathed myself, changed clothes and I didn't know where
I was going ... And when I noticed, I was again in the church where
I had been baptized seven years ago. Since that moment my life began to
change ...
    I did have a lot of support from all the brothers of the church ... they
took care of me like a baby and taught me really how to live the gospel.
After two months in church they conferred the Aaronic priesthood on me.
After three months in church they conferred the Melchizedek priesthood on
me ... and so they ... called me as president of the young men of the ward.

In the case of Guillermo, a very troubled childhood of drugs and alcohol was followed by a conversion at a young age (18). The church members
could not support him sufficiently, so he dropped out of the Mormon
Church and was inactive for many years. Again, when the drug problem
got out of hand and threatened to kill him, he appealed to God and had
a supernatural experience, after which God guided him back to the same
Mormon congregation that he had visited before. Now, however, he does
receive sufficient support from the members and has also been given an
important calling. Again, the crisis was caused by a combination of individual and social factors and resolved after receiving the support of church
members and becoming active in church.
    The conversion careers described here among the Charismatic Catholics,
Mormons, and Pentecostals are remarkably similar. In all the cases, the
contingency factor of the crisis appears as the starting point. The informants have a religious problem-solving perspective; some try to visit
curanderos, priests, and Umbanda leaders to find a solution. Charismatic
Catholics in Nicaragua stay in their church, because they are happy

with it. In the studies on Argentina, Guatemala, and Nicaragua, people who are dissatisfied with Catholicism are reported to be more open to experimentation by visiting other churches. In the end, a contingency social factor, a chance meeting with missionaries or the influence of a friend or neighbor, establishes the first contact with their new church. If they receive support from members, they will stay. But the support is often insufficient and the church demands are high, which sometimes leads to (temporary) disaffiliation. I return to this theme in the conclusion.

Pentecostal Disaffiliation

There are few comprehensive studies on religious disaffiliation in Latin America. Cantón's (1998) study of Guatemala provides no information on the informants' church commitment following their conversion. However, it is significant that the Pentecostal informants of Míguez (1997) in Buenos Aires were all designated Area Leaders or Visitors soon after their conversion and subsequent baptism into their church. The fact that these Pentecostals went from affiliation to conversion to confession in a relatively short time appears to have strengthened their church commitment, but Míguez provides no details to gauge how this process worked.

In 2000, a survey of over 2,400 Nicaraguans by the Dutch Reverend Henk Minderhout showed that the total Protestant church disaffiliation (or "desertion") was 27 percent of all Protestants. Among these ex-Protestants, 8 percent said that they had returned to the Catholic Church and 19 percent reported that they did not belong to any religion anymore.[24]

Jorge Gómez presents even more detailed information on disaffiliation in Costa Rica, based on three large surveys in 1989, 1991, and 1994. The total Protestant "apostasy" rate was 48 percent in 1989 and 53 percent in 1991. The 1989 survey showed that among these ex-Protestants, 62 percent had actually returned to the Catholic Church.[25] A full one-third had completely dropped out of any church and 6 percent had joined the Jehovah's Witnesses or the Mormon Church. Gómez reported that among those born into Catholicism, 12.5 percent deserted.[26]

Gómez has a very interesting comparison to offer about the main reasons for entering and leaving Protestant churches, based on the 1994 survey.[27] The main reasons for the original conversion were "the desire to become a new creature in Christ" (50 percent), being born into an evangelical family (11 percent), church recruitment through a friend or relative (10 percent), the attraction of evangelical preaching (7 percent), and being healed (6 percent). The main reasons for dropping out were: not being able to live up to the evangelical moral standards (29 percent), rejection of bad financial management in the Pentecostal church (13 percent), and the bad conduct of other members (9 percent) or of the pastor (8 percent).

The only book-length monograph on religious disaffiliation in Latin America is Kurt Bowen's study on Mexico. Bowen concluded that "conversion is often a process of encounter and retreat, which only after some time culminates in conversion. Altogether, 54 percent of converts identified one or another crisis in their lives that significantly affected their conversion decision."[28]

In typical fashion, Bowen dedicated more attention to why Mexicans joined Pentecostalism than to why they left it behind. Consider this story by a woman (37), who converted after seeing a leaflet advertising a Christian film during a campaign:[29]

> I like films of Christ. The first time I went, there was not a film. I felt deceived ... The pastor invited people to go forward to give themselves to Christ. I did not go ... After the film next time, he also made the call. I felt embarrassed, but my sister went up, so, with my children, we went up and delivered ourselves to Christ. I did not know anything of Christ. I did not know how to study the Bible. After the campaign we stopped attending, but some brothers came to visit us to teach us.

It is clear that some people may drift into a Pentecostal church after seeing a film or an evangelical television program, but their continued commitment would seem to depend on finding a community, on receiving support from like-minded people, and above all on receiving the attention of other members (for example, being visited by them).

Just like growth rates, the desertion rates were also very high in Mexican Pentecostal churches. According to Bowen, "68 per cent of those baptized in Evangelical churches in the 1980s had dropped out by the end of the decade."[30] Based on Bowen's extensive surveys in over forty congregations, the total disaffiliation rate in Pentecostal churches was 43 percent, meaning that less than half of all those who once belonged to a Pentecostal church actually stayed in it.[31]

Mormon Disaffiliation

The dropout rate for new Mormon converts in Latin America generally exceeds 50 percent.[32] One year after joining the Mormon Church, at best, half of the new converts remain active, meaning that they attend Mormon Church services at least once a month.

I have already noted that the conversion careers of Mormon entrepreneurs in Guatemala City showed a rapid change from (pre)affiliation to conversion to confession. Patricio and Guillermo both had a troubled childhood and adolescence, marked by alcohol and drug problems. Although they converted to the Mormon Church at a relatively young age, twenty-six and eighteen respectively, both were inactive for many years. They felt that members showed no interest in them during this time. When their alcohol problems got out of hand, they prayed to God, hoping for an intervention in their lives. Both had a supernatural experience that they interpreted as support for the veracity of the Mormon Church. They subsequently returned to church and this time they did receive support from members and leaders.

An important element in my informants' Mormon socialization was, again, the fact that they soon received one or more important "callings" (church assignments). The callings seemed to reinforce and sustain their commitment: "In a calling, members are forced to learn new things, like teaching, that they are not used to and do not know how to do well. They would like to shirk their responsibilities, but they are afraid of losing God's blessing—God's favor—if they fail, so they go on."[33] However, there is a risk to giving the new members a calling too soon. When they feel too uncertain of themselves, some may become inactive, as happened with another Mormon informant, Miguel.[34]

Catholic Disaffiliation

There is little literature on disaffiliation among Catholics, although most studies agree that nominal Catholics make up the bulk of all people identifying themselves as Catholic in surveys on religious affiliation. Based on a 1989 survey, Gómez reports that 13 percent of all reported Catholics in Costa Rica never go to church and that 25 percent go only very rarely.[35] Pablo (41, carpenter), an inactive Catholic who believed in being a Christian but not in going to church, told me: "In the Catholic Church they don't explain to you what it all means ... So you have to find a way to live well ... To apply the law which our Lord Jesus Christ taught us, to be good, to give up vices."[36]

The Catholic Charismatic Renewal movement has become an important vehicle for Catholics to become active in the church again, but in a very different way than before.[37] Although it usually occurred at a later time in their lives than with the Pentecostals and Mormons, Charismatic Catholics who were studied in Brazil and Nicaragua also had a personal meeting with Christ that then affected their entire life. Like the Pentecostals, they usually called it a conversion and it often happened during a spiritual retreat. They received the Holy Spirit in a way similar to the Pentecostals. Almost all the informants in Brouwer (2000) had been nominal Catholics, who became active again in the Catholic Church under the influence of certain events in their lives. These events were alcohol problems or a feeling of meaninglessness, similar again to those described by Pentecostal informants. However, it is not clear why these informants had become nominal Catholics in the first place.

In sum, the remarkable similarities in the conversion careers of Pentecostals, Charismatic Catholics, and Mormons also extend to the dynamics behind the processes of (temporary) disaffiliation. I now turn to a brief analysis of these conversion discourses, using the conversion career approach to shed more light on this phenomenon.

Conclusion

Sweeping generalizations that explain conversion in the context of Latin America should be met with skepticism. The available literature on conversion in Latin America remains limited and the conversion stories presented in this chapter come from different churches in seven countries: Chile, Brazil, Argentina, Nicaragua, Guatemala, Mexico, and Costa Rica. Even in these testimonials, essential information on the conversion careers of informants was often missing.[38] This was primarily due to the fact that conversion careers take place over time, include different levels of commitment, and frequently extend far beyond the particular time frame or interests of a given researcher. Most of the conversion narratives collected in Latin America, as in the North American and European literature on religious conversion (see Chapter 4), were collected among adolescents or people in their twenties and thirties.

Despite these limitations, I detect some important insights from the literature on conversion that lead to a more comprehensive and interdisciplinary approach to explaining and comparing conversion. I follow the conversion career approach to analyze the conversion narratives presented in this chapter. The conversion career approach goes beyond the Pauline idea of conversion as a once-in-a-lifetime experience, categorizing different levels of conversion (preaffiliation, affiliation, conversion, confession, and disaffiliation) and outlining the key factors that the approach identifies as essential in the conversion career (social, institutional, cultural, individual, and contingency factors).

First, during the *preaffiliation* situation of the informants, the impetus most informants mention is a contingency factor: a crisis. This can be of various sorts, although all of these crises touch upon the informant's personality. In the most extreme cases, the crisis involved drug or alcohol problems, often in combination with crime. These crises were related to the informant's social situation (poverty, child labor, absent fathers) or personality (machismo, insecurity). In other cases, the crisis was less extreme and related to illness, divorce, adultery, or poverty. Whatever its origin, the crisis always caused anxiety (Horacio and Elba), desperation (Carlos), and dissatisfaction with the current (religious) lifestyle.

It is important that most informants were at this time still adolescents or in their twenties and that all informants couched the crisis—and its possible solutions—in religious terms. Most informants had a nominal Catholic background. A few were active Catholics; some were seekers, always looking for God (Victor). When the crisis was at its worst, many experimented with different religious solutions: *curanderos*, Umbanda, Catholicism, or secular political philosophies such as Marxism. The vibrant religious markets all over Latin America allow lukewarm Catholics unprecedented opportunities for tuning into television and radio stations and moving from one church to another.[39] The preaffiliation level makes visible the reservoir of potential converts, but for affiliation and an actual conversion, much more is needed.

Second, a combination of social and contingency factors is decisive in determining the particular church that people will *affiliate* with. It could be a chance meeting with Mormon missionaries or the influence of a spouse, friend, or neighbor that serves to establish the first contact with the new church. In some cases, the influence of evangelical television programs is mentioned. Here institutional factors are important: the evangelization activities that a religious group employs to recruit new members, either by sponsoring television programs or by motivating their members to give their testimonies and to bring their family and friends to the church. Not surprisingly, the churches that put greater emphasis on their members participating in this type of evangelization activities—like most Pentecostal churches and the Mormon Church—generally achieve higher growth.

Social factors are principally responsible for the question of whether or not the informant will decide to actually affiliate with a new church. Here, most informants mention the importance of receiving the support of the "brothers" (and sisters, who are grammatically included in the Spanish word *hermanos*). New members need a lot of attention, nurturing, and counseling; this is mentioned in the conversion career scheme under "incorporating, creating, and shaping activities."[40] The crucial importance of social networks for Venezuelan evangelicals is demonstrated by David Smilde.[41]

Third, the actual *conversion* usually follows when the new church is seen as (contributing to) the solution to the original crisis. This can take many forms: the healing of an illness, giving a new purpose and meaning to one's life, overcoming alcohol problems, giving people peace and tranquility.

Even getting a job through another church member is often interpreted as a divine sign that conversion is the right choice.

Fourth, many of the informants in the literature fit in the highest level of the conversion career typology of religious activity: *confession*. In the conversion career approach, role learning is considered to be the basis of church commitment.[42] A good way to strengthen church commitment is to give the novice a voluntary church assignment. In a great many cases, the informants remained active in church while accepting important leadership or teaching responsibilities. However, there is always the danger that the informant still feels insecure and may feel pressured into accepting a task that they are not ready for yet. In that case, disaffiliation may follow.

Finally, *disaffiliation* also happens when the new members feel rejected or neglected by the other members of the church. Informants from the three groups mentioned that they remained active in church because "the brothers" visited them. However, because many congregations are big and the leaders overworked, one can safely assume that many people were not visited and hence dropped out after a while. This applied especially to people who converted very quickly, with only a rudimentary knowledge of the church's doctrine and rules of conduct. The fact that the consequences of conversion are rather limited in so many cases also suggests that many of these "conversions" are actually only a rather superficial form of affiliation and a temporary one at that.

In other cases, disaffiliation was caused by the high demands—in discipline, morality, time, and money—of the church in question. This was noted particularly in the literature on Pentecostal churches. It means that the same factors that were originally responsible for the success of Pentecostalism in Latin America also account for its high dropout rates. Salvation sometimes proves to be less secure than people had originally hoped, the high levels of commitment and high standards of conduct are difficult to maintain, and the organization of many Pentecostal churches would seem to stimulate schism rather than to control it. During this process, people may join various churches. But researchers should be wary of simply equating affiliation with conversion. For researchers who wish to understand both the process and effects of conversion in the context of Latin America, the distinction between conversion and affiliation is critical. In the concluding chapter, I show that this distinction is of equal importance all over the world.

6

Conclusion

To have a conversion experience is nothing much. The real point is to be able to keep on taking it seriously; to retain a sense of its plausibility. *This* is where the religious community comes in.

(*Peter L. Berger and Thomas Luckmann,* The Social Construction of Reality, *1967: 158*)

Introduction

In the introduction, I used the term "religious perspective" to analyze the unique window on the world that religion has to offer. All human beings need a philosophy, whether atheism or a religion, to give meaning to their lives, and it seems that any religion has the potential to make life meaningful for its adherents. I used the conversion career approach to analyze why people become and remain religiously active.

This conclusion presents the consequences of the conversion career approach for the religious organization and the converting subject and also addresses the religious factor in conversion. As Lewis Rambo put it succinctly: "The process of conversion is a product of the interactions among the convert's aspirations, needs, and orientations, the nature of the group into which he or she is being converted, and the particular social matrix in which these processes are taking place."[1] I end with an analysis of conversion patterns and some general conclusions and recommendations for future research on conversion.

Conversion and the Religious Organization

Chapter 3 argued that the so-called rational choice debate is moot. Even if people do *not* make rational choices concerning the religion they profess, religious organizations would still be competing for members against each other. The quintessential condition is not the *rationalist* actor or even the cost-benefit analysis, implicit or explicit, people make of the religious group(s) they visit.[2] The essence is religious liberty: the freedom to choose one's religion and the freedom to express that choice by publicly affiliating with, or perhaps just visiting, a particular religious group.

Religious freedom leads to religious pluralism, which in turn leads to interreligious competition for members. Religious organizations can compete against each other by using their unique histories,[3] their core beliefs and doctrines, their rules of conduct (for example, the *Word of Wisdom* in Mormonism), their morality, their special rituals (including conversion stories and testimonies), their specific forms of empowerment (for example, the use of the Holy Spirit in Pentecostalism), their theologies, their organizations, their leadership, their special religious experiences (such as speaking in tongues in Pentecostalism), their passionate prayers, their miraculous healings, their access to prosperity, and their special missionary programs and agents.

The religious organization by itself constitutes a major factor in the conversion process. The institutional factor includes not only the appeal of the organization and its doctrine, but also how it defines conversion. What are the organization's requisites for membership, conversion, and commitment? And how are these enforced?

Figure 6.1 summarizes the levels of religious participation in the conversion career approach. I added what I consider the *minimal* weekly participation requirements of the three religious organizations I refer to most in this book: Catholics, Pentecostals, and Mormons.[4] These are, of course, open to debate.

Chapter 1 argued that a sophisticated combination of socialization and role theory approaches is useful in analyzing the conversion process from the perspective of the religious organization. Long and Hadden defined socialization as "the social process of creating and incorporating new members of a group from a pool of nonmembers, carried out by members and their allies." This implies looking at the cultural and organizational factors in membership, acknowledging the fact that the church members define who is a novice, and analyzing the sorts of activities the participants carry out. Three activities constitute the tools of the trade for religious organizations to achieve this:

1. *Incorporating activities* include recruiting novices, certification (monitoring of novices), and placing novices in certain church positions (that is, voluntary assignments).
2. *Creating activities* include "displaying the requisites of membership for novices" by the established members (the role models).

Preaffiliation: life situation and worldview of person before affiliation.
Church terms: "visitor," "seeker," "unchurched Christian."
Minimum weekly participation requirements by religious organization: Roman Catholic
Church—0–1 hour, most Pentecostal groups—1 hour, Latter-day Saints (Mormons)—1–4
hours.

Affiliation: formal membership in a religious group, without a change of identity.
Church terms: "member," "baptized member."
Minimal weekly participation requirements by religious organization:
Roman Catholic Church—1–2 hours, most Pentecostal groups—2–4 hours,
Latter-day Saints (Mormons)—3–5 hours.

Conversion (in the limited sense of the conversion careers approach): a (radical) change of
identity, followed by a commitment to a (new) religious group.
Church terms: "convert," "full member," "baptized member."
Minimal weekly participation requirements by religious organization:
Roman Catholic Church—2–3 hours, most Pentecostal groups—2–5 hours,
Latter-day Saints (Mormons)—4–6 hours.

Confession: a core member identity with a high level of participation inside the (new) religious
community and a strong evangelism on the outside.
Church terms: "core member," "leader," "deacon," "missionary" (et cetera).
Minimal weekly participation requirements by religious organization:
Roman Catholic Church lay leaders—3–6 hours; Pentecostal pastors, deacons,
volunteer leaders—4–10 hours; Latter-day Saints (Mormons)—5–20 hours.

Disaffiliation: no church membership or visits.
Church terms: "inactive member," "seeker," "unchurched Christian."
General weekly participation in religious organization: 0 hours.

Figure 6.1   Levels and requirements of individual religious participation in the
conversion career approach

3. *Shaping activities* include shaping novices by the threat and application of sanctions.[5]

From the review of the literature in the preceding chapters, it appears that the successful religious organizations in the United States are especially strong in incorporating and shaping activities, while those in Latin America probably score better in incorporating and creating activities. This implies that the emphasis in successful religious organizations in the United States is more on commitment, whereas in Latin America the emphasis is more on participation (or on membership numbers). In the United States, the churches with expanding memberships tend to be evangelical, with a minority among them being (neo-)Pentecostals. In Latin America, the successful churches are overwhelmingly (neo-)Pentecostal, with a minority being evangelicals.

The three types of activities are closely connected to the organizational structure of the religious organization. Most successful churches in Latin America and the United States have a strong leadership that defines the particular membership profile of the organization—and hence its niche on the religious market—and the main methods it uses to compete for members with other religious organizations.[6]

Based on the findings of this book, religious organizations all over the world that want to increase their membership should:

1. Try to influence people's personalities as much as possible through primary and secondary religious socialization and religious education.
2. Try to strengthen the development of friendships among their members and the use of members' social networks to bring in as many visitors as possible.
3. Try to contain internal dissent and arguments with a minimum of force and power, always avoiding the risks of parsimony and hypocrisy.
4. Try to find the best possible match between the religious organization and the mentalities and personalities of (the majority of) its members.
5. Try to recruit as many missionary agents as possible—turning each member into a missionary—and try to accomplish as many contingency meetings with potential converts as is humanly possible; a sophisticated use of mass media is important here.
6. Try to use their own typical music, rituals, and sacraments as powerful experiences that induce and consolidate the conversion process.[7]

However, it is important to remember that religious freedom and religious pluralism are dynamic and exist in differing degrees all over the world. In the United States, religious freedom is among the oldest and strongest in the world and thus constitutes an important cultural factor in conversion. But even here, some religions receive more (tax) benefits than others and some religious groups are subject to more state harassment than others. In Western Europe, mainstream churches are often favored and even subsidized by the state. The religious market there is more regulated and religious groups may sometimes merge to form a cartel. The demand for organized religion—but probably not for spirituality and other free-flowing forms of religion[8]—seems to be lower in Western Europe than in the United States or Latin America. The religious monopoly of the Roman Catholic Church in most Latin American countries formally started eroding in the late nineteenth century.[9] Protestant missionaries were persecuted violently in some countries in Latin America until the 1950s and 1960s.[10] Finally, in most countries of the Middle East, no religious freedom exists at all. Islam forms a religious monopoly, protected by the nation-state, leaving Muslims there with religious options that are internal to Islam: inactivity, nominal activity, or (state-repressed) radicalism.

The Converting Subject

Contemporary conversion in the United States, Western Europe, and Latin America still happens mostly during adolescence and young adulthood, just as William James reported around 1900.[11] Most conversions still occur between the ages of fifteen and twenty-five. The literature is biased in select-ing informants overwhelmingly from this age category (see Chapter 1). Future research should aim for a more even spread of informants from all levels of the life cycle: adolescents, young married couples, people in their middle years, and the elderly. One cannot assume that conversion in youth will be the same as conversion at an older age.

Age is also relevant in influencing the subject's "structural availability":[12] how much freedom and time do people have to seek out religious groups and visit them? The converting subject nowadays has many ways to make first contact with the religious groups, but the main avenues are those based on one's social networks, on contacts with the mass media, or on chance encounters with missionary agents from religious groups (see Chapter 3). The informant's social network includes not only spouses and children, but also best friends, family members in the broadest sense (ranging from siblings and cousins to grandparents) and weaker ties[13] with neighbors, colleagues at work, street and neighborhood dwellers, friends, and acquaintances.

The mass media nowadays often bring both men and women in contact with religious groups: radio and television, the Internet, and, occasionally, newspapers and weekly magazines. Usually a program or article explicitly deals with the theme of religion, but occasionally it is sufficient just to hear compelling conversion stories on the radio or to see people's testimonies delivered on television. This makes people curious about the group, which provides the impetus to visit them, especially if one is accompanied by an acquaintance.

Chapter 3 argued that informants always make implicit or explicit cost-benefit analyses of the religious groups they are visiting (although I am wary of the concept of "rational choice," as mentioned earlier). People generally continue to visit the religious groups where they "felt at home." For people to feel at home in a religious group, various requirements have to coincide. If one or more fail to occur, disaffiliation is the most likely outcome. I give the requirements in the order of *decreasing* importance:

1. The new members got along well with members and leaders.
2. The new members felt they received sufficient attention and support from coreligionists.
3. The new members liked the religious group's code of conduct.
4. The new members liked the religious group's essential beliefs and doctrines.
5. The new members generally (with the exceptions often leading to disaffiliation) appreciated it when they were asked to perform in a special task as a volunteer.

Although one would expect to encounter gender differences in the conversion process, starting with the primary socialization in one's parental religion, the literature is curiously silent on this. The same applies for possible gender differences in the extent and use of social networks or gender differences in the telling of conversion stories.[14] A study among mostly Free Methodist undergraduate students in the United States found that men used more adventurous metaphors, while most women preferred peaceful metaphors to describe their conversion experience.[15] From the literature on conversion stories I analyzed in this book, however, no general conclusions on gender differences in the conversion career can be drawn.

Levels and Patterns of Religious Activity

The literature reviewed in this book made it hard to operationalize in detail the level of religious activity I designated as *preaffiliation*.[16] It became a highly heterogeneous "miscellaneous" category, including such different groups as people on a personal religious quest ("seekers"), people who were between religious affiliations, and people who were temporarily or permanently unchurched. Similarly, the *disaffiliation* level contained a wide spectrum: atheists, agnostics, unchurched religious believers, and inactive adherents who still identified themselves as members but who ceased to assist the meetings of their religious organization on any regular basis.

The people I locate at the *affiliation* level—that is, formal membership in a religious group that does not form an important element of one's identity—met the first two requirements I mentioned above. They got along well with and received sufficient attention from fellow group members and leaders. They generally liked the group's core doctrines and rules of conduct, although they often had no detailed knowledge of the beliefs and although their behavior did not always conform to the expected code of conduct. Moreover, they did not feel the need to become involved more deeply in the group through an assignment as a volunteer.

People who reported a *conversion* experience in the literature invariably conformed to the rules of conduct and were in a process of internalizing the core beliefs and practices. This process often took years, as was clear from frequent reports of periods of struggle and sometimes even temporary disaffiliation. Interestingly, in most cases of a "successful" conversion (that is, continued commitment to and involvement in the religious group) the paramount factor was involvement in a church assignment. In that sense, the *confession* level in my typology was a reliable indicator of a successful conversion. The confession level in the typology always followed the conversion level (defined as a change in religious worldview and identity); it never happened the other way around. Even so, most people who were currently at the confession level had gone through periods of inactivity in the past. They came back by holding on to factors 1, 2, or 5.

It is now possible to give a more specific version of the dynamics of people moving between the levels of religious activity: see Figure 6.2.

Chapter 1 identified and synthesized the various factors in the dynamic process from affiliation and conversion to confession: social, institutional, individual, cultural, and contingency factors (see Fig. 6.3 below). Although at least three of these will generally be relevant in any conversion process, there often is one factor that is dominant. The following are the three most common types of religious activity, defined by the dominant factor, as they

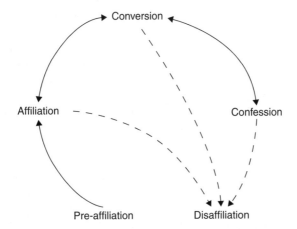

Figure 6.2 Movement between levels of religious activity in the conversion career approach

appeared in the literature—mainly on Christian groups—from the United States and Europe (Chapter 4) and Latin America (Chapter 5):

1. The *institutional affiliation* pattern referred to a type of religious affiliation influenced predominantly by institutional factors pertaining directly to the religious organization involved. Common elements were: doctrine, rules of conduct, organization, evangelization methods, and presence in the (mass) media. This type of "institutional affiliation" usually showed significant interaction with social and individual factors in the conversion process. In Latin America and the United States, cultural factors also influenced the level of religious involvement indirectly.[17]

2. The *social conversion* pattern: here, the religious conversion—understood throughout this book as a change in religious worldview and identity—was influenced predominantly by social factors, that is, the social networks the converting subject already belonged to or a new social network s/he was being drawn into. The "social conversion" usually showed significant interaction with institutional factors that defined the precise requirements for conversion to the perspective/doctrine of that particular religious group and with individual factors.

3. The *individual confession* pattern: Confession is a core member identity, characterized by a high level of participation inside the new religious group and a strong missionary zeal toward nonmembers. It was influenced predominantly by individual factors pertaining to a personal quest for meaning and religious expression. People at this level liked to base their lives on the "religious perspective," as I assumed in the introduction. The "individual confession" interacted mostly with institutional factors defining the requirements for confession and leadership in that particular religious group and to a lesser extent with social factors such as getting along with other group members and leaders. Cultural factors were an indirect influence on personality through primary and secondary socialization.

The Religious Factor in Conversion

Figure 6.3 is not meant to suggest that I repeated the mistake of most social scientists studying conversion by reducing it to an elaborate scheme of non-religious factors.[18] Rambo reminded us that for religious people, "the purpose of conversion is to bring people into relationship with the divine and provide them a new sense of meaning and purpose."[19] The "encounter with the holy" is the main religious factor in conversion and there were plenty of examples in the conversion stories of chapters 4 and 5. But they were always closely connected to the religious organization that people converted to.

Hence, it should come as no surprise that many converts to *Pentecostalism* had experienced haunting dreams and visions before converting or right after the moment they accepted Jesus Christ as their savior. Not all converts reported speaking (or singing) in tongues after their conversion, but some

Social factors
- The influence of relatives, friends, and/or acquaintances on joining or leaving a religious group (social networks).
- The influence of religious group members, including charismatic leaders,[a] through socialization and role learning.

Institutional factors
- Dissatisfaction with current religious group or with religious inactivity.
- The presence of and interreligious competition between different religious groups.
- Recruitment methods of these religious groups (evangelization, TV/radio messages, Internet).
- Appeal of their leaders, organization, practices, rituals, rules of conduct, ethics, values, and doctrine (interreligious competition factors).

Cultural and political factors
- Appeal of the culture politics of a religious group (its view on local culture and society; its view on local politics).
- Tension between religious group and society and/or a specific ethnic group or country.

Individual factors
- A religious worldview or need to become religiously involved (prior socialization).
- A personal need to give a concrete expression to feelings of meaning making or meaninglessness.
- A personal need to seek meaning and/or spirituality in a religious group.
- A personal need to give a concrete expression to feelings of meaning making or meaninglessness.
- A personal need to seek meaning and/or spirituality in a religious group.
- A personal need to change one's life situation.
- Certain character traits are conducive to religious participation (for example, anxiety, insecurity, sociability; cf. "convert personality").

Contingency factors
- An acutely felt crisis or turning point (for example, illness, alcohol problems, joblessness, marriage, divorce, migration).
- A religion-based or inspired solution to the crisis (for example, healing, a new job in church).
- A chance meeting with representatives of a religious group (for example, missionaries).
- A chance viewing of a (religious) program on television.

Figure 6.3   Factors in religious activity
[a]Cf. Rambo (1982).

did and it obviously was a powerful experience. Almost all Pentecostal converts were "seized by the Holy Spirit" or "filled by the Holy Spirit" at some point of their conversion career—usually in the beginning. Some of them had experienced "dancing in the Spirit" as well. Many Pentecostal converts heard the voice of God and described "a sense of warmth" and feelings of incredible joy, often leading them to cry. Ironically, many *deconversion* stories also stressed the feelings of enormous joy and relief that the ex-believers felt when they had the sudden moment of insight that the repressive religion they belonged to, usually their parental religion, was just—in the words of Ayaan Hirsi Ali—"humbug."

Charismatic Catholics typically equated the conversion moment with the moment they became fully aware of God's love for them. At that moment, they decided to dedicate themselves fully to Christ and aimed to live a different type of life, following Christ as their example and typically remaining active in meetings of the Catholic Charismatic Renewal afterward. Some described a deep longing for mass and the Eucharist. When they were seized by the Holy Spirit, they described similar feelings of warmth and joy as the Protestant Pentecostals above.

The *Mormon* converts expressed their joy at hearing about "a Christ of love" from the missionaries. They put themselves into God's hands, after their lives became bogged down in alcohol and family problems. Mormon converts did not describe religious experiences but typically stressed the support of the Mormon community in getting their lives in order and the comforting feeling that God was watching over them.

The *Muslim* converts typically felt attracted to the simplicity and the rational logic of Islam. They rarely discussed their feelings about religious experiences in Islam, although many also reported experiencing tremendous joy according to the general literature.[20]

General Conclusions and Recommendations

Finally, I present some general conclusions pertaining to all levels of religious participation that the conversion career approach distinguishes:

1. Childhood and adolescence continue to be important stages of the life cycle, influencing religious activity later in life. This could be called the vindication of William James, Erik Erikson, and perhaps to a certain extent even Sigmund Freud.
2. Conversion in the narrow sense of the conversion career approach always requires a change in religious worldview and *identity*. Empirical indicators of conversion as a "rupture with a former identity" and the "ubiquitous utilization of the convert identity in

all areas of life" are still relevant in contemporary studies of religious change worldwide.[21]

3. Hence, researchers should be wary of simply equating recruitment with conversion. For researchers who wish to understand both the process and effects of conversion all over the world, the distinction between affiliation and conversion is critical. To a large degree, this distinction gives us greater insights into the high religious mobility of many individuals.

4. Similar factors are involved in changes between religious activity levels: whether from affiliation to conversion, preaffiliation to conversion, or conversion to disaffiliation. The interconnectedness between individual and social factors was particularly striking throughout this book. I also find it remarkable that contingency factors cropped up often. Of course, what I call contingency will be called providence by believers.

5. The contemporary importance of religious seeking and especially religious shopping is directly related to the privatization of religion, the increased availability of options in the religious market, and the increased accessibility of these options through the modern mass media (especially radio, television, and the Internet). First contact with new religious groups is nowadays more often established through the modern mass media than through personal agents.[22] Although religious seekers and shoppers are the most visible category, they do not necessarily form a majority among all active believers. After all, most people stick to their parental religion (see Chapter 4). These people neither (re)affiliate nor (re)convert.[23]

6. The conversion process is primarily influenced by significant others (relatives, friends, and acquaintances) through the *social networks* to which the individual belongs (see chapters 4 and 5). It is clear from the literature that almost all people, men *and* women, are recruited to religious organizations through social networks. While studying the role of networks in religious recruitment, it is important to identify who are the first in a network to convert to a new religion. My impression is that the core members, people at the confession level of the conversion career, are often the *trendsetters* in being the first of a social network to convert.

7. As these people consider the pros and cons of membership in a religious organization, they always make an implicit or explicit rationalistic cost-benefit analysis.[24]

8. Recruitment to religious organizations is therefore influenced heavily by the competition happening between various religious groups in most parts of the world.[25] Whether one likes the term or

not, this religious competition means that a religious market is in fact already in operation. More research is needed to analyze how the religious market functions in different cultural contexts and how this is influenced by state regulation of religion.[26]

9. The methods by which religious organizations compete against each other on the local, sometimes regional, or even national religious market should be carefully described and analyzed: these include their recruitment strategies and the methods, sometimes including the cultural politics involving mainstream society, they employed to attract members and compete against other groups.

10. Hence, in a context of strong religious competition in most continents, particularly in North America and Latin America, it is all the more important that researchers of religion in the future should try to:

First, delineate in detail the various levels of religious participation they utilize in their studies of religion.

Second, systematize the variables impacting the various levels of conversion and disaffiliation.

Third, recognize the importance of subjective religious experience in the conversion process.

Fourth, plan their research to systematically gauge the influence of gender on conversion of both male and female informants.

Fifth, accomplish an even spread of informants from *all* levels of religious activity and *all* phases of the life cycle (adolescents, married people, mid-life persons, and old age).

Sixth, endeavor to collect the most complete data possible at various locations to fill in the full comparative model of the conversion career.

Notes

Introduction

1. Quoted in Campbell (2008: B9: Editorial).
2. This entire section consists of excerpts from Taseer (2005: 1–7).
3. Beeston is the suburb of Leeds, where three of the four London underground bombers worked or lived in July 2005.
4. *Fajr* is the morning prayer, the first of the five prayers that Muslims are required to say every day.
5. Hassan Butt possibly meant *denominations* here.
6. Richardson (1978, 1980) coined the term conversion career, but for him it only referred to serial conversions. I give new meaning to the conversion career concept in this book by distinguishing levels of religious participation, identifying five groups of factors involved, and synthesizing the relevant literature on conversion from anthropology, sociology, psychology, history, mission studies, religious studies, and theology (see below).
7. Cf. Droogers, Gooren, and Houtepen (2003).
8. Cf. Einstein (*Brands of Faith*, 2008), Moore (*Selling God*, 1994), and Roof (*Spiritual Marketplace*, 1999).
9. Richardson (1978, 1980) and Rambo (1993).
10. The roots of Pentecostalism can be traced to various revivals involving speaking in tongues in South India (1860s); Topeka, Kansas (1900); Wales (1904–1905); Azusa Street, Los Angeles (1906); Korea (1907–1908); and Chile (1909). Most historians consider the 1906 revival in Azusa Street to be the birth of Pentecostalism. It was led by the black preacher William Joseph Seymour, whose emphasis on the power of the Holy Spirit, combined with a tendency to include both black and white members in the group, caused him to be evicted from the small black Holiness church where he was preaching. Seymour subsequently started his own church (Anderson 2004: 35–43).
11. The Catholic Charismatic Renewal (CCR) started in the United States in 1967, when Catholic students at Duquesne University, Pennsylvania, were baptized in the Holy Spirit and received the charismata. The movement is part of the Roman Catholic Church, but has attracted little scholarly attention in Latin America.
12. The conversion stories from my 2005–2006 fieldwork in Nicaragua have not been fully processed yet, so I decided to save them for my next book: *Conversion Careers in Nicaragua*.
13. Heelas and Woodhead (2005).

14. Cf. Berger (1999), Goodstein (2005), and Meyer (2006). A program of an association of European research councils (NORFACE) was entitled "Re-Emergence of Religion as a Social Force in Europe?"
15. For instance, in Douglas (1982) and in Robertson and Chirico (1985).
16. Martin (1990) and Stoll (1990).
17. Van der Veer (1994).
18. Corten and Marshall-Fratani (2001) and Meyer (2004).
19. Berger (1967: 108–9).
20. An interesting example of coercive religion are the *pillarization* (from the Dutch word *verzuiling*) structures in the Netherlands that guided believers from a certain religion to their own schools, sports clubs, trade unions, banks, newspapers, political parties, and even universities (Lijphart 1968).
21. Berger (1967: 138–51). He admitted later that his early expectation that increasing pluralism would lead to increasing secularization was simply wrong (Berger 1997, 1999).
22. Berger (1967) and Wilson (1985: 19).
23. See also Chapter 3.
24. See, for example, the many case studies described in Richardson (2004).
25. Kelley (1972).
26. Finke and Stark (1992).
27. Einstein (2008). She also points out the close similarities between marketing recruitment models and religious conversion models.
28. Martin (1990) and Stoll (1990).
29. Cf. Sassen (2006).
30. Robertson and Chirico (1985: 222) offer the earliest theoretical analysis of the link between globalization and religion: "The virtually worldwide eruption of religious and quasi-religious concerns and themes cannot be exhaustively comprehended in terms of focusing on what has been happening sociologically within societies." Among the many other authors on this theme are Beyer (1994, 2006), Beyer and Beaman (2007), Corten and Marshall-Fratani (2001), Dempster et al. (1999), Huntington (1996), Kurtz (1995), Lechner (2000), Lehmann (2002), Poewe (1994), and Robertson (1992).
31. According to some researchers—for example, Beyer (2006)—a "global society" made up of global "religious communities" exists nowadays.
32. Cf. Hoover and Clarke (2002) and Meyer and Moors (2006).
33. Cf. Helle (1997: xii).
34. Marx (1847).
35. Stark and Finke (2000: 199–200).
36. Weber (1978 [1922]).
37. Geertz (1973).
38. This is one aspect of Weber's famous Protestant ethic thesis (Weber 1958) that has generated so much literature that it could serve almost as an academic discipline in its own right (see Gooren 1999).
39. I developed my first ideas of the "religious perspective," which echoes Geertz (1973: 110–13), before reading Simmel (1997). Georg Simmel likewise saw

religion as an attitude or a perspective that, like art, constitutes a "third realm" mediating between the subject and the object. See also Helle's Introduction in Simmel (1997: xi–xx).

40. Houtepen (2006: 21). Rambo (personal communication) correctly points out that the prophets limited conversion to the Jewish community—not the whole "inhabited earth."

41. Flinn (1999: 51–52). Cf. Peace (2004: 8) and Walls (2004: 3): "The word *shubh* occurs in the Hebrew Bible no less than 750 times with the sense of turning, or (in a causative form, with God as agent) in the sense of being turned, brought back, or restored."

42. Holland (2005: 1).

43. Hawkins (1985: 21, 45) correctly points out that Saint Paul and Saint Augustine both present the archetypical versions of the crisis conversion experience.

44. Richardson (1985) identified it as the origin of the "passive" convert approach to conversion.

45. Cf. Rambo (1993).

46. Houtepen (2006: 23).

47. Peace (2004: 6).

48. Houtepen (2006: 25).

49. Houtepen (2006: 27).

50. Hawkins (1985) analyzes John Bunyan (1628–1688) as an archetype of conversion concepts during the Reformation (cf. James 1958: 133, 154–56). *The Pilgrim's Progress* shows influences from both Luther and Calvin.

51. Flinn (1999: 70). John Wesley preached that "conversion results from a warming of the heart."

52. Caldwell (1985). My Oakland University colleague Andrea Knutson pointed out there also existed a more mystical conversion strain in the North American Puritan colonies (e-mail communication, November 1, 2007).

53. Lovelace (1990: 303). He quotes from the Puritan writer Phineas Fletcher (*Joy in Tribulation*, 1632).

54. Lovelace (1990: 304).

55. Edwards (1966 [1737]), Flinn (1999: 53), and Scheick (1974).

56. Flinn (1999: 53).

57. Edwards (1966 [1737]), quoted in Flinn (1999: 53).

58. Houtepen (2006: 27–28).

59. See, for example, Bushman's (2005) excellent biography of Joseph Smith and Shipps's (1985) history of Mormonism.

60. Bushman (2005: 150, 191, 310–11). He (2005: 319) calls the 1830s the "high point of visionary religion in American history," referring to Joseph Smith, the Adventist prophetess Ellen G. White, Emerson, and the Shakers. However, few of Smith's contemporaries had his knack for institution-building. The Mormon Church's many councils and quorums formed a "charismatic bureaucracy" from its early beginning (Bushman 2005: 258).

61. Bushman (2005: 114–15).

62. See, for example, the Mormon conversion stories in Davis et al. (1991), Eliason (1999), and Grover (2001). Contemporary Mormon conversion stories often have much in common with those from Pentecostals: see Chapter 4 and 5.

63. Flinn (1999: 62–63).

64. Some call the Christian revival that started in the 1980s the Fourth Awakening (Flinn 1999: 64).

65. "When the day of Pentecost had fully come, they [the Apostles] were all with one accord in one place. And suddenly there came a sound from heaven, as of a rushing mighty wind, and it filled the whole house where they were sitting. Then there appeared to them divided tongues, as of fire, and one sat upon each of them. And they were all filled with the Holy Spirit and began to speak with other tongues, as the Spirit gave them utterance" (Bible 1988, Acts 2: 1–4).

66. Flinn (1999: 66).

67. Flinn (1999: 65).

68. Peace (2004: 9).

69. Roald (2006: 49). See also Norris (2003: 174–75).

70. Nida (1958: 122): "In order to be accepted within the Evangelical community, he often symbolizes his break with the past by strong denunciation of his former friends, publicized breaking or burning of images, unnecessarily harsh denunciation of the Roman Catholic Church, and even unwarranted disrespect for the religious sentiments of conscientious people."

71. Kundera (1983: 308).

72. In the Netherlands, however, the deconversion story is clearly more prevalent. The fiction-writer couple Vonne van der Meer and Willem Jan Otten form an exception to this rule. Both converted to Roman Catholicism, and Otten (2003: 18–21; 2005) wrote extensively about his conversion experiences.

73. Pearce (1999).

74. Lewis (1955).

75. In 2007, the former British prime minister Tony Blair converted from the Anglican Church to the Roman Catholic Church. The U.S. president George W. Bush (2000–2008) converted to born-again evangelical Christianity after two decades of binge drinking (Stam 2003). Other famous converts among U.S. presidents include Jimmy Carter (1976–1980) and Bill Clinton (1992–2000). Perhaps Ronald Reagan (1980–1988) should also be included here (Morris 1999).

76. Dick, "What the Dead Men Say" (2002 [1964]): "Isn't it true that the half-lifer often finds himself in possession of a sort of insight, of a new frame of reference, a perspective, that he lacked while alive?" "I've heard psychologists say that," Gertrude agreed. "It's what the old theologists called *conversion*."

77. Douglas Coupland's novel *Hey Nostradamus* contains a haunting line written by one of the pupils, right before she was killed in a Canadian high school massacre similar to Columbine: "God is nowhere / God is now here."

78. The title explanation of DBC Pierre's quirky novel *Vernon God Little* reads: "'Don't be lookin up at no sky for help. Look down here, at us twisted dreamers.' He takes hold of my shoulders, spins me around, and punches me towards the mirror on the wall. 'You're the God. Take responsibility. Exercise

your power'" (Pierre 2003: 260). It is truly the beginning of Vernon's own paradigm shift (Pierre 2003: 33–34).

79. David Mitchell's *Cloud Atlas* contains intriguing references to future history "Pentecostal revolutions in North America" and to nineteenth-century converts and mission churches in the Pacific (Mitchell 2003: 343, 497 ff.).
80. McAdams (2006: 37–39).
81. McAdams (2006: 141–43).
82. I am not trained in psychology and see many pitfalls in evaluating the subjective psychological features of conversion. The fiction writer Orson Scott Card offers this warning: "the truth is that no person ever understands another, from beginning to end of life, there is no truth that can be known, only the story we imagine to be true, the story they tell us is true, the story they really believe to be true about themselves; and all of them lies" (Card, *Children of the Mind*, 1996: 140).
83. Cf. Rambo (1993).
84. Linde (1993: 9).
85. Rosenwald and Ochberg (1992: 2).
86. Popp-Baier (2002: 48–51).
87. See especially Snow and Machalek (1983, 1984), Stapels and Mauss (1987), and Stromberg (1990, 1993).
88. See Chapter 1 for more details on Mead's universe of discourse and on biographical reconstruction (Snow and Machalek 1983, 1984).
89. Popp-Baier (2002: 50), referring to Ricoeur (1991: 426).
90. Flinn (1999: 51) mentions "the mass conversions of whole peoples: the Slavs, missionized by Saint Cyril and Methodius, the Chinese by Buddhist missionaries, and Africans by Muslim missionaries." See also Hefner (1993) and Van der Veer (1996).
91. Stark (2005: 70–71) and Stark and Finke (2000: 126) maintain that there are "no credible accounts" of mass conversions, implying that these are mythical inventions to motivate missionaries.
92. Cf. Kose (1996), Posten (1992), and Woodberry (1992).
93. William James ([1902] 1958).

Chapter 1

1. No anthropologists are represented in this chapter, although Gerlach and Hine (1970) came close. Gooren (2010) analyzes in detail why anthropologists historically experienced problems in dealing with individual religious conversion.
2. Max Weber (for example, *The Social Psychology of the World Religions*, 1947: 277) shared with James a similar interest in "the religious virtuoso, the ascetic, the monk, the Sufi" (see also Weber 1947: 287–90).
3. See also O'Toole (2004) for the contemporary importance of William James.
4. In all fairness, Lofland (1977) later also recognized the limitations of the original process model of conversion (see also Lofland and Skonovd 1981).
5. Lewis R. Rambo, personal communication.

6. James T. Richardson, personal communication.

7. Hence for Richardson (1978, 1980), the term "conversion career" only referred to serial conversions. This book gives new meaning to the conversion career concept by distinguishing levels of religious participation, identifying five groups of factors involved, and synthesizing the relevant literature on conversion from anthropology, sociology, psychology, history, mission studies, religious studies, and theology (see Chapter 2).

8. See the many articles in Bromley and Richardson (1983) for critical overviews of the brainwashing approach to conversion from sociological, legal, and historical perspectives. See also Richardson (1993).

9. Roger Finke, personal communication at the annual meeting of the Society for the Scientific Study of Religion (SSSR), Kansas City, October 24, 2004.

10. Cf. Droogers, Gooren, and Houtepen (2003).

Chapter 2

1. Cf. Meyer (2006).

2. See Chapter 1; cf. Lofland and Stark (1965) or Lofland (1977).

3. See, for example, Brusco (1995), Goldin and Metz (1991), Gooren (1999), Lancaster (1988), Mariz (1994), and Martin (1990, 2002). See also Chapter 5.

4. Chapter 3 connects the conversion career approach to religious market theory.

5. Snow and Machalek (1984: 173).

6. Snow and Machalek (1984: 173–74).

7. See Gooren (2010).

8. Some important authors on conversion to Islam are Bourque (2003), Kose (1996), Mansson-McGinty (2006), Posten (1992), van Nieuwkerk (2006), and Wohnrab-Sahr (1999). Gaudeul (1999) wrote on conversion from Islam to Christianity.

9. See Gooren (2006b) for the review of conversion literature. Important inspirations for both the levels of religious activity and the factors in conversion were Bromley and Shupe (1979), Gooren (2001b), Long and Hadden (1983), and especially Rambo (1993).

10. Some reviewers balked at the term "confession" and suggested "commitment" instead. But peoples at the conversion or even affiliation levels can also be fully committed to their faith and religious group.

11. Probably 90 percent or more of the conversion literature in psychology and sociology deals with individual religious change among adolescents or young adults (Gooren 2006b).

12. Snow and Machalek (1983) and Paloutzian et al. (1999).

13. Droogers, Gooren, and Houtepen (2003: 6).

Chapter 3

1. Warner (2002) uses the term "new paradigm," but he refers more to religious competition than to religious markets; he seems wary of the rational choice elements. Stark and Finke (2000: 27ff.) also use the term paradigm. I prefer

the more neutral term *model*, since I advocate a stricter use of the term paradigm.

2. The criticisms of secularization theory by Stark and Finke (2000: 27, 57) are aimed especially at Dobbelaere (1987) and Wilson (1982). See also Wilson (1985) and Dobbelaere (2000).
3. Berger (1967: 50).
4. Stark and Finke (2000: 114–38).
5. Stark and Finke (2000: 38).
6. Bankston (2003: 158).
7. Spickard (1998). Cf. Weber (1978).
8. Stark and Finke (2000: 119–20).
9. Iannaccone (1990).
10. Stark and Finke (2000: 114) call this *reaffiliation*; Rambo (1993, 13) calls it *institutional transition*.
11. Bankston (2002).
12. Bankston (2002), Johnson (2002), and Neitz and Mueser (1997).
13. Bankston (2003), Hamberg and Petterson (2002), Neitz and Mueser (1997), and Spickard (1998).
14. Neitz and Mueser (1997).
15. Sherkat and Wilson (1995).
16. Hamberg and Petterson (2002).
17. Stark and Finke (2000: 38).
18. Iannaccone (1997).
19. Spickard (1998: 108).
20. Bankston (2003: 160).
21. Robbins (2001: 336).
22. For example, Bankston (2002: 313) and Hamberg and Petterson (2002: 92).
23. Bankston (2003: 165).
24. Stark and Finke (2000: 86).
25. Berger (1967: 134).
26. Berger (1967: 137; emphases in original).
27. Berger (1997).
28. Stark and Bainbridge (1987).
29. For example, Iannaccone (1990, 1992a, 1992b, 1997).
30. For example, Stark and Finke (2000, 2002). See also Finke and Stark (1992).
31. For example, Warner (2002).
32. Stark and Finke (2000: 143–44).
33. Stark and Finke (2000: 145).
34. Stark and Finke (2000: 205–7).
35. Stark and Finke (2000: 156–57).
36. Stark and Finke (2000: 162).
37. Stark and Finke (2000: 163).
38. Stark and Finke (2000: 230).
39. Stark and Finke (2000: 196; emphasis in original).
40. Stark and Finke (2000: 195).
41. Stark and Finke (2000: 198).

42. Stark and Finke (2000: 211–12). They suggest that these niches exist all over the world.
43. Droogers, Gooren, and Houtepen (2003: 4).
44. For example, Pentecostal churches in Guatemala attract many people (especially women, but also many men recovering from an alcoholic past) who reject the custom of *machismo* (Gooren 1999). See also Brusco (1995).
45. Stark and Finke (2000: 107–12). See also Stark and Bainbridge (1987) and Sengers (2003, 42–43).
46. Cf. Olson (2002: 134).
47. Gooren (2000, 2001a, 2001b).
48. Stark and Finke (2000: 193).
49. Olson (2002: 134).
50. Stark and Finke (2000: 199).
51. Stark and Finke (2000: 199–200).
52. Stark and Finke (2000: 193).
53. Bankston (2002).
54. Olson (2002: 134).
55. Olson (2002: 148).
56. Olson (2002: 141).
57. Olson (2002: 143–44).
58. Olson (2002: 154).
59. Cf. Davie (1994, 2000).
60. Stark (2005). See Gooren (2007d) for a criticism of Stark's use of Mormonism.
61. Stark (1984, 1990, 1996, 2005).
62. Gooren (1999: 66, 2000, 2001) and Knowlton (2005).
63. Stark and Finke (2000: 114).
64. Stark and Finke (2000: 115).
65. Roger Finke, personal communication, Annual Meeting of the Society for the Scientific Study of Religion (SSSR), Kansas City, October 24, 2004.
66. Stark and Finke (2000: 117).
67. Stark and Finke (2000: 117).
68. See, for example, Chesnut (2003), Davie (1994, 2000), Gooren (1999), Martin (2002), and Roof (1999).
69. Stark and Finke (2000: 122).
70. Stark and Finke (2000: 119).
71. Stark and Finke (2000: 125).
72. Stark and Finke (2000: 120).
73. Stark and Finke (2000: 121).
74. Stark and Finke (2000: 123).
75. O'Connell (1990). However, Vande Berg and Kniss (2008) show that Indian immigrants in major cities of the United States are more responsive to joining the Hare Krishna movement, ISKCON.
76. Bruce (1999: 2002).
77. Bruce (2002: 180).
78. Bruce (2002: 177–78).

79. Chaves and Gorski (2001: 279).
80. See, for example, Chesnut (2003), Gill (1998), Gooren (2001b), Jelen (2002), and Míguez (1997).
81. See, for example, Chesnut (2003) and Gill (1998).
82. Stark and Finke (2000: 193).
83. See, for example, Bernice Martin (2006). Religious competition, however, lies at the heart of the analysis of Pentecostalism as a "global option" in David Martin's *Pentecostalism: The World Their Parish* (2002: 173–74).
84. Earlier I used the concept of *culture politics* to describe and analyze this process in different continents (see above and Droogers, Gooren, and Houtepen 2003: 4).
85. See the Introduction, and, for example, Houtepen (2006).
86. I owe thanks to Armand Mauss for this suggestion.
87. Olson (2002: 148).
88. Stark and Finke (2000: 107–12).
89. Gooren (2000, 2001a, 2001b).
90. Stark and Finke (2000: 117).

Chapter 4

1. For a historical approach to "archetypical" conversions, see Hawkins, *Archetypes of Conversion: The Autobiographies of Augustine, Bunyan, and Merton* (1985). Chapter 5 analyzes conversion careers in Latin America to correct for a possible "Western" (or rather "Northern") bias.
2. Cf. Hadden (1987), "Towards Desacralizing Secularization Theory."
3. Two cases I know from direct experience are my own parents, who both grew up as Dutch Roman Catholics. My mother, born in 1934, stopped going to Mass in the 1980s. My father, who was born in (Dutch) Indonesia in 1930, kept going to Mass until the 1990s, but until his death in 2008 only supported his parish financially without ever attending anymore.
4. According to Rambo (1993: 13), his typology of conversion "portrays the nature of conversion in terms of *how far someone has to go socially and culturally in order to be considered a convert*" (emphasis in original).
5. Chapter 5 analyzes various Latin American cases of mainstream Catholics, who experienced a similar revitalization of their parental religion through the Catholic Charismatic Renewal.
6. In the remainder of the book, Neitz even omits her informants' names from the interview excerpts.
7. See Bibby and Brinkerhoff (1973, 1994) and Brinkerhoff and Bibby (1985).
8. Roof's "spiritual marketplace" is, of course, a synonym for the religious market (see Chapter 3).
9. *Be Here Now* (1971) is a book by the American guru Baba Ram Das (also known as Richard Alpert).
10. The *Shahada* is the Muslim declaration of belief in the oneness of God and the acceptance of Muhammad as his prophet. The declaration reads "La illaha ill Allah, Muhammadur Rasul Allah" or "There is no God but Allah,

Muhammad is the Messenger of Allah" in English. Non-Muslims wishing to convert to Islam do so by a public recitation of this creed in the presence of three Muslims.

11. Hermansen (2006: 256–57).
12. Cf. Chapter 3.
13. Hermansen (2006) contains various stories of similar conversion careers among U.S. Muslims, moving from intellectual curiosity to mystical Sufi Islam.
14. Erhard Seminars Training (EST) was an intense course to achieve personal transformation (Bartley 1978).
15. Cf. Douglas Coupland, *Generation X: Tales for an Accelerated Culture* (1991).
16. Cf. Snow and Machalek (1983, 1984) and Staples and Mauss (1987).
17. Stromberg (1990: 55; 1993: xvi) uses a detailed system of transcription symbols, which—though scholarly sound—alas render his interview excerpts hard to read. I have limited myself to the conversion story, putting the two emphases in italics.
18. Cf. Geertz (1973: 93–94).
19. Cf. Snow and Machalek (1983, 1984) and Staples and Mauss (1987). See also Chapter 1.
20. Mansson-McGinty (2006: 96–97).
21. Mansson-McGinty (2006: 99, 101–2).
22. Mansson-McGinty (2006: 99).
23. A story that exactly resembles that of the Reverend Cantrell can also be found in Harding (1987: 177), but as one long text without the paragraphs.
24. Compare Decoo (1996) with Chapter 5 on Mormon conversion and disaffiliation processes in Latin America.
25. The LDS Church refers to the Church of Jesus Christ of Latter-day Saints, which is commonly known as the Mormon Church. Decoo grew up as a Roman Catholic in the Dutch-speaking part of Belgium.
26. Taseer (2005: 1–7).
27. Butt (2007a).
28. Butt (2007b).
29. Cragun (2006: 10) aims for consensus in exiting terminology, by proposing the following terms. *Apostates* are individuals who leave religions, regardless of where they end up. *Deconverts* have renounced the beliefs and/or values that accompanied their former conversion ("secular disaffiliation"). *Disengagers* are individuals who discontinue their activity in a religious group but continue to self-identify as members. *Dropouts* are people who leave a religion and do not reaffiliate or identify with another religion. Where I use the term seeker, Cragun prefers *switcher*: someone who leaves a religion and reaffiliates or identifies with another religion.
30. Interestingly, Hirsi Ali's autobiography *Infidel* (2007) is entitled *Mijn vrijheid* ("My Freedom") in Dutch, which shows that she is aiming for different audiences in the Netherlands and in the English-speaking world.
31. Ayaan's complete deconversion story can be found in Chapter 14 of *Infidel*, which is entitled "Leaving God" (Hirsi Ali 2007: 261–82).
32. Hirsi Ali (2007: 269).

33. Ibid.
34. Hirsi Ali (2007: 271).
35. Ibid.
36. These conclusions would motivate her to make the short film "Submission" with Theo van Gogh, who was afterward assassinated by a Muslim radical in Amsterdam in 2004. Hirsi Ali became the object of numerous death threats, limiting her freedom and leading to a life with bodyguards needed around the clock.
37. Hirsi Ali (2007: 271–73).
38. Hirsi Ali (2007: 281).
39. Hirsi Ali (2007: 281).
40. Hirsi Ali (2007: 261).
41. Hirsi Ali (2007: 282).
42. Albrecht et al. (1988), Bahr and Albrecht (1989), Francis and Brown (1991), Hadaway and Roof (1988), Hunsberger (1980), Hunsberger and Brown (1984), Martin et al. (2003), and Regnerus and Uecker (2006); cf. Cragun (2006: 23–25).
43. Heelas and Woodhead (2005).
44. Cf. Kilbourne and Richardson (1988: 15) and Richardson (1985: 175–76). See also Chapter 1.
45. Cf. Douglas Coupland, *Generation X: Tales for an Accelerated Culture* (1991).
46. James (1958 [1902]); see also Chapter 1.
47. Cf. Einstein (2008).
48. Stark and Finke (2000: 115); see also Chapter 1.

Chapter 5

1. See, for example, Brouwer (2000), Burdick (1993), Cantón (1998), Ireland (1991), and Míguez (1997).
2. See, for example, Brusco (1995), Lalive (1969), and Mariz (1994).
3. Willems (1967: 125–31).
4. Willems (1967: vi–vii, 125–31).
5. Willems (1967: 127).
6. Willems (1967: 130–31).
7. See Míguez (1997: 103–6). Míguez (1997: 28) acknowledges the problems of "representivity and generalization" in ethnographic research. He interviewed members and leaders of the Pentecostal *Centro Cristiano* in a representative suburb of Buenos Aires, Argentina.
8. Umbanda is an Afro-Brazilian religion in which clients pay for the services of mediums, who are taken over by West African spirits and deities. "Umbanda is a clear case of syncretism in which discrete religious traditions—Catholicism, Macumba, and Spiritism—merged and coalesced to form a new religion" (Chesnut 2003: 104).
9. Míguez (1997: 107–9).
10. Cantón (1998: 134).

11. Cantón (1998: 148–60). Her twenty-three key informants, selected at random, come from seventeen different congregations in various Guatemalan towns and cities. Eight are Pentecostals and one is a Charismatic Catholic (Cantón 1998: 136).
12. Cantón (1998: 168).
13. Cantón (1998: 189–96); translation mine.
14. For the role of conversion in the Catholic Charismatic Renewal, see Brouwer (2000), Chesnut (2003), Cleary (2007), and Neitz (1987: 63). See Bryant et al. (forthcoming), Davies (2000), Davis et al. (1991), Gooren (1999), and Bushman (2005) for the role of conversion in Mormonism.
15. Brouwer (2000: 35).
16. Brouwer (2000: 36).
17. Brouwer (2000: 25–26). Brouwer conducted a community study in a Charismatic parish and an independent Pentecostal church in the provincial town Masaya.
18. Brouwer (2000: 28); translation mine.
19. Brouwer (2000: 30–31); translation mine.
20. Brouwer (2000: 32).
21. See Gooren (1999). On the peculiarities of Mormonism, see, for example, Davies (2003). On Mormonism in Latin America, see Gooren (1999: 63–68) or Gooren (2000).
22. Gooren (1999: 153–54).
23. Gooren (1999: 155–56, 163).
24. Interview with the Reverend Henk Minderhout, the Dutch director of the Nicaraguan In-Depth Evangelization Institute (INDEF: Instituto Nicaraguense de Evangelización en Fondo), Managua, June 15, 2005.
25. See Gómez (1998: 30). Gómez (1998: 11–17) used statistical materials from various Censuses and from three Consultoría Interdisciplinaria en Desarrollo [English: Interdisciplinary Development Consultants] (CID)/Gallup polls that are based on over 1,200 arbitrarily interviewed people from all over Costa Rica. In addition, Gómez selected a sample of fifty churches from sixteen different denominations, where he conducted survey research. In these sample churches, he also conducted over 500 interviews with leaders and members.
26. Gómez (1998: 42).
27. Gómez (1998: 58–59, 75).
28. Bowen (1996: 95).
29. See Bowen (1996: 99). Bowen (1996: 9) conducted three extensive surveys and interviews of members and leaders in the forty-three congregations he studied. This extensive statistical material was compared to secondary materials and census data and complemented with participant observation. The samples are not random, but they are representative of the population (Bowen 1996: 11).
30. Bowen (1996: 225).
31. Bowen (1996: 70–71, 218–19).
32. Gooren (1999: 66), Grover (1985: 137–39), and Knowlton (2005: 54).
33. Gooren (1999: 169).
34. Gooren (1999: 170).

35. Gómez (1998: 32).
36. Gooren (1999: 152).
37. Brouwer (2000) and Chesnut (2003).
38. The available data are biased toward religious seekers and shoppers and confessing leaders.
39. See Chesnut (2003) and Gooren (2003, 2006a). Radio is more important as a religious recruitment mechanism in Latin America, television seems to be of equal importance all over the world, whereas the Internet is more important in the United States than in Latin America (see Chapter 4).
40. Long and Hadden (1983).
41. Smilde (2007).
42. Cf. Bromley and Shupe (1979).

Chapter 6

1. Rambo (1993: 7).
2. Gooren (2006a).
3. The unique histories of religious groups often include persecution. See, for example, Mormons in the nineteenth-century United States (Bushman 2005; Shipps 1985) or in 1980s Nicaragua (Gooren 2007c); see also the persecution stories of the early Protestant missionaries in Latin America (Nida 1958; Saler 1965; Gill 1998).
4. The literature I used throughout this book was curiously silent on the concrete question of how many hours active believers of religious organizations actually spent on church matters (cf. Gooren 1999: 195–97, 212).
5. Long and Hadden (1983: 5–7).
6. The relationship between leadership and interreligious competition remains undeveloped in the literature, even in Stark and Finke (2000). Rambo (1982) addressed it in the conversion literature.
7. No. 6 was suggested by Lewis Rambo, personal e-mail, January 5, 2007.
8. Heelas and Woodhead (2005).
9. Gill (1998).
10. Gill (1998).
11. James (1958 [1902]).
12. Snow and Phillips (1980) and Rambo (1993: 60). Rambo (1993: 61–62) additionally mentions emotional, intellectual, and religious availability.
13. Cf. Granovetter (1973).
14. "One area that has not been researched, even though literature on religious conversion and on gender and clergy is abundant, is the area of gender differences in the telling, or communication, of religious stories" (Knight et al. 2005: 113).
15. Knight et al. (2005: 126 ff.).
16. See Figure 6.1 above for definitions of the various levels of religious activity in the conversion career approach: preaffiliation, affiliation, conversion, confession, and disaffiliation.

17. In the United States, the main cultural factors influencing conversion were education and region of the country; in Latin America, *machismo* comes to mind (Brusco 1995; Mariz and Campos Machado 1997; Gooren 1999).
18. Cf. Droogers (1994).
19. Rambo (1993: 10).
20. See van Nieuwkerk on the anthropology of Islam (2010), Bourque (2003), and Hermansen (2006).
21. Travisano (1970: 598, 605).
22. Cf. Einstein (2008).
23. Stark and Finke (2000: 115).
24. Gartrell and Shannon (1985), Gooren (1999), and Stark and Finke (2000).
25. Gooren (2006a).
26. Chesnut (2003), Gill (1998), and Stark and Finke (2000).

References

Albrecht, Stan L., Marie Cornwall, and Perry H. Cunningham. 1988. Religious leave-taking: Disengagement and disaffiliation among Mormons. In *Falling from the faith: Causes and consequences of religious apostasy*, ed. David G. Bromley, 62–80. Newbury Park, CA: Sage.

Austin-Broos, Diane. 2003. The anthropology of conversion: An introduction. In *The anthropology of religious conversion*, ed. Andrew Buckser and Stephen D. Glazier, 1–12. Lanham, MD: Rowman and Littlefield.

Bahr, Howard M., and Stan L. Albrecht. 1989. Strangers once more: Patterns of disaffiliation from Mormonism. *Journal for the Scientific Study of Religion* 28 (2): 180–200.

Bankston III, Carl L. 2002. Rationality, choice, and the religious economy: The problem of belief. *Review of Religious Research* 43 (4): 311–25.

———. 2003. Rationality, choice, and the religious economy: Individual and collective rationality in supply and demand. *Review of Religious Research* 45 (2): 155–71.

Bartley, William Warren. 1978. *Werner Erhard—The transformation of a man: The founding of EST*. New York: Clarkson N. Potter.

Berger, Peter L. 1967. *The sacred canopy: Elements of a sociology of religion*. Garden City, NY: Doubleday.

———. 1997. Epistemological modesty: An interview with Peter Berger. *Christian Century* 114 (October 29): 972–75, 978.

———, ed. 1999. *The desecularization of the world: Resurgent religion and world politics*. Washington, D.C.: Ethics and Public Policy Center.

———, and Thomas Luckmann. 1967. *The social construction of reality: A treatise in the sociology of knowledge*. Garden City, NY: Anchor Books / Doubleday.

Beyer, Peter. 1994. *Religion and globalization*. London and New York: Routledge.

———. 2006. *Religions in global society*. London and New York: Routledge.

———, and Lori Beaman, eds. 2007. *Religion, globalization, and culture*. Leiden, the Netherlands: Brill.

Bibby, Reginald W., and Merlin B. Brinkerhoff. 1973. The circulation of the saints. *Journal for the Scientific Study of Religion* 12: 273–83.

———. 1994. Circulation of the saints, 1966–1990. *Journal for the Scientific Study of Religion* 33: 273–80.

Bourque, Nicole. 2003. How Deborah became Aisha: The conversion process and the creation of female Muslim identity. Paper presented at the symposium on gender and conversion to Islam, Nijmegen (the Netherlands), May 16–17.

Bowen, Kurt. 1996. *Evangelism and apostasy: The evolution and impact of evangelicals in Mexico*. Montreal: McGill-Queen's University Press.

Brinkerhoff, Merlin B., and Reginald W. Bibby. 1985. Circulation of the saints in South America. *Journal for the Scientific Study of Religion* 28: 151–67.

Bromley, David G., and James T. Richardson, eds. 1983. *The brainwashing/deprogramming controversy: Sociological, legal, and historical perspectives*. Lewiston, NY: Edwin Mellen.

Bromley, David G., and Anson D. Shupe. 1979. "Just a few years seem like a lifetime": A role theory approach to participation in religious movements. In *Research in social movements, conflicts, and change, volume 2*, ed. Louis Kriesberg, 159–85. Greenwich, CT: Jai Press.

Brouwer, Janneke. 2000. *Nieuwe scheppingen in Christus: Bekeringsverhalen van protestante evangélicos en katholieke carismáticos in Masaya, Nicaragua*. MA thesis, cultural anthropology, Utrecht University, Utrecht.

Brown, Dan. 2003. *The Da Vinci code*. London: Corgi.

Bruce, Steve. 1999. *Choice and religion: A critique of rational choice theory*. Oxford: Oxford University Press.

———. 2002. The poverty of economism or the social limits on maximizing. In *Sacred markets, sacred canopies: Essays on religious markets and religious pluralism*, ed. Ted G. Jelen, 167–85. Lanham, MD: Rowman and Littlefield.

Brusco, Elizabeth E. 1995. *The reformation of machismo: Evangelical conversion and gender in Colombia*. Austin: University of Texas Press.

Bryant, Seth, Henri Gooren, Rick Phillips, and David Stewart Jr. Forthcoming. Conversion and retention in Mormonism. In *The Oxford handbook of religious conversion*, ed. Lewis R. Rambo and Charles E. Farhadian. New York: Oxford University Press.

Burdick, John. 1993. *Looking for God in Brazil*. Berkeley, CA: University of California Press.

Bushman, Richard Lyman. 2005. *Joseph Smith: Rough stone rolling—A cultural biography of Mormonism's founder*. New York: Alfred A. Knopf.

Butt, Hassan. 2007a. The network: Interview with Hassan Butt. *CBS News*. March 25. Web. Available at http: www.cbsnews.com/stories/2007/03/23/60 minutes/printable2602308.shtml. Accessed on July 7, 2008.

———. 2007b. My plea to fellow Muslims: You must renounce terror. *The Observer*. July 1.

Caldwell, Patricia. 1985. *The Puritan conversion narrative: The beginnings of American expression*. Cambridge: Cambridge University Press.

Campbell, Colleen Carroll. 2008. Religious commitment in a conversion-prone culture. *St. Louis Post-Dispatch*, B9 (Editorial).

Cantón Delgado, Manuela. 1998. *Bautizados en fuego: Protestantes, discursos de conversión y política en Guatemala (1989–1993)*. Antigua Guatemala / South Woodstock, VT: CIRMA/Plumsock Mesoamerican Studies.

Card, Orson Scott. 1996. *Children of the mind*. New York City: Tor.

Chaves, Mark, and Philip S. Gorski. 2001. Religious pluralism and religious participation. *Annual Review of Sociology* 27: 261–81.

Chesnut, R. Andrew. 1997. *Born again in Brazil*. New Brunswick, NJ: Rutgers University Press.

———. 2003. *Competitive spirits: Latin America's new religious economy*. New York: Oxford University Press.

Cleary, Edward L. 2007. The Catholic Charismatic Renewal: Revitalization movements and conversion. In *Conversion of a continent: Religious change in Latin America*, ed. Timothy J. Steigenga and Edward L. Cleary, 153–73. New Brunswick, NJ: Rutgers University Press.

Coleman, Simon. 2000. *The globalization of Charismatic Christianity: Spreading the gospel of prosperity*. Cambridge: Cambridge University Press.

———. 2003. Continuous conversion? The rhetoric, practice, and rhetorical practice of Charismatic Protestant conversion. In *The anthropology of religious conversion*, ed. Andrew Buckser and Stephen D. Glazier, 15–27. Lanham, MD: Rowman and Littlefield.

Coupland, Douglas. 1991. *Generation X: Tales for an accelerated culture*. New York: St. Martin's.

———. 2003. *Hey Nostradamus*. London: Flamingo.

Cragun, Ryan. 2006. Religious change and religious exiting: A test of a unified role theory. Draft Chapter 1 of PhD dissertation, University of Cincinnati (forthcoming). An excerpt was presented at the annual meeting of the Society for the Scientific Study of Religion (SSSR), October 19–21, in Portland, OR, as "Pushing for consensus: Religious exiting terminology."

Davie, Grace. 1994. *Religion in Britain since 1945: Believing without belonging*. Oxford: Blackwell.

———. 2000. *Religion in modern Europe: A memory mutates*. Oxford: Oxford University Press.

Davies, Douglas J. 2003. *An introduction to Mormonism*. Cambridge: Cambridge University Press.

Davis, Troy, Richard Nelson, and David Salmons. 1991. *Our miraculous heritage: Amazing conversion stories from the early church*. Orem, UT: Cedar Fort.

Dean, Kenda Creasy. 2007. Book review of *Branded: Adolescents converting from consumer faith* [2005] by Katherine Turpin. *Theology Today* 64 (3): 403–6.

Decoo, Wilfried. 1996. Feeding the fleeting flock: Reflections on the struggle to retain church members in Europe. *Dialogue* 29 (1): 97–118.

Dick, Philip K. 2002 [1964]. What the dead men say. In *Minority report*, 131–89. London: Gollancz.

Dobbelaere, Karel. 1987. Some trends in European sociology of religion: The secularization debate. *Sociological Analysis* 48: 107–37.

———. 2000. Toward an integrated perspective of the processes related to the descriptive concept of secularization. In *The secularization debate*, ed. William H. Swatos and Daniel V. A. Olson, 21–39. Lanham, MD: Rowman and Littlefield.

Douglas, Mary. 1982. The effects of modernization on religious change. *Daedalus* 3 (1): 1–19.

Downton, James V., Jr. 1980. An evolutionary theory of spiritual conversion and commitment: The case of Divine Light Mission. *Journal for the Scientific Study of Religion* 19 (4): 381–96.

Droogers, André. 1994. The normalization of religious experience: Healing, prophesy, dreams, and visions. In *Charismatic Christianity as a global culture*, ed. Karla O. Poewe, 33–49. Columbia, SC: University of South Carolina Press.

———. 2003. The power dimensions of the Christian community: An anthropological model. *Religion* 33: 263–80.

———. 2006. *Het gedwongen huwelijk tussen Vrouwe Religie en Heer Macht*. Amsterdam: Vrije Universiteit, valedictory lecture, June 23.

Droogers, André, Henri Gooren, and Anton Houtepen. 2003. *Conversion careers and culture politics in Pentecostalism: A comparative study in four continents*. Proposal submitted to the thematic program "The Future of the Religious Past" of the Netherlands Organization for Scientific Research (NWO).

Edwards, Jonathan. 1966 [1737]. *Basic writings*. Edited by Ola Winslow. New York: New American Library.

Einstein, Mara. 2008. *Brands of faith: Marketing religion in a commercial age*. New York: Routledge.

Eliason, Eric A. 1999. Toward the folkloristic study of Latter-Day Saint conversion narratives. *BYU Studies* 38 (1): 137–50.

Farouky, Jumana. 2006. Allah's recruits: Why more and more Westerners are converting to Islam and, in some cases, pursuing an extremist path. *Time* 168 (9): 36, August 28.

Finke, Roger, and Rodney Stark. 1992. *The churching of America, 1776–1990: Winners and losers in our religious economy*. New Brunswick, NJ: Rutgers University Press.

Flinn, Frank K. 1999. Conversion: Up from evangelicalism or the pentecostal and charismatic experience. In *Religious conversion: Contemporary practices and controversies*, ed. Christopher Lamb and M. Darroll Bryant, 51–72. London: Cassell.

Francis, L. J., and L. B. Brown. 1991. The influence of home, church, and school on prayer among sixteen-year-old adolescents in England. *Review of Religious Research* 33 (2): 112–24.

Freston, Paul. 1993. Brother votes for brother: The new politics of protestantism in Brazil. In *Rethinking protestantism in Latin America*, ed. Virginia Garrard-Burnett and David Stoll, 66–110. Philadelphia, PA: Temple University Press.

———. 2001. *Evangelicals and politics in Asia, Africa and Latin America*. Cambridge: Cambridge University Press.

Gartrell, C. David, and Zane K. Shannon. 1985. Contacts, cognitions, and conversion: A rational choice approach. *Review of Religious Research* 27 (1): 32–48.

Gaudeul, Jean-Marie. 1999. *Called from Islam to Christ: Why Muslims become Christians*. Crowborough, UK: Monarch.

Gerlach, Luther P., and Virginia H. Hine. 1970. *People, power, change: Movements of social transformation*. Indianapolis and New York: Bobbs-Merrill.

Gill, Anthony. 1998. *Rendering unto Caesar: The Catholic Church and the state in Latin America*. Chicago: University of Chicago Press.

Goffman, Erving. 1959. *The presentation of self in everyday Life*. Garden City, NY: Doubleday.

————. 1963. *Stigma: Notes on the management of spoiled identity.* Englewoods Cliffs, NJ: Prentice-Hall.

Goldin, Liliana R., and Brent Metz. 1991. An expression of cultural change: Invisible converts to protestantism among highland Guatemala Mayas. *Ethnology* 30 (4): 325–38.

Gómez, Jorge I. 1998 [1996]. *El crecimiento y la deserción en la iglesia evangélica costarricense.* San José (Costa Rica): IINDEF.

Goodstein, Laurie. 2005. More religion, but not the old-time kind. *New York Times*, January 9.

Gooren, Henri. 1999. *Rich among the poor: Church, firm, and household among small-scale entrepreneurs in Guatemala City.* Amsterdam: Thela [Latin America Series, number 13].

————. 2000. Analyzing LDS growth in Guatemala: Report from a *barrio. Dialogue* 33 (2): 97–115.

————. 2001a. The dynamics of LDS growth in Guatemala, 1948–1998. *Dialogue* 34 (3 and 4): 55–75.

————. 2001b. Reconsidering protestant growth in Guatemala, 1900–1995. In *Holy saints and fiery preachers: The anthropology of protestantism in Mexico and Central America*, ed. James W. Dow and Alan R. Sandstrom, 169–203. Westport, CT: Greenwood/Praeger.

————. 2005a. The conversion careers approach: Why people become and remain religiously active. Paper presented at the Society for the Scientific Study of Religion (SSSR) meeting, Rochester, New York, November 4–6.

————. 2005b. Towards a new model of conversion careers: The impact of personality and situational factors. *Exchange* 34 (2): 149–66.

————. 2006a. The religious market model and conversion: Towards a new approach. *Exchange* 35 (1): 39–60.

————. 2006b. Towards a new model of religious conversion careers: The impact of social and institutional factors. In *Paradigms, poetics and politics of conversion*, ed. Wout J. van Bekkum, Jan N. Bremmer, and Arie Molendijk, 25–40. Leuven: Peeters.

————. 2007a. Conversion careers in Latin America: Entering and leaving church among Pentecostals, Catholics, and Mormons. In *Conversion of a continent: Religious change in Latin America*, ed. Timothy J. Steigenga and Edward L. Cleary, 52–71. New Brunswick, NJ: Rutgers University Press.

————. 2007b. Reassessing conventional approaches to conversion: Towards a new synthesis. *Journal for the Scientific Study of Religion* 46 (3): 337–53.

————. 2007c. Latter-day Saints under siege: The unique experience of Nicaraguan Mormons. *Dialogue* 40 (3): 134–55.

————. 2007d. Review of *The Rise of Mormonism* (2005) by Rodney Stark. *Mormon Social Science Association (MSSA) Newsletter* 28 (1): 3–9.

————. 2008. The Mormons of the world: The meaning of LDS membership in Central America. In *Revisiting Thomas F. O'Dea's The Mormons: Contemporary Perspectives*, ed. Cardell K. Jacobson, John P. Hoffman, and Tim P. Heaton, 362–88. Salt Lake City: University of Utah Press.

————. Forthcoming. The anthropology of conversion. In *The Oxford handbook of religious conversion*, ed. Lewis R. Rambo and Charles E. Farhadian. New York: Oxford University Press.

Granovetter, Mark. 1973. The strength of weak ties. *American Journal of Sociology* 78 (6): 1360–80.

Greil, Arthur L. 1977. Previous dispositions and conversion to perspectives of social and religious movements. *Sociological Analysis* 38 (2): 115–25.

————, and David R. Rudy. 1984. What have we learned from process models of conversion? An examination of ten case studies. *Sociological Focus* 17 (4): 305–23.

Grover, Mark L. 1985. *Mormonism in Brazil: Religion and dependency in Latin America*. PhD dissertation, Indiana University, Bloomington, IN.

————. 2001. One convert at a time. *BYU Speeches*. Web. Available at http://speeches.byu.edu/reader/reader.php?id=713. Accessed on May 24, 2007.

Hadaway, C. Kirk, and Wade Clark Roof. 1988. Apostasy in American churches: Evidence from National Survey Data. In *Falling from the faith: Causes and consequences of religious apostasy*, ed. David G. Bromley, 29–46. Newbury Park, CA: Sage.

Hadden, Jeffrey K. 1987. Toward desacralizing secularization theory. *Social Forces* 65 (3): 587–611.

Hamberg, Eva, and Thorleif Petterson. 2002. Religious markets: Supply, demand, and rational theories. In *Sacred markets, sacred canopies: Essays on religious markets and religious pluralism*, ed. Ted G. Jelen, 91–114. Lanham, MD: Rowman and Littlefield.

Harding, Susan F. 1987. Convicted by the Holy Spirit: The rhetoric of fundamental Baptist conversion. *American Ethnologist* 14 (1): 167–81.

————. 1992. The afterlife of stories: Genesis of a man of God. In *Storied lives: The cultural politics of self-understanding*, ed. George C. Rosenwald and Richard L. Ochberg, 60–75. New Haven, CT and London: Yale University Press.

Hawkins, Anne Hunsaker. 1985. *Archetypes of conversion: The autobiographies of Augustine, Bunyan, and Merton*. London and Toronto: Associated University Presses.

Hays, Bonnie B. 2005. *I met God in Florida*. Web. Available at http://www.chnetwork.org/bhconv.htm. Accessed on October 27.

Heelas, Paul, and Linda Woodhead. 2005. *The spiritual revolution: Why religion is giving way to spirituality*. Oxford: Blackwell.

Hefner, Robert W., ed. 1993. *Conversion to Christianity: Historical and anthropological perspectives on a great transformation*. Berkeley, CA: University of California Press.

Heirich, Max. 1977. Change of heart: A test of some widely held theories about religious conversion. *American Journal of Sociology* 83 (3): 653–80.

Helle, Horst Jürgen. 1997. Introduction. In *Essays on Religion*, ed. Georg Simmel, xi–xx. New Haven, CT: Yale University Press.

Hermansen, Marcia. 2006. Keeping the faith: Convert Muslim mothers and the transmission of female Muslim identity in the West. In *Women embracing Islam: Gender and conversion in the West*, ed. Karin van Nieuwkerk, 250–75. Austin: University of Texas Press.

Hirsi Ali, Ayaan. 2006. *The caged virgin: An emancipation proclamation for women and Islam*. New York: Free Press.

———. 2007. *Infidel*. New York: Free Press.

Hoge, Dean R. 1981. *Converts, dropouts, returnees: A study of religious change among Catholics*. New York: Pilgrim.

Holland, Clifton L. 2005. *A brief study of apostasy and conversion*. Web. Available at http://www.prolades.com. Accessed on October 6.

Holy Bible. 1988. Nashville: Gideons International.

Hoover, Stewart M., and Lynn Schofield Clark, eds. 2002. *Practicing religion in the age of the media: Explorations in media, religion and culture*. New York: Columbia University Press.

Horton, Robin. 1971. African conversion. *Africa* 41: 85–108.

———. 1975a. On the rationality of conversion: Part one. *Africa* 45: 219–35.

———. 1975b. On the rationality of conversion: Part two. *Africa* 45: 373–99.

Houtepen, Anton. 2006. Conversion and the religious market: A theological perspective. *Exchange* 35 (1): 18–38.

Hunsberger, B. 1980. A reexamination of the antecedents of apostasy. *Review of Religious Research* 21 (2): 158–70.

———, and L. B. Brown. 1984. Religious socialization, apostasy, and the impact of family background. *Journal for the Scientific Study of Religion* 23 (3): 239–51.

Huntington, Samuel P. 1996. *The clash of civilizations and the remaking of world order*. New York: Simon and Schuster.

Iannaccone, Laurence R. 1990. Religious practice: A human capital approach. *Journal for the Scientific Study of Religion* 29 (3): 297–314.

———. 1992a. Sacrifice and stigma. *Journal of Political Economy* 100 (2): 271–91.

———. 1992b. The consequences of religious market structure. *Rationality and Society* 3: 156–77.

———. 1997. Rational choice: Framework for the scientific study of religion. In *Rational choice theory and religion: Summary and assessment*, ed. Lawrence A. Young, 25–45. New York: Routledge.

Ireland, Rowan. 1991. *Kingdoms come: Religion and politics in Brazil*. Pittsburgh, PA: Pittsburgh University Press.

James, William. 1958 [1902]. *The varieties of religious experience: A study in human nature*. New York: New American Library.

Jawad, Haifaa. 2006. Female conversion to Islam: The Sufi paradigm. In *Women embracing Islam: Gender and conversion in the West*, ed. Karin van Nieuwkerk, 153–71. Austin: University of Texas Press.

Jelen, Ted. 2002. Reflections on the "new paradigm": Unfinished business and an agenda for research. In *Sacred markets, sacred canopies: Essays on religious markets and religious pluralism*, ed. Ted G. Jelen, 187–203. Lanham, MD: Rowman and Littlefield.

Jeremias, Luis. 2006. *Luis Jeremias*. Web. Available at http://www.infidels.org/electronic/email/ex-tian/Luis_Jeremias.html. Accessed on August 29.

Johnson, D. Paul. 2002. From religious markets to religious communities: Contrasting implications for applied research. *Review of Religious Research* 44 (4): 325–40.

Kahn, Peter J., and A. L. Greene. 2004. "Seeing conversion whole": Testing a model of religious conversion. *Pastoral Psychology* 52 (3): 233–58.

Kilbourne, Brock, and James T. Richardson. 1988. Paradigm conflict, types of conversion, and conversion theories. *Sociological Analysis* 50 (1): 1–21.

Knight, David A., Robert H. Woods, Jr., and Ines W. Jindra. 2005. Gender differences in the communication of Christian conversion narratives. *Review of Religious Research* 47 (2): 113–34.

Knowlton, David. 2005. How many members are there really? Two censuses and the meaning of LDS membership in Chile and Mexico. *Dialogue* 38 (2): 53–78.

Kose, Ali. 1996. *Conversion to Islam: A study of native British converts*. London: Kegan Paul.

Kox, Willem, Wim Meeus, and Harm 't Hart. 1991. Religious conversion of adolescents: Testing the Lofland/Stark model of religious conversion. *Sociological Analysis* 52 (3): 227–40.

Kuhn, Thomas. 1970. *The structure of scientific revolutions*. Chicago: University of Chicago Press.

Kundera, Milan. 1983. *The unbearable lightness of being*. London: Faber and Faber.

Kurtz, Lester R. 1995. *Gods in the global village*. Thousand Oaks, CA: Pine Forge.

Lalive d'Epinay, Christian. 1969. *Haven of the masses: A study of the pentecostal movement in Chile*. London: Lutterworth.

Lancaster, Roger N. 1988. *Thanks to God and the revolution: Popular religion and class consciousness in the new Nicaragua*. New York: Columbia University Press.

Leatham, Miguel C. 1997. Rethinking religious decision-making in peasant millenarianism: The case of Nueva Jerusalén. *Journal of Contemporary Religion* 12 (3): 295–309.

Lechner, Frank J. 2000. Global fundamentalism. In *The globalization reader*, ed. Frank Lechner and John Boli, 338–41. Oxford: Blackwell.

Lehmann, David. 2002. Religion and globalisation. In *Religions in the modern world*, ed. Linda Woodhead and Paul Heelas, 299–315. London: Routledge.

Leonard, Karen I., Alex Stepick, Manuel A. Vásquez, and Jennifer Holdaway, eds. 2005. *Immigrant faiths: Transforming religious life in America*. Lanham, MD: Altamira.

Lewis, C. S. 1955. *Surprised by joy: The shape of my early life*. San Diego, CA: Harcourt Brace Jovanovich.

Lewis, Sinclair. 1927. *Elmer Gantry*. New York: Penguin Signet Classic.

Lifton, Robert Jay. 1961. *Thought reform and the psychology of totalism: A study of "brainwashing" in China*. New York: W. W. Norton.

Lijphart, Arend J. 1968. *The politics of accommodation: Pluralism and democracy in the Netherlands*. Berkeley, CA: University of California Press.

Linde, Charlotte. 1993. *Life stories: The creation of coherence*. New York: Oxford University Press.

Locks, Steve. 2000. *Asymmetry of conversion*. Web. Available at http://www.users.globalnet.co.uk/~slocks/conversion_asymmetry.html. Accessed on August 29, 2006.

Lofland, John. 1977. Becoming a world-saver revisited. *American Behavioral Scientist* 20 (6): 805–18.

————, and Norman Skonovd. 1981. Conversion motifs. *Journal for the Scientific Study of Religion* 20 (4): 373–85.

Lofland, John, and Rodney Stark. 1965. Becoming a world-saver: A theory of conversion to a deviant perspective. *American Sociological Review* 30 (6): 862–75.

Long, Theodore E., and Jeffrey K. Hadden. 1983. Religious conversion and the concept of socialization: Integrating the brainwashing and drift models. *Journal for the Scientific Study of Religion* 22 (1): 1–14.

Lovelace, Richard C. 1990. The anatomy of Puritan piety: English Puritan devotional literature, 1600–1640. In *Christian spirituality: Post-reformation and modern*, ed. Louis Dupré and Don E. Saliers, 294–323. London: SCM Press.

Manson-McGinty, Anna. 2006. *Becoming Muslim: Western women's conversions to Islam*. New York: Palgrave Macmillan.

Mariz, Cecília Loreto. 1994. *Coping with poverty: Pentecostal churches and Christian base communities in Brazil*. Philadelphia, PA: Temple University Press.

————, and María das Dores Campos Machado. 1997. Pentecostalism and women in Brazil. In *Power, politics, and pentecostals in Latin America*, ed. Edward Cleary and Hannah Stewart-Gambino, 41–54. Boulder, CO: Westview.

Martin, Bernice. 2006. Pentecostal conversion and the limits of the market metaphor. *Exchange* 35 (1): 61–91.

Martin, David. 1990. *Tongues of fire: The explosion of pentecostalism in Latin America*. Oxford: Blackwell.

————. 2002. *Pentecostalism: The world their parish*. Oxford: Blackwell.

Martin, Todd F., James M. White, and Daniel Perlman. 2003. Religious socialization: A test of the channeling hypothesis of parental influence on adolescent faith maturity. *Journal of Adolescent Research* 18 (2): 169–87.

McAdams, Dan P. 2005. *The redemptive self: Stories Americans live by*. New York: Oxford University Press.

Mead, George Herbert. 1934. *Mind, self, and society*. Chicago: University of Chicago Press.

Menon, Kalyani Devaki. 2003. Converted innocents and their trickster heroes: The politics of proselytizing in India. In *The anthropology of religious conversion*, ed. Andrew Buckser and Stephen D. Glazier, 43–53. Lanham, MD: Rowman and Littlefield.

Meyer, Birgit. 2004. "Praise the Lord … ": Popular cinema and pentecostalite style in Ghana's new public sphere. *American Ethnologist* 31 (1): 92–110.

————. 2006. *Religious sensations: Why media, aesthetics and power matter in the study of contemporary religion*. Amsterdam: Vrije Universiteit, valedictory lecture, October 6.

————, and Annelies Moors, eds. 2006. *Religion, media, and the public sphere*. Bloomington, IN: Indiana University Press.

Míguez, Daniel. 1997. *"To help you find God": The making of a pentecostal identity in a Buenos Aires suburb*. PhD dissertation, Vrije Universiteit, Amsterdam.

Mitchell, David. 2003. *Cloud atlas*. London: Sceptre.

Moore, R. Laurence. 1994. *Selling God: American religion in the marketplace of culture*. Oxford: Oxford University Press.

Morris, Edmund. 1999. *Dutch: A memoir of Ronald Reagan.* New York: Random House.

Neitz, Mary Jo. 1997. *Charisma and community: A study of religious commitment within the Charismatic Renewal.* New Brunswick, NJ: Transaction.

———, and Peter R. Mueser. 1997. Economic man and the sociology of religion: A critique of the rational choice approach. In *Rational choice theory and religion: Summary and assessment,* ed. Lawrence A. Young, 105–18. New York: Routledge.

Nida, Eugene A. 1958. The relationship of social structure to the problems of evangelism in Latin America. *Practical Anthropology* 5 (3): 101–23.

Nock, Arthur Darby. 1933. *Conversion.* New York: Oxford University Press.

Norris, Rebecca S. 2003. Converting to what? Embodied culture and the adoption of new beliefs. In *The anthropology of religious conversion,* ed. Andrew Buckser and Stephen D. Glazier, 171–81. Lanham, MD: Rowman and Littlefield.

O'Connell, Joseph T. 1990. Do bhakti movements change Hindu social structures? The case of Caitanya Vaisnavas in Bengal. In *Boeings and bullock-carts, volume 4,* ed. B. L. Smith, 39–63. Delhi: Chanakya.

Olson, Daniel V. A. 2002. Competing notions of religious competition and conflict in theories of religious economies. In *Sacred markets, sacred canopies: Essays on religious markets and religious pluralism,* ed. Ted G. Jelen, 133–65. Lanham, MD: Rowman and Littlefield.

Omenyo, Cephas N. 2002. *Pentecost outside pentecostalism: A study of the development of Charismatic Renewal in the mainline churches in Ghana.* Zoetermeer: Boekencentrum.

———. 2005. From the fringes to the centre: Pentecostalization of the mainline churches in Ghana. *Exchange* 34 (1): 39–60.

O'Toole, Roger. 2004. Review article: William James and the varieties of contemporary religion. *Journal of Contemporary Religion* 19 (2): 231–39.

Otten, Willem Jan. 2003. *De bedoeling van verbeelding: Zomerdagboek,* 18–21. Amsterdam/Antwerp: De Prom.

———. 2005. Een bekering vormt het mooiste verhaal [A conversion is the most beautiful story]. *Tertio* 276: 8–10.

Paloutzian, Raymond F., James T. Richardson, and Lewis R. Rambo. 1999. Religious conversion and personality change. *Journal of Personality* 67 (6): 1047–79.

Peace, Richard V. 2004. Conflicting understandings of Christian conversion: A missiological challenge. *International Bulletin of Missionary Research* 28 (1): 8–14.

Pearce, Joseph. 1999. *Literary converts: Spiritual inspiration in an age of unbelief.* London: Harper Collins.

Peterson, Anna L., Manuel A. Vásquez, and Philip J. Williams, eds. 2001. *Christianity, social change, and globalization in the Americas.* New Brunswick: Rutgers University Press.

Pierre, DBC. 2003. *Vernon God Little.* London: Faber and Faber.

Poewe, Karla O., ed. 1994. *Charismatic Christianity as a global culture.* Columbia, SC: University of South Carolina Press.

Popp-Baier, Ulrike. 2002. Conversion as a social construction: A narrative approach to conversion research. In *Social constructionism and theology,* ed. C. A. M. Hermans, G. Immink, A. de Jong, and J. van der Lans, 42–61. Leiden, the Netherlands: Brill.

Posten, Larry. 1992. *Islamic Daiwah in the West: Muslim missionary activity and the dynamics of conversion to Islam*. Oxford: Oxford University Press.

Price, Robert M. 1997. *From fundamentalist to humanist*. Web. Available at http://www.infidels.org/library/modern/robert_price/humanist.html. Accessed on August 29, 2006.

Rambo, Lewis R. 1982. Charisma and conversion. *Pastoral Psychology* 31: 96–108.

———. 1992. The phenomenology of conversion. In *Handbook of religious conversion*, ed. H. Newton Malony, 229–58. Birmingham, AL: Religious Education Press.

———. 1993. *Understanding religious conversion*. New Haven, CT and London: Yale University Press.

———. 1999. Theories of conversion: Understanding and interpreting religious change. *Social Compass* 46 (3): 259–71.

Read, David H. C. 1992. The evangelical protestant understanding of conversion. In *Handbook of religious conversion*, ed. H. Newton Malony and Samuel Southard, 137–43. Birmingham, AL: Religious Education Press.

Regnerus, Mark, and Jeremy E. Uecker. 2006. Finding faith, losing faith: The prevalence and context of religious transformations during adolescence. *Review of Religious Research* 47 (3): 217–37.

Richardson, James T., ed. 1978. *Conversion careers: In and out of the new religions*. Beverly Hills: Sage.

———. 1980. Conversion careers. *Transaction: Social science and modern society* 17 (3): 47–50.

———. 1985. The active vs. passive convert: Paradigm conflict in conversion/recruitment research. *Journal for the Scientific Study of Religion* 24 (2): 163–179.

———. 1993. A social psychological critique of "brainwashing" claims about recruitment to new religions. In *The handbook of cults and sects in America*, ed. David G. Bromley and Jeffrey K. Hadden, 75–94. Greenwich, CT: Jai Press.

———, ed. 2004. *Regulating religion: Case studies from around the globe*. London: Kluwer Academic / Plenum Publishers.

———, and Mary Stewart. 1978. Conversion process models and the Jesus movement. In *Conversion careers: In and out of the new religions*, ed. James T. Richardson, 24–42. Beverly Hills: Sage.

Ricoeur, Paul. 1991. Life: A story in search of a narrator. In *A Ricoeur reader: Reflection and imagination*, ed. M. J. Valdés, 59–91. New York: Harvester/Wheatsheaf.

Roald, Anne Sofie. 2006. The shaping of a Scandinavian "Islam": Converts and equal gender opportunity. In *Women embracing Islam: Gender and conversion in the West*, ed. Karin van Nieuwkerk, 48–70. Austin: University of Texas Press.

Robbins, Thomas. 2001. The elementary firms of religion. *Review of Religious Research* 42 (3): 334–36.

Robertson, Roland. 1992. *Globalization: Social theory and global culture*. London: Sage.

————, and JoAnn Chirico. 1985. Humanity, globalization, and worldwide religious resurgence: A theoretical exploration. *Sociological Analysis* 46 (3): 219–42.

Roof, Wade Clark. 1999. *Spiritual marketplace: Baby boomers and the remaking of American religion*. Princeton, NJ: Princeton University Press.

Rosenwald, George C., and Richard L. Ochberg, eds. 1992. *Storied lives: The cultural politics of self-understanding*. New Haven, CT: Yale University Press.

Saler, Benson. 1965. Religious conversion and self-aggrandizement: A Guatemalan case. *Practical Anthropology* 13: 107–14.

Sargant, William W. 1957. *Battle for the mind: A physiology of conversion and brainwashing*. London: Heinemann.

Sargeant, Kimon Howland. 2000. *Seeker churches: Promoting traditional religion in a nontraditional way*. New Brunswick, NJ: Rutgers University Press.

Sassen, Saskia. 2006. *Territory, authority, rights*. Princeton, NJ: Princeton University Press.

Scheick, William. 1974. Family, conversion, and the self in Jonathan Edwards' *A Faithful Narrative of the Surprising Work of God*. *Tennessee Studies in Literature* 19: 29–89.

Sengers, Erik. 2003. *"Al zijn wij katholiek, wij zijn Nederlanders": Opkomst en verval van de katholieke kerk in Nederland sinds 1795 vanuit rational-choice perspectief* ["Although we are Catholic, we are Dutch": Rise and fall of the Catholic Church in the Netherlands since 1795 from a rational-choice perspective]. Delft: Eburon.

Sherkat, Darren E., and John Wilson. 1995. Preferences, constraints, and choices in religious markets: An examination of religious switching and apostasy. *Social Forces* 73 (3): 993–1026.

Shipps, Jan. 1985. *Mormonism: The story of a new religious tradition*. Urbana and Chicago: University of Illinois Press.

Simmel, Georg. 1997. *Essays on religion*. New Haven, CT: Yale University Press.

Smilde, David. 2007. *Reason to believe: Cultural agency in Latin American evangelicalism*. Berkeley, CA: University of California Press.

Smith, Christian (with Melissa Lundquist Denton). 2005. *Soul searching: The religious and spiritual lives of American teenagers*. New York: Oxford University Press.

Snow, David A., and Richard Machalek. 1983. The convert as a social type. In *Sociological theory*, ed. Randall Collins, 259–89. San Francisco: Jossey-Bass.

————. 1984. The sociology of conversion. *Annual Review of Sociology* 10: 167–90.

Snow, David A., and Cynthia L. Phillips. 1980. The Lofland-Stark conversion model: A critical reassessment. *Social Problems* 27 (4): 430–47.

Spickard, James V. 1998. Rethinking religious social action: What is "rational" about rational-choice theory? *Sociology of Religion* 59 (2): 99–115.

Stam, Juan. 2003. Bush's religious language. *The Nation*. December 22. Web. Available at http://www.thenation.com/doc/20031222/stam/print. Accessed on July 17, 2008.

Staples, Clifford L., and Armand L. Mauss. 1987. Conversion or commitment? A reassessment of the Snow and Machalek approach to the study of conversion. *Journal for the Scientific Study of Religion* 26 (2): 133–47.

Stark, Rodney. 1984. The rise of a new world faith. *Review of Religious Research* 26 (1): 18–27.

———. 1990. Modernization, secularization, and Mormon success. In *In Gods we trust—Second edition*, ed. Thomas Robbins and Dick Anthony, 210–18. New Brunswick, NJ: Transaction.

———. 1996. So far, so good: A brief assessment of Mormon membership projections. *Review of Religious Research* 38 (2): 175–78.

———, and William Sims Bainbridge. 1987. *A theory of religion*. New York: Peter Lang.

———, and Roger Finke. 2000. *Acts of faith: Explaining the human side of religion*. Berkeley, CA: University of California Press.

———. 2002. Beyond church and sect: Dynamics and stability in religious economies. In *Sacred markets, sacred canopies: Essays on religious markets and religious pluralism*, ed. Ted G. Jelen, 31–62. Lanham, MD: Rowman and Littlefield.

———. (Reid Neilson, ed.). 2005. *The rise of Mormonism*. New York: Columbia University Press.

Steigenga, Timothy J. 2001. *The politics of the spirit: The political implications of pentecostalized religion in Costa Rica and Guatemala*. Lanham, MD: Lexington.

Straus, Roger A. 1979. Religious conversion as a personal and collective accomplishment. *Sociological Analysis* 40 (2): 158–65.

Stromberg, Peter G. 1990. Ideological language in the transformation of identity. *American Anthropologist* 92 (1): 42–56.

———. 1993. *Language and self-transformation: A study of the Christian conversion narrative*. Cambridge: Cambridge University Press.

Taseer, Aatish. 2005. Dying to kill: Interview with a British Jihadist. *Prospect* 113 (August). Available at http://www.prospect-magazine.co.uk. Accessed on August 24, 2005.

Travisano, Richard V. 1970. Alternation and conversion as qualitatively different transformations. In *Social psychology through symbolic interaction*, ed. G. P. Stone and H. A. Faberman, 594–606. Waltham, MA: Ginn-Blaisdell.

Turner, Victor W. 1969. *The ritual process: Structure and anti-structure*. London: Routledge and Kegan Paul.

Ullman, Chana. 1989. *The transformed self: The psychology of religious conversion*. New York: Plenum Press.

Vande Berg, Travis, and Fred Kniss. 2008. ISKCON and immigrants: The rise, decline, and rise again of a new religious movement. *The Sociological Quarterly* 49: 79–104.

van der Veer, Peter, ed. 1996. *Conversion to modernities: The globalization of Christianity*. New York: Routledge.

———. 2006. Conversion and coercion: The politics of sincerity and authenticity. In *Cultures of conversions*, ed. Wout J. van Bekkum, Jan N. Bremmer, and Arie Molendijk, 1–14. Leuven: Peeters.

van Gennep, Arnold. 1960. *The rites of passage*. London: Routledge and Kegan Paul.

van Nieuwkerk, Karin, ed. 2006. *Women embracing Islam: Gender and conversion in the West*. Austin: University of Texas Press.

————. Forthcoming. The anthropology of conversion to Islam. In *The Oxford handbook of religious conversion,* ed. Lewis R. Rambo and Charles E. Farhadian. New York: Oxford University Press.

Vásquez, Manuel A., and Marie F. Marquardt. 2003. *Globalizing the sacred: Religion across the Americas.* New Brunswick, NJ: Rutgers University Press.

Walls, Andrew F. 2004. Converts or proselytes? The crisis over conversion in the early church. *International Bulletin of Missionary Research* 28 (1): 2–6.

Warner, R. Stephen. 2002. More progress on the new paradigm. In *Sacred markets, sacred canopies: Essays on religious markets and religious pluralism,* ed. Ted G. Jelen, 1–29. Lanham, MD: Rowman and Littlefield.

————, and Judith G. Wittner, eds. 1998. *Gatherings in diaspora: Religious communities and the new immigration.* Philadelphia: Temple University Press.

Weber, Max. 1947 [1922–1923]. The social psychology of the world religions. In *From Max Weber: Essays in sociology,* ed. H. H. Gerth and C. Wright Mills, 267–301. London: Kegan Paul.

————. 1958 [1904–1905]. *The protestant ethic and the spirit of capitalism.* New York: Scribner.

————. 1978 [1922]. *Economy and society: An outline of interpretive sociology.* Two Volumes. Berkeley, CA: University of California Press.

Willems, Emilio. 1967. *Followers of the new faith: Culture change and the rise of protestantism in Brazil and Chile.* Nashville, TN: Vanderbilt University Press.

Wilson, Bryan R. 1982. *Religion in sociological perspective.* Oxford: Oxford University Press.

————. 1985. Secularization: The inherited model. In *The sacred in a secular age,* ed. Phillip E. Hammond, 9–20. Berkeley, CA: University of California Press.

Wohlrab-Sahr, Monika. 1999. *Konversion zum Islam in Deutschland und den USA.* Frankfurt: Campus.

Woodberry, J. Dudley. 1992. Conversion in Islam. In *Handbook of religious conversion,* ed. H. Newton Malony and Samuel Southard, 22–40. Birmingham, AL: Religious Education Press.

Index

active seekers   25–6, 28, 32, 34, 36,
    39, 40
Acts of the Apostles (Bible)   10–11
Acts of Faith (2000)   66
adolescence   4, 20, 23, 33, 41–2, 45,
    51, 76, 83, 90, 95, 102, 106–8,
    110, 112, 115, 117, 119, 122,
    126–8, 135, 140, 142, 148n11
Adventism   58, 145n60
affiliation   4, 25, 31, 34, 37, 40,
    48–50, 52, 85, 110, 128, 133,
    136–7
    level of religious activity in   50,
        133, 136–7
    and welfare states   4
Afghanistan   1, 5, 8, 101
    See also Taliban
Africa   5, 43
age bias   42
agnostics   7
Al Qaeda   6
Alcoholics Anonymous   123
alcoholism   52, 105, 119, 121–3,
    126–8, 139–40, 150n44
Alley, Kirsty   16
alternation   24
analogical reasoning   32–3, 44–5, 47
Anglicanism   1, 146n75
apostasy   10, 30, 37, 49–50, 68, 102,
    124
Argentina   117, 124, 127, 153n7
The Atheist Manifesto (1995)   104
atheists   7, 103–5, 111
Azusa Street, Los Angeles
    (1906)   143n10

Baba, Meher   88–9, 95
Baha'i faith   84–5
Bainbridge, William Sims   57
Bankston III, Carl L.   54, 56
Baptists   58, 108
Be Here Now (1971)   82
Belgium   100, 152n25
Berger, Peter   6, 56–7, 131, 144n21
Berlin Wall, fall of   7
Bin Laden, Osama   3, 103–4
biographical reconstruction   17, 39,
    44, 64, 86
Blair, Tony   146n75
Book of Acts,
    See also Acts of the Apostles
"born again,"   7, 32, 69, 108–10,
    146n75
Bowen, Kurt   125, 154n29
brainwashing model   25, 29–30, 34,
    39, 45–6, 148n8
Brazil   116, 126, 127, 153n8
British Muslims   1–3, 100–2
Bromley, David   19, 28, 30, 34, 37, 41,
    42, 46–7, 148n9
Bromley/Shupe approach   19, 28,
    30, 34, 37, 41, 42, 46–7,
    148n9
Brouwer, Janneke   120, 122, 126–7,
    154n17
Brown, Dan   16
Bruce, Steve   66
Buddhism   23, 31, 49, 62, 78–9
Bunyan, John   145n50
Bush, George W. (2000–2008)
    146n75

Bushman, Richard Lyman   145n59,60
Butt, Hassan   1–4, 17–18, 94, 100–2,
    143n5

The Caged Virgin (2006)   103
Californian Episcopalian Church
    73–4, 76
Calvin, John   12, 145n50
Calvinism   15, 17
Cane Ridge Revival (Kentucky)
    (1805)   14
Cantón, Manuela   115, 118–19, 124,
    154n11
Card, Orson Scott   147n82
Carter, Jimmy (1976–1980)   146n75
Catholic Charismatic Renewal
    (CCR)   4, 5, 49, 72–3, 76,
    91–2, 111, 118, 120–4, 140,
    143n11, 154n14
  Latin American conversions   120–2
  See also Precious Blood
Catholic Pentecostals (Michigan)   27
Catholicism   1, 5, 11–12, 15, 27,
    62, 66, 79–80, 83–5, 91–4,
    105–6, 108, 110–12, 126–8, 134,
    146n75, 151n3
  and conversion   11–12, 15–16,
    79–80, 83–5, 126
  and Latin America   126
Central Intelligence Agency (CIA)   5
Charisma and Community
    (1987)   72–3
Charles F. Parham's Bible school
    (Topeka, Kansas)   14
Chaves, Mark   66
childhood   49, 51, 69, 79–83, 88–9,
    95, 108–12, 115, 123, 126, 140
Chile   116, 127, 143n10
church attendance   6–7
Church of Jesus Christ of Latter-day
    Saints (LDS)   13, 100, 152n25
Clinton, Bill (1992–2000)   146n75
coercive religion   6, 144n20
Coleman, Simon   75
commitment indicators   45

committed converts   18, 38–9, 69,
    86–102, 111
  and gender   84–5
  and "miracles,"   90–2
  and psychological motives   87–94
  and social factors   86–7
communism   2, 5, 7, 101
confessing leaders   18, 69, 96–102,
    112
  and family   100
  and meaning   96–9
  and radical Islam   100–2
confession   4, 16, 25, 45, 49–50,
    96–102, 120, 129, 133, 137–8,
    148n10
  individual confession pattern   138
  and Latin America   129
  level of religious activity in   51, 137
  See also confessing leaders
conservative religions   58
Constantine I   11
continuous conversion   75–6
conversion
  active. See active seekers
  versus alternation   24
  appeal of   1–18
  approaches to. See conversion
    approaches
  and celebrities   16
  and commitment. See committed
    converts
  and context   38–40, 65
  continuous. See continuous
    conversion
  and crisis. See crisis; turning-point
    experience
  defined   3, 25, 36, 49–50, 53, 85
  factors in. See conversion factors
  and gender. See gender
  as "heartfelt,"   12, 145n51
  history of   10–14
  and identity. See identity
  indicators of. See conversion
    indicators
  instantaneous   21

and language 86–7, 96
level of. *See* religious activity levels
life cycle approach. *See* life cycle
migration. *See* migration
in modern fiction. *See* fiction
and narratives. *See* biographical
    reconstruction
as a paradigm shift 27–8, 34
passive. *See* passive seekers
and pathology 21, 45
and personality. *See* personality
as quest. *See* quest
rational choice approach. *See*
    rational choice approach
versus recruitment. *See* recruitment
and religious experience. *See*
    religious experience
religious factor in 138–40
and the religious organization. *See*
    religious organization
role theory of. *See* role theory
    approach
and social networks. *See* social
    networks
styles. *See* conversion styles
and the subject. *See* converting
    subject
and testimony. *See* testimony
theology's effect on 39
universal models of 41
and "universe of discourse." *See*
    "universe of discourse"
volitional. *See* volitional conversion
and young adults. *See* young adults
See also conversion career
conversion approaches 19–48
    critique of 40–2, 43–8
    and disciplinary biases 41–2, 45–6
    exploration of 19–40
    need for new 43–5
    synthesis of 46–8
    See also conversion career
conversion career 3–4, 16–18, 43–5,
    48–52, 67, 143n6, 147n82
    definition of 48, 67

figure for 50
as framework 3–4
as heuristic tool 4, 18
levels of. *See* conversion career levels
life cycle approach. *See* life cycle
    approach
need for 43–5
processes of 4
psychological aspects of 17,
    147n82
as self-narratives 17
types of. *See* conversion career types
conversion career levels 48–51
    See also affiliation; confession;
        conversion; disaffiliation;
        preaffiliation
conversion career types 18, 69
    See also committed converts;
        confessing leaders; disillusioned
        disaffiliates; parental religion;
        religious seekers and shoppers
conversion factors
    contingency factors 18, 23, 34–5,
        44–5, 48, 52, 79, 110–12, 115,
        118–20, 123–4, 127–8, 134, 137,
        139, 141
    cultural and political factors 8, 18,
        29, 44, 47–8, 51, 52, 55, 115,
        132, 137, 139
    individual factors 18, 27, 42, 44–5,
        48, 52, 76, 85, 92, 102, 105, 112,
        115, 119, 138
    institutional factors 18, 34, 41–2,
        44, 48, 51, 76, 85, 92, 102, 105,
        111–12, 115, 118, 128, 132,
        138–9
    social factors 18, 29, 34–5, 44, 48,
        51, 68, 76, 82, 85–7, 92, 105,
        109–12, 115, 119, 123–4, 128,
        138–9, 141
conversion indicators 30–3, 44–5,
    47, 133
    See also analogical reasoning;
        convert role; master attribution
        scheme

conversion styles
  and Catholicism 11–12, 15
  in Christianity 5, 10–11
  communal 11–14
  evangelical 14
  forced 11, 17
  mass 11, 14, 147n91
  modern 15
  and Mormonism 13
  and Pentecostalism 14
  and Protestantism 12–13, 15,
    146n70
  and Puritanism 12–13
convert role 30–3, 45, 87–90
the converting subject 135–6
Converts, Dropouts, Returnees
  (1981) 79–80
cost-benefit analysis 15, 47, 67,
  82–3, 132, 135, 141
Costa Rica 4, 124, 126, 127, 154n25
Coupland, Douglas 16, 146n77
Cragun, Ryan 152n29
"creating" activities 29–30 , 47, 128,
  132
crisis 38–9, 41, 45, 52, 76, 98–9, 102,
  110, 127–8
  See also turning-point experience
Cruise, Tom 16
cults 30, 45, 88–9, 95
culture politics 51, 59, 67, 139,
  151n84
curanderos 123, 128
Czech Republic 15

Da Vinci Code 16, 53
Dawkins, Richard 105
Dean, Kenda Creasy 43
Deconversion. *See* disaffiliation
Dick, Philip K. 16, 146n76
disaffiliation 4, 10, 15–16, 18, 28–9,
  34, 39, 41, 49–50, 69–70,
  102–11, 124–7, 129, 136
  and affiliation 49
  and education 111
  importance of 28

  and lack of detailed literature
    69–70
  in Latin America 124–7, 129
  level of religious activity in 51,
    136
  in modern fiction 15–16
  See also disillusioned disaffiliates
disciplinary bias 41–2, 45–6
disillusioned disaffiliates 18, 69,
  102–10
  Islam to atheism 103–5
  and secular disaffiliation 106–8
  and secular humanism 108–10
  and spiritual disaffiliation 105–8
dissatisfaction 49
Divine Light Mission (DLM) 35, 41
Dominican Republic 16
drift model. *See* "social drift" model
drug usage 1, 33, 78, 88, 90, 92, 95,
  119, 122–3, 126–7
Durkheim, Émile 9
Dutch Labor Party 103

Edwards, Jonathan 13
Elmer Gantry (1927) 15
Emerson, Ralph Waldo 145n60
"emic" accounts 33
Episcopalians 58, 73–4, 76, 109, 111
EST 83–5
evangelical Christians 7, 14, 45, 77,
  86, 89–90, 117–18, 133–4,
  146n75

"faith branding," 7
fiction and conversion 15–16
Finke, Roger 9, 19, 35–7, 42,
  53–68, 147n9, 148n9,1,
  149n2,4,5,8,17,24,32–41,
  150n42, 155n6
Finney, Charles (1792–1875) 13
First Epistle to the Corinthians 14
First Great Awakening (U.S.)
  (1730–1750) 13
Fletcher, Phineas 12, 145n53
Flinn, Frank K. 14, 147n90

forced conversions   11, 17
free-riders   57
Freud, Sigmund   112
From Fundamentalist to Humanist   108

Gartrell, C. David   19, 35–7
Geertz, Clifford   9, 144n39
gender   24, 39, 42, 47, 55, 58–9, 94–5, 103–5, 136, 142, 155n14
Generation X   78, 85, 111
genital mutilation   103
Germany   103
global religious networks   8
globalization   4, 7–8, 18, 39, 44, 75–6, 110, 144n30
Goffman, Erving   26
Gómez, Jorge   124, 126, 154n25
Gooren, Henri   36, 47–8, 144n38, 147n1, 148n9,11, 150n44, 151n84, 154n21, 155n39,3,4, 156n17
Gorski, Philip S.   66
Graham, Billy   14
Great Awakening. *See* First Great Awakening
Greene, A. L.   39, 40
Greil, Arthur   19, 26–7, 30, 40
Greil/Rudy approach   40
Guatemala   4, 119, 122, 124–7, 150n44, 154n11
Guerra, Juan Luis   16

Hadden, Jeffrey   19, 29–30, 34, 41, 132
Harding, Susan   96–9
Hare Krishna   45, 58, 65, 150n75
Hawkins, Anne Hunsaker   145n50
Heirich, Max   19, 27–8, 37
Hermans, W. F.   15
Hindu fundamentalism (India)   5, 49, 54
Hirsi Ali, Ayaan   103–5, 143, 152n30, 153n36
Hizb ut-Tahrir   1

Hoge, Dean R.   79–80
Holiness movement   14, 17
Holy Spirit   11, 14, 91, 97–9, 106–8, 117, 121, 126, 132, 140, 143n10,11, 146n65
Horton, Robin   45
Houtepen, Anton   13
human capital   55, 57
Hutchinson, Christopher   105

Iannaccone, Laurence R.   55, 57
iconic reasoning   32, 47
identity   24–7, 31–3, 39, 46–9, 75, 86, 99, 110, 140–1
    and affiliation   48
    change   24–6, 31–3, 45–6
    and conversion   49
    theory   39
    See also convert role; "spoiled" identity
Imitatio Christi   12
immigration   8, 150n75
"incorporating activities,"   29–30, 47, 128, 132
India   5, 49, 54, 65
individual confession pattern   138
Infidel (2007)   103
institutional affiliation   138
institutional transition   49
intensification   49, 71–2
Internet   7–8, 111, 135, 155n39
Iranian Revolution (1979)   5, 8
Islam
    as brotherhood   2
    conversion from   103–5
    conversion to   1–4, 45, 82–3, 94–5, 140
    and fundamentalism   1–3, 54
    niche of   58
    recruitment to   17
    and religious freedom   135
    as way of life   2
Islamic fundamentalism   5–6
Islamic radicalism   1–3, 100–2
Israel, ancient   10, 145n40

James, William (1842–1910)   19–23,
    31, 34, 39, 41–2, 45–6, 112, 135,
    140, 147n2
  and the divided self   20–2
  and religious experience   20–3
  and "sick souls,"   21
  two types of conversion   21
Jehovah's Witnesses   7, 58, 124
Jesus Movement   33
Jewish Christians   24–5, 112
Jewish Unitarians   24
John Paul II   5
Judaism   2, 4
Judaism, orthodox   4, 58, 90

Kahn, Peter J.   40
Kenya   103
Khomeini, Ruhollah Mousavi   5
Kniss, Fred   150n75
Knutson, Andrea   145n52
Koran   2, 103–4
Korean War   46
Kox, Willem   23–4, 25
Kundera, Milan   15
Kuhn, Thomas   19, 34, 67

Latin America   43, 44, 64, 113,
    115–29, 133–5
  conversion experience   128–9
  and Protestantism   44
  and religious affiliation   64
  religious participation   133
  and religious pluralism   44
  religiosity of   43
  See also Catholic Charismatic
    Renewal; Latin American
    conversion careers;
    liberation theology;
    machismo
Latin American conversion
    careers   115–29
  approach to   115–16
  Catholic   126
  Charismatic Catholic   120–2
  conclusions about   127–9

Mormon   122–4, 125–6
Pentecostal   116–20, 124–5
Leatham, Miguel C.   37
Lebanon   5
Lewis, C. S.   15
liberal religions   58
liberation theology   9, 74, 108–9
life cycle approach   4, 25, 27, 31, 39,
    48, 51, 115, 135, 140, 142
  See also adolescence; childhood;
    marriage; young adults
Lofland, John   19, 21–8, 30, 33–4,
    36–7, 39–41, 44–7, 63,
    147n4
Lofland/Stark process model   19,
    21–8, 30, 33–4, 36–7, 39–41,
    44–7, 63, 147n4
  criticisms of   23
  influence of James on   22–3
  motivational model   22, 28
  and social networks   23
  typology of religious
    commitment   22
Long, Theodore   19, 29–30, 34, 41,
    132
Long/Hadden approach   19, 29–30,
    34, 41, 132
  See also creating; incorporating;
    shaping activities
Lovelace, Richard C.   12–13
Luckmann, Thomas   131
Luther, Martin   12, 145n50
Lutherans   58

Machalek, Richard   19, 30–3, 39, 41,
    42, 45–7
machismo   67, 150n44, 156n17
Madonna (pop star)   16
Malinowski, Bronisław Kasper   45
marriage   36, 51–2, 64–5, 72–6, 82,
    95, 115
Martin, Bernice   151n83
Martin, David   151n83
Marx, Karl   9, 119, 128
mass conversions   11, 14, 147n91

mass media 8, 18, 25–6, 52, 110–13, 135, 155n39
master attribution scheme 31–3
Mauss, Armand L. 32, 45
McAdams, Dan P. 16
McRae, John 105
Mead, George Herbert 17, 24
meaning, and religion 9, 54, 96–8
Meeus, Wim 23–4, 25
membership 6–8, 26–7, 47, 52, 62, 68, 132–4, 139, 142
  increasing 68, 134
  and religiosity 62
  versus recruitment 26–7
  See also religious market model
metanoia 10, 46
Methodism 12, 17, 58, 96–8, 136
methodology 3–5, 16–18, 52
Mexico 125, 127
Middle East 6, 8, 95, 101, 135
migration 8, 36, 52, 64–5, 139
Míguez, Daniel 117–18
Minderhout, Henk 124
Minjung theology (South Korea) 9
missionary agents 4, 16, 49, 50, 59, 62, 132–5, 138
"missionary atheism," 103–5
Mitchell, David 16, 147n79
moderate religions 58
Moon, Sun Myung 22, 45
Moral Majority movement 5
Mormonism 4, 5, 7, 8, 13, 35, 58, 62–3, 100, 122–6, 132, 140, 145n59,60, 154n14,21, 155n39
  Latin American conversions 122–6
  and missionary work 62
  and polygamy 13

narrative theory 17, 39
  See also biographical reconstruction
Neitz, Mary Jo 72–3
neopaganism 80–2
Netherlands 15, 23, 103, 144n20, 151n3

New Age groups 58, 79–83
New Religious Movements (NRMs) 4, 7, 17, 35, 41, 45–6
Nicaragua 116, 120–4, 126–7, 143n12, 155n3
Nichiren Shoshu of America (NSA) 23, 31
Nock, Arthur Darby 31, 46

occult 80–1
Olson, Daniel V. A. 61–2, 67–8
Ozman, Agnes 14

Pakistan 100
parental religion 18, 69, 70–6, 80–2, 95–6, 102, 110–11, 136
  and Pentecostalism 74–6
  rebirth through television 72–3
  recovery of tradition 73–4
  teenager and trauma 70–2
passive seekers 11, 23, 25, 27, 28, 34, 39, 145n44
  See also brainwashing model
Pauline conversion 11, 21, 34, 48, 86–7, 127, 145n43,44
Pentecostalism 4, 5, 7, 8, 14–16, 18, 27, 52, 58, 66, 72, 74–6, 106–8, 116–20, 123–7, 129, 132–3, 139–40, 143n10, 150n44, 151n83
  birth of 143n10
  continuous conversion in 75–6
  and globalization 8
  Latin American conversions 116–20, 124–5, 129
  and parental religion 74–6
  roots of 143n10
  as strict religion 58
personality 3, 21, 23, 27, 28, 30, 34, 39–40, 87–90, 134
Philipse, Herman 104
Phillips, Cynthia L. 64, 155n12
Pierre, DBC 16, 146n78
Pietism 12, 17
The Pilgrim's Progress (1678) 145n50

pillarization (Netherlands)   144n20
Poland   5
polygamy   13
Popp-Baier, Ulrike   17
Popper, Karl   67, 105
Portugal   106–8
preaffiliation   3, 25, 40, 48, 50,
    117–18, 127–8, 133, 136
    and Latin America   127–8
    level of religious activity in   50,
    133, 136
    See also crisis; turning-point
    experience
Precious Blood   72–3
Presbyterianism   58, 105, 110
Price, Robert   108–10
privatization of religion   4, 6–7, 112,
    141
process models, See Stark/Lofland
    process model
Protestant Reformation (1517–1648)
    12, 17
Protestant work ethic   9, 144n38
Protestantism   12–13, 15, 22, 23, 135,
    146n70
psychology of religion   34, 45
The Psychology of Religion (1899)   20
Puritanism   12–13, 17, 145n52

quest   38–9, 73–4

Rambo, Lewis R.   4, 19, 37–41, 42,
    49, 131, 138–9, 145n40, 151n4,
    155n12
    interdisciplinary model of   37–40
    See also institutional transition;
    intensification; tradition
    transition
rational choice approach   26, 35–7,
    42, 53–5, 57, 66–8, 131–2, 135,
    148n1
reaffiliation   36, 63–5, 71–6, 110
Reagan, Ronald (1980–1988)   5, 7,
    146n75
"reawakening" stories   71–6

recruitment   1, 8, 17, 23, 26, 28–30,
    35–7, 40, 47–8, 51, 65–6, 101,
    119, 124, 128, 132, 134, 139,
    141–2, 144n27, 155n39
The Redemptive Self: Stories Americans
    Live By (2006)   16
religious activity levels   51–2, 133,
    136–9, 141
religious capital   55, 65, 67
religious commitment   22, 38–9, 45, 62
religious competition   6–8, 47, 52,
    56–62, 68, 132, 134, 139, 142,
    151n83
    See also membership; religious
    market
religious demand   60–1, 63, 65–8
religious economy   6–7, 54, 57–63
    See also religious demand
religious experience   4–5, 20–3, 46
religious freedom   7, 54, 60, 132,
    134–5
religious fundamentalism   5–6, 8, 49,
    54, 69, 96, 108–10
religious market   6–7, 9, 36, 44, 47–8,
    52, 53–68, 112, 134, 142
religious market model   53–68
    and congregation size   57
    and conversion   63–5
    criticisms of   54–5
    as degrading   66–7
    and diversity   62
    as local phenomenon   60
    at the macro-level   59–63
    at the meso-level   56–9
    as metaphor   66
    at the micro-level   54–6
    niches   56, 58–9, 68
    and pluralism   54, 56, 58, 60, 66
    and the rationalist actor   54–6
    and religious freedom   54, 132
    as supply-side model   55–6, 60–3,
    65–8
    and sustainability   61
    and tension   57–9, 68
    See also religious competition

religious market theory   4, 18
religious opposition   61
religious organization   11–14, 40,
    56–63, 68, 131–5, 142, 155n6
  and competition   56–62, 68, 142
  and conversion   131–5
  and leadership   134, 155n6
religious perspective   8–9, 144n39
religious pluralism   6–7, 17, 43–4,
    53–4, 56, 58–60, 66, 132, 134,
    144n21
religious seekers   11, 18, 23, 25–6, 28,
    30, 39, 47, 64, 69, 73–85, 111,
    141, 145n44
  and conversion   64
  and Generation X   78, 85, 111
  profile of   77
  and "seeker churches,"   77–8
  and shoppers   18, 69, 75–85, 111,
    141
  and tourism   79
  See also active seekers; passive
    seekers
religious tourism   79
"revitalization" stories   71–6
Richardson, James T.   4, 19, 33–5,
    143n6, 145n44, 148n7
  and "conversion career,"   33–4, 148n7
Robbins, Thomas   56
role learning   47
role theory approach   28, 31–2, 34,
    132
Roof, Wade Clark   73–4, 77–9, 105–6,
    109
Rudy, David R.   40

Saint Paul conversion   10–11, 21, 34,
    48, 86–7, 127, 145n43,44
Saudi Arabia   103
Scientology   16–17, 78–9, 81–2
Second Great Awakening (U.S.)
    (1790–1840s)   13, 14
secularization   4, 6–7, 53–4, 56–7,
    60–1, 63, 66, 70, 144n21, 149n2
  definition of   6

"old paradigm,"   53–4, 56–7, 60–1,
    63, 66, 70
  and pluralism   144n21
seekers. *See* religious seekers
September 11, 2001   2–3, 6, 46, 103–5
7 July 2005 London bombings   1, 101
Seymour, William Joseph   143n10
Shahada   82, 151n10
Shakers   145n60
Shannon, Zane K.   19, 35–7
"shaping" activities   29–30, 47, 72,
    128, 133
Shari'a law   2, 101
shubh   10, 145n41
Shupe, Anson   19, 28, 30, 34, 37, 41,
    42, 46–7, 148n9
Siebelink, Jan   15
Simmel, Georg   144n39
Smilde, David   128
Smith, Christian   70–2
Smith, Joseph   13, 145n59,60
Snow, David A.   19, 23, 30–3, 39, 41,
    42, 45–7
Snow/Machalek approach   19, 30–3,
    39, 41, 42, 45–7
social capital   55
social conversions   95, 111–12, 138
"social drift" model   29–30
social networks   23, 25–8, 30, 32,
    34–6, 41–2, 44–5, 47, 51, 55,
    57, 63–4, 68, 85, 111, 118, 128,
    134–6, 138–9, 141
  as reward for conversion   63–4
  and trendsetters   141
socialization   26–7, 29–30, 33–6, 38,
    40–2, 47, 51–2, 55–6, 58, 70–2,
    76, 85, 90, 94–9, 109–11, 126,
    132, 134, 136, 138–9
  and confessing leaders   96–9
  and parental religion   70–2
sociologists of religion   45
Somalia   103
Soul Searching (2005)   70–2
Southern Hemisphere   5, 7, 8, 41
Soviet Union   2, 101

speaking in tongues (*glossolalia*)
13–14, 42, 72, 92, 95, 106,
112, 121, 132, 139–40, 143n10,
146n65
Spickard, James V.   54–5, 68
Spiritual Marketplace (1999)   77–9
spirituality   5, 52, 82–3, 111, 118,
134, 139
"spoiled" identity   26–7, 46–7
Staples, Clifford L.   32–3, 45
Star Trek   78–9
Starbuck, Edwin D.   20
Stark, Rodney   9, 19, 21–8, 30, 33–7,
39–42, 44–7, 53–68, 147n91,
148n1, 149n2, 150n42, 155n6
Stark/Finke approach   9, 19, 35–7, 42,
53–68, 147n91, 148n1, 149n2,
150n42, 155n6
defined   36–7
See also rational choice approach
Stevens, Cat   16
Stewart, Mary White   33
Straus, Roger   19, 25–6, 34
strict religions   58
Stromberg, Peter G.   86–7, 96,
152n17
The Structure of Scientific Revolutions
(1962)   19
Sufi Islam   82–3
Sweden   75–6, 94–5, 110
Swedish Pentecostal "Faith"
ministry   75–6

't Hart, Harm   23–4, 25
't Hart, Maarten   15
Taliban   6, 101
Taseer, Aatish   1–3
television   7–8, 72–3, 111, 118, 135,
155n39
terrorism   1–3, 6, 100–2
See also September 11, 2001; 7 July
2005 London bombings
testimony   16, 31, 68
theologians   46
A Theory of Religion (1987)   57

Third Great Awakening (1850–1900)
14, 15
Thomas à Kempis   12
Tillich, Paul   108–9
Tolkien, J. R. R.   15
tradition transition   49
The Transformed Self (1989)   83
Travisano, Richard   19, 24–5, 32, 34,
40, 46
See also "universes of discourse"
Travolta, John   16
turning-point experience   23, 76, 85,
102, 110, 111, 120

Ullman, Chana   83–5, 90–2
ultraliberal religions   58
ultrastrict religions   58
Umbanda   118, 123, 128, 153n8
The Unbearable Lightness of Being
(1984)   15
Unification Church (UC)   17, 22, 28,
29, 35, 41, 45
United States
baby boomers   73–4
capitalism, and terrorism   2
church attendance rates (1970s)
6, 7
and conversion   4, 41, 63
conversion careers   102
convert demographics   30–1
and reinvention of self   16
and religion   43, 64, 133–4
universal conversion models   41
"universe of discourse,"   17, 24, 31,
44, 147n88
ut-Tahrir, Hiz   101

Vande Berg, Travis   150n75
The Varieties of Religious Experience
(1958)   20
volitional conversion   21, 34
voluntarism   35, 40

Warner, R. Stephen   148n1
Washington State University   32

Waugh, Evelyn   15
Weber, Max   6, 54–5, 68, 144n38,
     147n2
welfare states   7
Wesley, John   145n51
Western Europe
   church attendance rates (1970s)
     6, 7
   and conversion   4, 41
   conversion careers   102
   and religion   61, 64, 134
   as secular   43
White, Ellen G.   145n60

Wicca   80
Wilde, Oscar   15
Willems, Emilio   116–17
Winfrey, Oprah   16
Witnesses   8
Wolkers, Jan   15
Word of Life   75–6
World Council of Churches   7

young adults   27–31, 36, 42, 65, 80,
     135, 148n11

Zelezak, Betty   72–3